The Crown's Servants

Gerald Edward Aylmer 1926–2000

The Crown's Servants

*Government and Civil Service
under Charles II, 1660–1685*

G. E. AYLMER

OXFORD

UNIVERSITY PRESS

OXFORD
UNIVERSITY PRESS

Great Clarendon Street, Oxford OX2 6DP

Oxford University Press is a department of the University of Oxford.
It furthers the University's objective of excellence in research, scholarship,
and education by publishing worldwide in

Oxford New York

Auckland Bangkok Buenos Aires Cape Town Chennai
Dar es Salaam Delhi Hong Kong Istanbul Karachi Kolkata
Kuala Lumpur Madrid Melbourne Mexico City Mumbai Nairobi
São Paulo Shanghai Singapore Taipei Tokyo Toronto

with an associated company in Berlin

Oxford is a registered trade mark of Oxford University Press
in the UK and in certain other countries

Published in the United States
by Oxford University Press Inc., New York

British Library Cataloguing in Publication Data

Data available

Library of Congress Cataloging in Publication Data

Aylmer, G. E.
The crown's servants: government and civil service under Charles II, 1660–1685/
G.E. Aylmer.
p. cm.
Includes index.
1. Civil service—Great Britain—History—17th century. 2. Great Britain—
Politics and government—1600-1688. I. Title.
JN425.A94 2002   351.41′09′032—dc21   2001055717
ISBN 0-19-820826-X

1 3 5 7 9 10 8 6 4 2

Typeset in Sabon by
Cambrian Typesetters, Frimley, Surrey
Printed in Great Britain
on acid-free paper by
Biddles Ltd, Guildford and King's Lynn

Preface

THIS BOOK IS a study of English central government and the royal court under Charles II (1660–1685). It deals with the structures of government and its methods, as well as with the personnel and their conditions of service. I desired to carry my earlier studies forward into the later seventeenth century, to see how much had changed and how much had remained the same since 1615–1642, and how completely the return of the monarchy in 1660 undid the changes brought about under the Republic since 1649. It is intended both as a sequel to my two earlier studies of royal officials under Charles I (1625–1642), and of office-holders under the Commonwealth and the Protectorate (1649–1660), and as a contribution in its own right to later seventeenth-century history and to the longer-term development of English central government, and all those who served in it.

I have tried to explain the purpose and scope of this book in the Introduction. In the course of its preparation, which has occupied me on and off since 1989, I have incurred many obligations.

I am grateful to the Leverhulme Trust, which awarded me an Emeritus Fellowship. This covered my travel and other expenses during the years 1993–6, and was particularly welcome at a time when neither academic salaries nor pensions kept pace with such costs.

I am very grateful to Sir John Sainty, KCB, Professor Paul Slack, Sir Keith Thomas, and Professor Austin Woolrych for their encouragement in the early stages of my research, and for their constant support thereafter.

I have been helped by numerous individuals, many of whom I thank in the Acknowledgements, and to the publishers' reader, who by convention must remain anonymous, but to whom my gratitude is not thereby the less. I am also grateful to Ms Ruth

Parr, Mr Michael Watson, and Ms Kay Rogers, editors at the Oxford University Press.

I am most grateful for permission to reproduce the picture of the Royal Palace of Whitehall survey in the Institute of Historical Research (a generous gift to the Institute from Professor Joyce Youings), and to Mr Derek Kendall for photographing it.

Once again, I thank my wife who has been a critical reader of early drafts, has helped with the preparation of the index, and has provided support and every encouragement at all stages.

Needless to say, I alone am responsible for all the mistakes and the imperfections which remain.

G.E.A.

11 December 2000

POSTSCRIPT

Gerald Aylmer completed the text of *The Crown's Servants* and delivered it to his publishers in December 2000; a very few days after writing the above Preface he died suddenly in Oxford on 17 December 2000.

I have made the selection of illustrations on his behalf. I am grateful to the institutions and individual copyright-holders for their permission to reproduce these, as acknowledged in the List of Illustrations.

I wish to thank Howard Colvin, Anne Laurence, Paul Slack and Brian Smith for their help; also the Ashmolean Museum, the Bodleian Library, the British Library, the Courtauld Institute of Art, the Museum of London, the National Portrait Gallery, the National Trust, and their staff, in particular Nicholas Mayhew, Jon Whiteley, Julian Brooks, Susan Harris, Melanie Blake, Andrew Batt, and Matthew Bailey.

I am greatly indebted to Keith Thomas for all his help in the final stages of preparation for publication of Gerald Aylmer's last book.

Ursula Aylmer

July 2001

Acknowledgements

In addition to those to whom I record my gratitude in the Preface, I would like to thank the following for their help:

John Baker
Andrew Barclay
Toby Barnard
Robert Beddard
Sarah Bendall
Colin Brooks
Robert Bucholz
Mary Clapinson
Roderick Clayton
Ron Clayton
The late Donald Coleman
Howard Colvin
Jacqueline Cox
Neil Cuddy
David Davies
Michael Duffy
Richard Dunn
John Ferris
Ruth Fisher
Dorothy Gardener
Mark Goldie
Sarah Griffin
John Habakkuk
Stuart Handley
Paul Hardacre
Barbara Harvey
David Hayton
Frances Henderson

Henry Horwitz
Margaret Hunt
Joanna Innes
Anne Laurence
Paul Langford
Rod Mather
Nicholas Mayhew
Oliver Millar
John Miller
David Mitchell
John Morrill
Mark Nicholls
Jane Ohlmeyer
Arthur Owen
Michael Perceval-Maxwell
Jacob Price
Marian Roberts
Stephen Roberts
Henry Roseveare
Ian Roy
Conrad Russell
Derek Sayer
Kevin Sharpe
The late Robert Somerville
The late Lionel Stones
John Twigg
David Underdown
Blair Worden

viii   *Acknowledgements*

Librarians, archivists, and staffs of:

Bodley, including Rhodes House, Radcliffe Science, and Law
libraries
History Faculty Library, Oxford
Public Record Office
Historic Manuscripts Commission, National Register of
Archives
London Library
British Library, MSS Room
National Trust, Kedleston Hall Archives
Post Office Archives, Mount Pleasant, London
House of Lords Record Office
Goldsmiths' Company library
Inner Temple library
Cambridge University Library, Dept. of MSS and University
Archives
King's College, Cambridge, Dept. of Archives
Family Records Centre
Cornwall Record Office
Dorset Record Office
Herefordshire Record Office
Hertfordshire Record Office
Somerset Record Office
North Yorkshire Record Office
West Sussex Record Office
West Yorkshire Archive Service
National Library of Scotland
Royal Bank of Scotland, Archives Dept.

Beinecke Rare Book and Manuscript Library, Yale University,
New Haven, Conn.
Isabella Stewart Gardner Museum, Boston, Mass.
Public Library, East Hampton, Long Island, NY

I would also like to thank the following owners of manuscripts:
Lord Egremont and Leconfield
Mrs Alison McCann
Professor Walker
Lord and Lady Wemyss

Contents

List of Illustrations

List of Tables

List of Abbreviations

Am. Hist. Rev.	*The American Historical Review*
Amer. J. Legal Hist.	*American Journal of Legal History*
Aylmer, *King's Servants*	G. E. Aylmer, *The King's Servants. The Civil Service of Charles I, 1625–1642* (London, 1961; 2nd edn., 1974)
Aylmer, *State's Servants*	G. E. Aylmer, *The State's Servants. The Civil Service of the English Republic, 1649–1660* (London, 1973)
BL	British Library
Bodl.	Bodleian Library, Oxford
Bodl. Libr. Rec.	*Bodleian Library Record*
Bull. IHR	*The Bulletin of the Institute of Historical Research*
Cal. Clar. St. Ps.	*Calendar of Clarendon State Papers*, i, ed. O. Ogle and W. H. Bliss (Oxford, 1872); ii, ed. W. Dunn Macray (Oxford, 1869); iii, ed. W. Dunn Macray (Oxford, 1876); iv, ed. F. J. Routledge (Oxford, 1932); v, ed. F. J. Routledge (Oxford, 1970)
Camb. Hist. J.	*Cambridge Historical Journal*
Complete Baronetage	G. E. Cokayne (ed.), *Complete Baronetage* (5 vols., Exeter, 1900–1909; repr. 1983)
Complete Peerage	G. E. Cokayne (ed.), *Complete Peerage of England, Scotland, Ireland, Great Britain and the United Kingdom*, rev. G. H. White (13 vols., Stroud and New York, 1910–1959)
CSPC Am WI	*Calendar of State Papers, Colonial Series. (i) America and West Indies*
CSPD	*Calendar of State Papers Domestic* (of Charles II unless otherwise specified)

CTB	*Calendar of Treasury Books*
DNB	Sir Leslie Stephen and Sir Sidney Lee (eds.), *Dictionary of National Biography from the Earliest Times to 1900*, rev. edn. (22 vols., Oxford, 1963)
Econ. Hist. Rev.	*The Economic History Review*
Eng. Hist. Rev.	*The English Historical Review*
GLC	Greater London Council
Hist. J.	*The Historical Journal*
Hist. Parl.	B. D. Henning (ed.), *History of Parliament: The House of Commons, 1660–1690* (3 vols., London, 1983)
Hist. Res.	*Historical Research*
HLRO	House of Lords Records Office, London
HMC	Historical Manuscripts Commission
IHR	Institute of Historical Research, University of London
J. Hist. Sociol.	*Journal of Historical Sociology*
J. Soc. Army Hist. Res.	*Journal of the Society of Army Historical Research*
Keeler, *The Long Parliament*	Mary Frear Keeler, *The Long Parliament, 1640–1641: A Biographical Study of its Members* (American Philosophical Society, Philadelphia, 1954)
LCC	London County Council
N&Q	*Notes and Queries*
NLS	National Library of Scotland
PCC	Prerogative Court of Canterbury
PRO	Public Record Office
RHS	Royal Historical Society
TRHS	*Transactions of the Royal Historical Society*
Wing, *STC 1641–1700*	Donald Wing, *et al.* (eds.), *Short-Title Catalogue of Books Printed in England, Scotland, Ireland, Wales and British America, and of English Books Printed in Other Countries, 1641–1700* (3 vols., New York, 1945–51)

1. Introduction

HISTORIANS SHOULD START by telling their readers what they are trying to do, and why this might be of interest to anyone besides themselves. This book is primarily a study of the men (and the very few women) who staffed the central government and the royal court from the restoration of the monarchy at the end of May 1660 to the death of King Charles II at the beginning of February 1685. But before attempting to present any kind of group portrait of Charles's servants, they must be set in their proper historical context. For this purpose we shall look first at the institutions of government, together with its methods and procedures, next at the terms and conditions of service in it; then at its members both collectively and as individuals. Finally we shall consider the policies, tasks, successes and failures of the regime, relating this to the process of state formation, and the impact of state on society. As in my earlier studies of Charles I's servants (1625–42) and those of the English Republic (1649–60),[1] this book therefore has two main aims: to provide a fuller understanding of English history over a limited span of time, namely during the reign of Charles II, and to relate this to longer-run continuities and changes in the English state.

Under a system of personal monarchy, when the king was still the head of government as well as the formal head of state, a change of reign was bound to have political and administrative consequences. In the belief of literal-minded royalists, and for some (but not all) legal purposes, Charles II's reign had begun when his father was executed on 30 January 1649. But, although there was a royal government in exile during the 1650s, it was not effectively the government of England as that

---

[1] Aylmer, *King's Servants*; id., *The State's Servants*.

is normally understood. So the restoration of the monarchy and the House of Lords in May 1660, and the King's return to a country which he had left as a defeated and hunted fugitive in the autumn of 1651, is a sensible starting point. However, the Restoration was not like the normal beginning of a reign or even of a dynasty. Charles arrived home with many obligations and commitments in his baggage; and, as we shall see, this was reflected in appointments to office at every level and in almost every branch of his government. At the same time, 1660 marked the swing of an ideological as well as a political pendulum in the country's history, away from Puritanism, republicanism, and military rule: for someone living in later twentieth-century Britain it has sometimes been all too tempting to see a parallel with 1979. Indeed emotionally, as a matter of empathy with one's subject, this feeling may be irresistible, but rationally it must not be allowed to dictate our agenda. *Caveat lector.*

So in one sense this book is a sequel to two others, written in the late 1950s and early 1970s respectively. This might seem to make it an easier undertaking; in some respects this is so, in others not. The guides, lists, and other ancillary aids to research, including those now online, make the location of relevant printed and manuscript sources much more expeditious. I think here particularly of the Institute of Historical Research series (mostly edited by J. C. Sainty), *Office-holders in Modern Britain,* several of which run from 1660;[2] other invaluable lists also compiled by Sir John Sainty;[3] various publications of the Royal Historical Society, notably its *Annual Bibliography of British and Irish History,* founded and for many years edited by

[2] J. C. Sainty, *Office-holders in Modern Britain,* i, *Treasury Officials, 1660–1870* (London, 1972); ii, *Officials of the Secretaries of State, 1660–1782* (London, 1973); iii, *Officials of the Boards of Trade, 1660–1870* (London, 1974); iv, *Admiralty Officials, 1660–1870* (London, 1975); vii, *Navy Board Officials, 1660–1832,* comp. J. M. Collinge (London, 1978); xi and xii, *Officials of the Royal Household, 1660–1837,* pts. i–ii, comp. Sainty and R. O. Bucholz (London, 1997–8).
[3] Sainty, *Officers of the Exchequer* (List and Index Society, spec. ser. 18 (1983)); id., *A List of English Law Officers, King's Counsel and Holders of Precedence* (Selden Soc., suppl. ser., 7 (1987)); id., *The Judges of England, 1272–1990* (Selden Soc., suppl. ser., 10 (1993)).

the late Sir Geoffrey Elton;[4] the computerized, online indexes to the guides and calendars of collections, held by the Royal Commission on Historical Manuscripts for the National Register of Archives. There are magnificent editions of texts, which were either not relevant for 1625–42 and 1649–60 or else not published in the 1950s to early 1970s: E. S. de Beer's edition of *Evelyn's Diary*, C. H. Josten's *Elias Ashmole*, and the Robert Latham–William Matthews' edition of the *Diary of Samuel Pepys*.[5] There are biographical dictionaries, above all, *The History of Parliament. The House of Commons, 1660–1690*, edited by B. D. Henning,[6] and in a different genre the latest edition of Howard Colvin's *Dictionary of British Architects*;[7] Michael Hunter's *The Royal Society and its Fellows, 1660–1700* is another very useful compilation.[8] Numerous other guides and handbooks could also be mentioned (and will be acknowledged where appropriate). As against all this, the actual business of research in libraries and record offices has changed in ways which not everyone finds to be wholly for the better. For example, the wills proved in the Prerogative Court of Canterbury are far more accessible than when they were in Somerset House, though scarcely more so than after their transfer to the Public Record Office (then still in Chancery Lane). There is an invaluable alphabetical index of testators from 1701–49 in printout, following on from those already published in conventional

---

⁴ Var. ed. and publishers, 1976 on. Note also Gary M. Bell, *A Handlist of British Diplomatic Representatives, 1509–1688* (RHS, 1990); E. L. C. Mullins, *Texts and Calendars, ii, An Analytical Guide to Serial Publications, 1957–1982* (RHS, 1983), continued online by the Royal Commission on Historical Manuscripts.

⁵ E. S. de Beer (ed.), *The Diary of John Evelyn* (6 vols., Oxford, 1955); C. H. Josten (ed.), *Elias Ashmole (1617–1692): His Autobiographical and Historical Notes, His Correspondence and Other Contemporary Sources Relating to His Life and Work* (5 vols., Oxford, 1966) (cont. pag.); Robert Latham and William Matthews (eds.), *The Diary of Samuel Pepys* (11 vols., London, 1970).

⁶ *Hist. Parl.*

⁷ Howard Colvin, *A Biographical Dictionary of British Architects, 1600–1840*, 3rd edn. (New Haven, Conn. and London, 1995).

⁸ Michael Hunter, *The Morphology of an Early Scientific Institution. The Royal Society and its Fellows, 1660–1700* (British Society for the History of Science Monographs, 4 (1982); repr. with corr., 1985).

form, for the years down to 1700, by the British Records Society. However, these wills have to be read on microfilm either in the Public Record Office at Kew or in a separate repository on the borders of Islington and Clerkenwell. Likewise, the main run of the State Papers Domestic can no longer be consulted in the originals but only on film. The quality and condition of the films as well as of some reading machines sometimes make the text more difficult to read than in the original manuscripts. Most libraries and record offices are more open and accessible, in the sense of being reader-friendly, and have much better finding aids than was the case forty years ago; this is most notably true of the Public Record Office itself. On the other hand, the pressures of security, conservation, and staff shortages sometimes make access to their holdings more, not less, restricted. In my list of acknowledgements at the beginning of this book I have tried to thank those librarians, archivists, and others who have helped me, often when they have been working under difficult conditions themselves.

Turning to the writings of other historians, there is an enormous contrast with the 1950s, even with the 1960s. In the preparation of my first book, when I had read C. V. Wedgwood's *Strafford* and *The King's Peace*; H. R. Trevor-Roper's *Archbishop Laud* and *The Gentry, 1540–1640*; Christopher Hill's *Economic Problems of the Church: From Archbishop Whitgift to the Long Parliament*; D. Brunton and D. H. Pennington, *Members of the Long Parliament*; M. F. Keeler, *The Long Parliament. A Biographical Dictionary*; and the early articles by Lawrence Stone, I could hardly be said to have been swamped or overwhelmed with parallel and related works by my immediate seniors. I was of course aware of the highly relevant and valuable work in progress by my contemporaries, Robert Ashton and Valerie Pearl, whose first books appeared almost simultaneously with my own.[9] When I was near to the completion of my book on the republic and its

[9] R. Ashton, *The Crown and the Money Market, 1603–1640* (Oxford, 1960); V. Pearl, *London and the Outbreak of the Puritan Revolution: City Government and National Politics, 1625–1643* (Oxford, 1961).

officers, I had the advantage of David Underdown, *Pride's Purge*, equipped, like Brunton and Pennington, with admirable biographical appendices, although unfortunately I was too early for Blair Worden's *The Rump Parliament* and for Austin Woolrych's *Commonwealth to Protectorate*.[10] Not a great deal of work by the so-called Revisionists (Conrad Russell, John Morrill, Anthony Fletcher, Kevin Sharpe, Jonathan Clark, Mark Kishlansky, and many others) had yet appeared. No doubt with excessive vanity, I had thought of myself as mildly revisionist, in relation to the interpretations of the seventeenth century associated with my own much-loved erstwhile tutor, Christopher Hill. But in the full flood tide of revisionism (*c.* 1972–90) it became quite clear to me that I was—after all—an old Whig (and one with some residual Leveller leanings too), even if in the jargon of the trade a splitter rather than a lumper.

Beginning work on the post-Restoration period from the later 1980s has been academically speaking to move into another world. If I were to start listing the books and articles by historians whose works are of direct relevance to this book, my problem would be where to stop. A large bibliographical essay does not seem to be in order here. At the risk of offending historians of real quality from whose work I have profited and whom I hold in high respect, it would, however, be wrong not to single out a few, extending in date of publication from the 1950s to the 1990s, which have been of particular help to me: Andrew Browning on *Thomas Osborne, Earl of Danby*; J. P. Kenyon's *Sunderland*; Kenneth Haley, *The First Earl of Shaftesbury*; the books by S. B. Baxter and Henry Roseveare on the Treasury, C. D. Chandaman, *The English Public Revenue 1660–1688*; H. M. Colvin and others on *The King's Works, 1660–1832*; John Western's *Monarchy and Revolution*; Christopher Clay on *The Career of Sir Stephen Fox*; and Alan Marshall's *Intelligence*

---

[10] David Underdown, *Pride's Purge: Politics in the Puritan Revolution* (Oxford, 1971); Blair Worden, *The Rump Parliament, 1648–1653* (Cambridge, 1974); Austin Woolrych, *Commonwealth to Protectorate* (Oxford, 1982).

and Espionage.[11] This highly selective listing is emphatically not meant to imply that these are the best books on English history from 1660 to 1688 written in the last fifty years, only that they are amongst those which have been of most help to me in my current work. Many others will be cited in later references.

It may well be asked why I have chosen the dates 1660–85. This is a considerably longer span of time than those covered in my two previous studies (1625–42 and 1649–60). And the number of individuals involved is correspondingly much larger; the sequence of changes in domestic affairs and in foreign relations is obviously likewise lengthier and more complex. I had at first thought of stopping at 1678 or 9, which would have made a better chronological balance with my earlier books; it also marks one of the three or four most obvious turning points within Charles II's reign. But three old friends whose judgements I value and respect all independently advised me to carry the work forward to the death of Charles. (I will not embarrass them by giving their names here.) Then, it may reasonably be asked, why not round out the so-called Stuarts by coming on another few years to 1688–9? This, after all, was the greatest political upheaval since 1660, some would say since 1649, even if it was not quite the great constitutional turning point portrayed in classic Whig historiography. But James's reign, although brief, none the less introduced so many new issues and so many new faces, that I decided it would upset the balance of my researches; besides, to include the servants of more than one monarch would be to introduce further difficulties. Charles II

---

[11] Andrew Browning, *Thomas Osborne, Earl of Danby and Duke of Leeds, 1632–1712* (3 vols., Glasgow, 1951); J. P. Kenyon, *Robert Spencer Earl of Sunderland, 1641–1702* (London, 1958); K. H. D. Haley, *The First Earl of Shaftesbury* (Oxford, 1968); Stephen B. Baxter, *The Development of the Treasury, 1660–1702* (London, 1957); Henry Roseveare, *The Treasury: The Evolution of a British Institution* (London, 1969); id., *The Treasury, 1660–1870: The Foundations of Control* (London, 1973); C. D. Chandaman, *The English Public Revenue, 1660–1688* (Oxford, 1975); Colvin, *et al. The History of the King's Works, v, 1660–1782* (London, 1976); J. R. Western, *Monarchy and Revolution: The English State in the 1680s* (London, 1972); Christopher Clay, *Public Finance and Private Wealth: The Career of Sir Stephen Fox, 1627–1716* (Oxford, 1978); Alan Marshall, *Intelligence and Espionage in the Reign of Charles II, 1660–1685* (Cambridge, 1994).

may not have been in every respect an admirable person, but by the standards of his time he was definitely a successful king; his brother categorically was not. So, open to criticism as this may be, 1660–85 it is.

The sequence and content of the chapters which follow are, I hope, reasonably self-evident. The institutional structure of government is surveyed first, with rather more attention being paid to those who staffed its various branches than in the comparable chapters of the book's predecessors. The institutions are divided under the headings of the central executive, the royal household, revenue and financial bodies, other departments of state, the law courts, and parliament. The inclusion of Ireland and the crown colonies, or plantations, is explained, and I hope justified; likewise the exclusion of Scotland. An alternative chronology of the reign is offered for the purposes of its administrative history, and the role of the monarch himself is very briefly noted. Full consideration is given to the changes since before the Civil War, as well as to the heritage of republican and Cromwellian rule. The boundaries of the subject are defined and, it is to be hoped, sufficiently explained.

The terms and conditions of service, the rewards and other attractions of office, both the fruits of success and the penalties of failure, comprise the core of Chapter 3. Whether the all-pervasive phenomenon of patronage, so often decisive for entry into and promotion within the king's service, meant the same thing in 1670 as it had done in 1570, or even in 1620, and as it would do in 1720 or in 1770—to take arbitrary fifty-year intervals—is an especially difficult and debatable issue.[12] Along with patronage, appointment and entry to office by means of patrimony and purchase, promotion, retirement, and dismissal will be discussed, together with the different types of tenure on which offices were held, the continued existence of reversions, the oaths and tests imposed on office-holders, the forms of remuneration both legitimate and unacceptable. In assessing the social and economic significance of office-holding, the demographical and economic

---

[12] I am grateful to Prof. Paul Langford for helpful suggestions about patronage in the eighteenth century.

context is shown to be at least as important as the constitutional, political, religious, and cultural aspects of the time, especially for making comparisons here with the situation under Charles I before the Civil War. For the economic and demographic background, I have necessarily relied on the work of other historians, who have written about population, prices and wages, landownership, and alternative opportunities for investment. However, as was also true both earlier and later, the reasons for being in the royal service were never exclusively material, in the sense of pursuing money and wealth; loyalty, ambition, the quest for status and reputation could be equally if not more compelling motives.

Chapter 4 opens with a short explanation of why it would not be meaningful to treat all royal office-holders, at every level and in all branches of government, over the whole twenty-five-year period, as a single population for statistical purposes. After some discussion of method and of particular sources which are available, we then proceed by taking three successive collective portraits or profiles of those holding a range of representative posts in 1663, 1673, and 1683 respectively. The turnover of office-holders between these dates will be related to their age, premature deaths, both violent and from disease and epidemics, also dismissal and voluntary retirement. The information to be presented, and where possible put on a numerical basis, will include family background, geographical origins, education and training, activities before 1660 (except for those who were too young for this to be relevant), age at first entry to office, the duration of such service, subsequent promotion or dismissal, final places of residence on retirement or death, and social rank or status attained. By the time that we reach the 1680s and those in post only a year or so before the King's own death, it becomes of increasing interest to trace their careers forward, to see how they fared under Charles's successors, first James II, then William II and Mary II, and Anne, and in the case of the youngest or longest lived even into Hanoverian times. Naturally many of the same individuals appear in two if not all three of the groups to be analysed in this way. A few have been included because of their exceptional interest, or because their careers are unusually well documented. Overall we shall be dealing with hundreds rather than thousands of people: I had nearly said of men, but there are a very few women too, though—perhaps to the disappointment of some readers—royal mistresses do not qualify unless they held some other position as well, such as being a Lady of the Bedchamber to the Queen. Family values could hardly mean the same thing under a monarch who had no legitimate but numerous illegitimate issue, as they might have done under say George III or Victoria.

More human interest will then be provided by a series of career studies, though not of course full-scale biographies, grouping individuals together in what I hope are fairly straight-forward categories. Here we are very much at the mercy of surviving original sources, whether correspondence, diaries, or other personal written remains. Some of those whose careers challenge comparison with that of Samuel Pepys as administrators, such as William Clarke, George Downing, Stephen Fox, and William Blathwayt, do not seem to have been diarists or autobiographers. Others who did leave ample personal as well as official records behind them, like Elias Ashmole, John Evelyn, Roger Whitley, and John Potenger were not in the same league as Crown servants. The great philosopher John Locke was only very briefly in the service of Charles II as opposed to that of William III, the same being true of the one-time Leveller John Wildman. Our only identified centenarian, Richard Bulstrode, was indeed an author, but it must be admitted not a very exciting one. Among the governmental and court families whom we shall meet are those at the very top, including privy councillors and great officers of state: the Howards, the Hamiltons, the Butlers, the Boyles, the Berkeleys; and at the middling levels those such as the Progers, the Mays, the Wynnes, the Wyndhams, and the Killigrews, besides members of the great legal dynasties. A summary attempt will then be made to characterize the Crown's servants under Charles II, in however broad and impressionistic a manner, to conclude this chapter, with a final reminder about the general method involved, its advantages and limitations.

Chapter 5 includes a modest attempt to meet the charge often brought against administrative historians, that they view society exclusively from the top down. In trying to counteract this, I have attended to such aspects of social life as law and order and popular disturbance, tax collection and resistance to it, and compulsory service both at sea and in the royal dockyards. Compared with my previous books, more emphasis has been laid on the symbols and insignia of state authority: coins, medals, flags, ceremonies, and the like, also the royal healing power. Such symbols included the pomp of the half-yearly assizes, with the judges travelling round the counties conducting trials some of which ended in public hangings.

The limitations of the regime can be seen most clearly in finance and military planning. While war, trade, and colonization are not my subjects here, the role of courtiers and administrators was none the less important, and sometimes decisive in how such activities worked out. How well served was the king? At times I have been tempted to reflect: better than he realized, or deserved to be. Whether the government should be given credit for such modest increase in national wealth as may have come about remains open to argument. This was not a fair or a just society, but it may have been no worse than most before the nineteenth or even the twentieth centuries, and a good deal better than many others.

The Conclusion thus offers a general appraisal of the English state, the government of Charles II and those who served in it. This is partly a matter of comparisons, however general and superficial, with other countries at this time, as well as with English government earlier and British later. This leads the author on to say farewell to his subject, covering some sixty years of English history, which has occupied his time on and off for fifty years, making it a conclusion to three books as well as to one.

2. The Structure of Government: Institutions and Personnel

INSTITUTIONAL HISTORY HAS a bad name, for being dull and old fashioned. Yet it would be absurd to start discussing the crown and its servants without some notion of the king's government, its different branches and their respective functions.

I. THE POLITICAL CONTEXT

It is a mistake to think of a ministry, a team of government ministers and their supporters, in the modern sense. Great officers of state, other privy councillors, middling and lesser officials were all still individually the king's servants. None the less, the government of Charles II's early years, from the time of his return until the mid- or even later 1660s, can reasonably be thought of as a coalition. It was dominated by royalists, both those who had been in exile with the royal family, such as Edward Hyde, Edward Nicholas, and the Marquis of Ormonde, and those who had sat it out at home under the Commonwealth and the Cromwellian Protectorate, like the Earl of Southampton and the Marquis of Hertford. But there were other important elements in the king's government, reflecting the fact that the Restoration was not a re-conquest: the king had been invited back by many who had fought against his father in the 1640s, or else had supported the great usurper, Oliver Protector even more recently than that. There were two distinct groups among these non-royalists: the ex-Cromwellians, of whom George Monck and Edward Montagu were the most immediately important, and Anthony Ashley Cooper (if only briefly a Cromwellian) in the long run the most politically interesting;

and the moderate, Presbyterian, and other anti-republican parliamentarians who had been in opposition from the winter of 1648–9 until February 1660, such as the Earl of Manchester, Lord Robartes, Denzil Holles, and Arthur Annesley.

The distribution of major offices reflected this. Hyde, soon to be Earl of Clarendon, was already Chancellor of the Exchequer, but was quickly promoted to be Lord Chancellor, being succeeded at the Exchequer by Ashley Cooper. After a very short interval under Lords Commissioners, Southampton became Lord Treasurer. Sir John Culpepper (or Colepeper as it is often spelt), another leading Cavalier politician from the 1640s, was Master of the Rolls, but died almost at once, to be succeeded, rather surprisingly by Harbottle Grimston, an ex-parliamentarian, who had a reversion to the post from long before. Besides being Lord General and Master of the Horse, George Monck, the foremost single instrument of the King's restoration, over and above the Dukedom of Albemarle and the Garter, was offered the Lord Lieutenancy of Ireland in absentia, with Robartes in charge as Lord Deputy. When this arrangement proved mutually unacceptable, James Butler the Marquis of Ormonde became Lord Lieutenant, combining this with being Lord Steward of the Household, where the ex-parliamentarian Manchester held the next most senior post as Lord Chamberlain. Hertford, having been recreated Duke of Somerset, became First Gentleman of the Bedchamber and Groom of the Stole; but he too died before the year was out and was succeeded by another ex-Cavalier soldier, John Grenville, shortly to be created Earl of Bath. Edward Nicholas retained the Secretaryship of State to which he had first been appointed as far back as 1641; after a little fumbling and hesitation, the other Secretaryship went to a tepid ex-parliamentarian turned royalist, William Morrice, who was connected by marriage with Monck. The King's brother James Duke of York took up the post of Lord Admiral to which he had been appointed as a child by his father back in the 1630s, with Edward Montague, shortly to become Earl of Sandwich, as Vice-Admiral. Other ex-parliamentarians who got places on the restored Privy Council were the Earl of Northumberland, the Earl of Leicester, Viscount Saye and Sele, Lord Robartes, Denzil Holles, Ashley Cooper, and Arthur Annesley. In the case of the first three there was an element of tokenism in this.[1] At the same time several impeccably royalist peers became councillors without gaining any major office; it is tempting but possibly misleading to equate them with modern ministers without portfolio.

Many historians have pointed out that a kind of generation gap soon opened up within Charles's government, and that this was actually to prove of more political consequence than the distinctions between ex-Cavaliers and ex-Roundheads. We shall return to that when considering changes of policy and personalities from 1663–4 and after.

II. THE CENTRAL EXECUTIVE

This is a modern, not a contemporary term.[2] As defined here, it consisted of the Council and its staff, of whom the four Clerks in ordinary were the most senior and important, together with the two Secretaries of State and their under-secretaries and subordinate clerks. It used to be argued that one of the ways in which Clarendon was backward-looking involved the Council. He was supposed to have wanted the King to rely on it for both advice and action, including the social paternalism which he supposed to have characterized its activities before the Civil War. In fact the Privy Council of James and Charles I, unlike that of Elizabeth I, had been too large to be an effective executive body. With more than twenty-five and often over thirty members, it had always included a number of aristocratic passengers who were poor attenders and took little part in its business. There is a conceptual confusion here, whether or not

---

[1] I am grateful to Prof. Lord Russell for the suggestion that Northumberland and Saye were restored to the Council because they were thought too dangerous to be left out; but of the three Saye, the ablest and most formidable, was seventy-eight years old, Leicester sixty-five, and Northumberland it is true only fifty-eight, but a spent force, politically speaking.

[2] Aylmer, *King's Servants*, 8, 13–26.

it existed in Clarendon's mind is not clear, between wanting the king to be well counselled, to draw on the advice of a wide range of the most loyal and influential of his subjects, and the more specific role of the Council as an institution. After 1660 as before 1640–2, much of the real work was done by council committees. Among these the secret committee on foreign affairs enjoyed a recognized primacy; those historians who have seen this body as the forerunner of the later Cabinet Council, and so eventually of the modern Cabinet, are probably correct. There was a marked tendency to proliferation, and in 1668 the standing committees were reorganized. But the number of councillors continued to creep up, and had reached forty by 1678–9. There was then what seemed at the time, and still looks like, a genuine reform with numbers being slashed to a ceiling of thirty. In fact this action, proposed so it was always said by Sir William Temple, a distinguished diplomat but never himself a great minister of state, is in practice inseparable from the political interplay at that time between the King and his leading critics, notably Ashley Cooper, by then Earl of Shaftesbury, and is therefore better considered in relation to those political changes during the reign which had administrative consequences.[3]

There are some unexpected examples of active, conscientious privy councillors. William Lord Craven, son of a very wealthy London merchant, had gained some military experience on the Continent before the time of the Civil War. Although heavily penalized financially himself by the victorious parliamentarians, he had helped to finance the royalist cause in exile. Craven was soon rewarded with an earldom and was a privy councillor from 1666 to 1679 and again from 1681 to 1689. Although he never held a major office of state, he was clearly regarded by the King as absolutely loyal and trustworthy. He attended a stag-

---

[3] Dorothy Margaret Gardener, 'The Work of the English Privy Council, 1660–1679 (with Respect to Domestic Affairs)', Univ. of Oxford D.Phil. thesis (1992) is much to be preferred to the older works on the Council and the cabinet by E. R. Turner. For a clear, brisk summary see Howard Tomlinson, 'Financial and Administrative Developments in England, 1660–1688', in J. R. Jones (ed.), *The Restored Monarchy, 1660–1688* (London and Basingstoke, 1979); alternatively Lionel K. J. Glassey, 'Politics, Finance and Government', in id. (ed.), *The Reigns of Charles II and James VII and II* (Basingstoke, 1997).

gering 92 per cent of all the possible meetings during the first period when he was a councillor; the next highest scorer was Henry Bennet Lord Arlington (Secretary of State and then Lord Chamberlain) with 73 per cent. The cynic might wonder whether this was because Craven had nothing better to do with his time, or whether as a nouveau riche he felt a continuing need to justify and ingratiate himself with the King, though in fact he was also an inveterate housebuilder and an active philanthropist. Craven succeeded George Monck Duke of Albemarle as colonel of the Coldstream Guards and as Lord Lieutenant of Middlesex, and served as acting commander-in-chief of the forces in the London area on several occasions. By contrast, Henry Pierrepont Marquis of Dorchester, a councillor from 1660 to 1679, could only manage 34 per cent of possible attendances.[4] As to the supposed social paternalism, the general view would now be that there was less difference between the pre-Civil War and post-Restoration councils than such a misunderstanding both of Clarendon and of the actual reality would suggest.

At the core of the central executive, the two Secretaries of State still divided overseas responsibilities between southern and northern Europe. The senior or southern one had charge of communications with the vice-regal regime in Ireland for all except financial matters. Domestic duties were split more haphazardly; when the King was out of town, it was normal for one Secretary to be with him and for the other to mind the shop in Whitehall. Petitions to the King were meant to come through one of the four Masters of Requests, whose judicial duties had ceased to exist, but petitioners often contrived to bypass the duty Master, going straight to a Secretary of State or even—in theory improperly—reaching the King via some other minister of state, councillor, or court favourite. Once received petitions

---

[4] For Craven and Dorchester see *DNB*; *Complete Peerage*; J.C. Sainty, *Office-holders in Modern Britain, Admiralty Officials, 1660–1870* (London, 1975), 20, 118; Gardener, 'English Privy Council', app. 2, pp. 226, *et seq.* I have compiled comparable figures from 1679 to the end of the reign from the Council registers (PRO, PC 2/67–70); Craven was not quite so regular in his attendance, being by then in his seventies.

were normally referred to one of the crown law officers (the Attorney- or Solicitor-General) if the contents seemed to raise constitutional or judicial issues, to the Treasury if they involved crown finance, and to the Surveyor-General if they touched on the crown's rights as a landlord, or anything involving tenancies and ownership of property. Since a great deal of land had changed hands during the Interregnum and much of it was returned to its previous owners in 1660–2, the Surveyor-General, Sir Charles Harbord, a veteran from the 1630s, was for a time one of the busiest, most influential men in the administration. All this must be seen in the context of a monarch who, in the words of an eminent mid-twentieth-century historian, 'although he was capable of strenuous work in an emergency, in ordinary times . . . lacked application.'[5]

Returning to the Secretaries, there was no one in this period comparable in political stature to Thomas Cromwell, William and Robert Cecil, and Francis Walsingham earlier or to the elder William Pitt later. None the less there were two occasions when one of the Secretaries was either the chief minister or the first among equals, what would later come to be called a 'Prime Minister': Arlington in the late 1660s to early 1670s and Robert Spencer Earl of Sunderland in 1679–81 and again from 1683. Clarendon was unquestionably chief minister as Lord Chancellor from 1660 to his fall in 1667; so was Thomas Osborne, Earl of Danby, as Lord Treasurer from 1673 to 1679. Of more consequence perhaps to historians than to contemporaries, the ex-Queen's College Oxford don, Joseph Williamson who was under-secretary from 1660 to 1674 and then Secretary of State 1674–9, was a most assiduous gatherer of intelligence and other information and a compulsive record keeper. Like his great Tudor predecessors in the Secretary's office, he evidently believed that knowledge is power. He insisted on regular, not to say constant, reports from a wide range of correspondents, some to do with counter-intelligence, many of a straightforward

---

[5] G. N. Clark, *The Later Stuarts* (Oxford, 1934 and later edns.), 2 and n. 1, citing Clarendon, the French ambassador Comminges, Bishop Burnet, Pepys, Halifax, and Evelyn.

factual nature, such as shipping news from round the coasts, in times of both peace and war; a vast number of these have survived in the state papers domestic.[6] Although Sir Leoline Jenkins, a distinguished civil lawyer from Glamorgan, Secretary from 1680 to 1684, had some of the same attributes, he was so taken up with the political opposition to the King and its extremist, conspiratorial, even terrorist dimension, that he failed to revive Williamson's more routine information network. Thus the fact that Arlington was not interested in the details of administration, still less in systematic archive management, did not matter so much to posterity because of Williamson's presence; by contrast, the same insouciance on the part of Sunderland and the palpable incompetence of the Earl of Conway (Secretary 1681–3) proved more damaging to the survival of such records. In this respect, Henry Coventry, younger son of Charles I's Lord Keeper, Secretary 1672–9, could be said to have come somewhere in between.

Appointed by the king and answerable to one or other Secretary of State, English diplomatic representatives abroad may be thought of as a projection of the central executive. Compared with early Stuart times, the ambassadors accredited to the King of France and to the States-General of the United Netherlands were relatively more important, while the Madrid embassy counted for somewhat less than it had done then. There were still only Residents or Agents (of sub-ambassadorial status) in the capitals of the many European states. It was no doubt in character that Charles made frequent use of temporary envoys, Ambassadors, and lesser agents extraordinary. At times there was no regular Ambassador in ordinary even in Paris; how far this reflected royal parsimony, cutting public expenditure, how far indecisiveness and procrastination, is not clear. To have had no minister of senior rank continuously resident in Paris, Madrid, the Hague, Brussels, or Lisbon, as was the case in the years 1681–6, is a remarkable comment on the conduct of

---

[6] See the excellent article by Alan Marshall, 'Sir Joseph Williamson and the Conduct of Administration in Restoration England', *Hist. Res.*, 69 (1996), 18–41, also his monograph, already cited, *Intelligence and Espionage in the Reign of Charles II, 1660–1685* (Cambridge, 1994).

foreign relations. The argument about savings to the public purse is strengthened by there having been an Ambassador to the Sublime Porte in Constantinople without a break, since it was the Levant Company which met the bill for this mission. Diplomacy at the routine level may be distinguished from the conduct of foreign policy, alike in the kind of people whom the Crown employed and in their rank, status, and emoluments. For example, Richard Bulstrode, Agent in Brussels from 1674–1689, reported back regularly but was never one of the inner circle of royal policy-makers. There were also numerous Consuls of varying interest and importance stationed in the trading ports of both southern and northern Europe. They were particularly important in the Mediterranean where there were no English diplomats except in Constantinople and northern Italy.[7]

The more routine side of processing outgoing royal letters and grants involved the Signet Office which came under the Secretaries of State. The Privy Seal office, normally under the Lord Privy Seal, enjoyed a key role in authorizing royal expenditure; the Great Seal, under the Lord Chancellor or Lord Keeper, who was at the same time the head of the legal side of government and the senior judge in the court of Chancery, was the ultimate body authorizing grants of offices and privileges and royal charters. Clarendon's successor, Orlando Bridgeman, Lord Keeper 1667–72, was a distinguished lawyer with limited political ambitions; by contrast Shaftesbury, Lord Chancellor 1672–3, was an immensely ambitious politician, who adapted outstandingly well to his novel judicial responsibilities, as even his political opponents admitted. His successors, Daniel Finch (created Earl of Nottingham), Lord Keeper and then Lord Chancellor 1673–82, and Francis North (who became Lord Guildford), Lord Keeper 1682–5, were by contrast career lawyers who transformed themselves into major political

---

[7] Unfortunately excluded from Gary M. Bell's *A Handlist of English Diplomatic Representatives, 1509–1688* (RHS, 1990) (but see p. 4); likewise from the valuable study by Phyllis S. Lachs, *The Diplomatic Corps under Charles II and James II* (New Brunswick, NJ, 1965), 31–2 and 215 n. 21. The article by Violet Barbour (*Am. Hist. Rev.*, 33 (1927–8)), cited there, still holds the field.

figures. Two of the three successive Lords Privy Seal of the reign were ex-parliamentarians from earlier days. Lord Robartes, who held the post from 1661 to 1673, had his tenure suspended and was replaced by three Commissioners during his short and markedly unsuccessful viceroyalty in Ireland (1669–70). His successor, Arthur Annesley, Earl of Anglesey, 1673–82, was a kind of opposition figure within the inner circle of government, a cultivated but unlikeable figure whom we shall meet again in other connections. Finally, George Savile, Earl and later Marquis of Halifax, 1682–5, was a rival to both Sunderland and Clarendon's younger son, Laurence Hyde Earl of Rochester, for the first place during the King's last years. Among the ablest and in some ways the most attractive of all Charles's ministers, Halifax somehow lacked the drive and application needed to reach the very summit in politics. What we know about the Privy Seal office, apart from its rather dull formal records, comes from three sources. Samuel Pepys was Lord Sandwich's deputy as one of the four Clerks there from 1660 to 1663;[8] Sir Edward Dering Bart., one of the three Commissioners during Robartes's absence, was another compulsive compiler of auto-biographical fragments, though not a systematic diarist or memoir writer;[9] Lord Anglesey, an unreconstructed Puritan from the 1640s and 1650s, kept a diary for parts of his career, which exemplifies marvellously well both the admirable and the unattractive aspects of his personality, indeed of puritanism in a wider sense.[10] Apart from the interest which these three sources impart, the Privy Seal Office was not particularly dynamic or important. Nor had those in charge of the Signet and Great Seals any scope for independent action, other than on the initia-tive of their respective heads. In the exercise of royal patronage, including appointments to office, the people who really

[8] Robert Latham and William Matthews (eds.), *The Diary of Samuel Pepys* (11 vols, London, 1970), x, *Companion* and xi, *Index*, for entries in vols. i–iii.
[9] Maurice F. Bond (ed.), *The Diaries and Papers of Sir Edward Dering Second Bart., 1644 to 1684*, HRLO occ. pub. 1 (London, 1976)).
[10] BL Add.MS 40,860 (printed in HMC, 52, *Fitzherbert and Other Collections* (1893), 261–78, for 1667 and 1671–5, and Add. MS 18,730, for 1675–84).

mattered were the Secretaries of State, the crown law officers, the Surveyor-General, the Treasury, and occasionally the Lord Chancellor (or Lord Keeper). At an informal level, as we shall see, the picture looks rather different; here we move into a back-stairs world of patrons, favourites, mistresses, and cronies. Looking at the central executive as a whole, over the twenty-four years and eight months of the King's reign, changes among the individuals at the top and in the wider political context were of more consequence than any institutional developments.

III. THE ROYAL HOUSEHOLD

This was still the largest central department, even if it was smaller and less costly than it had been under Charles I. Its structure had changed very little, if at all, except for the disappearance of purveyance as a means of supplying foodstuffs and other goods at less than market prices. In the Household the accession of James II was more of a break, seeing substantial cuts in numbers of staff and in costs; this reduction survived James's own overthrow by William of Orange and then the Hanoverian Succession in 1714, although size and expenditure crept up again during William's reign.[11]

Its two main branches were the Chamber, or Household 'above stairs', and the Household 'below stairs'. Putting it very simply, the former was concerned with ceremonial and personal attendance on the monarch, the latter with supply and the provision of services, but this has to be qualified in various ways. Security came under the Chamber, in so far as the Gentlemen Pensioners and the Yeomen of the Guard were both part of the Lord Chamberlain's department, while other

[11] Aylmer, 'The Last Years of Purveyance, 1610–1660', *Econ. Hist. Rev.*, 2nd. ser., 10 (1957), 81–93; R. O. Bucholz, *The Augustan Court: Queen Anne and the Decline of Court Culture* (Stanford, Calif., 1993); Andrew Barclay, 'The Impact of James II upon the Departments of the Royal Household', Univ. of Cambridge Ph.D. thesis (1993); Bucholz, Introduction to J. C. Sainty, *Office-Holders in Modern Britain*, xi, *Officials of the Royal Household, 1660–1837*, pt. i: Department of the Lord Chamberlain and Associated Offices, comp. Sainty and Bucholz (London, 1997).

offshoots of the Chamber such as the Jewel House, the King's Goldsmith, and the various Wardrobes had responsibilities for the supply as well as the care and maintenance of *objets*, fittings and furnishings, liveries, and clothing. Among the largest and most costly of these sub-departments, the Great Wardrobe suffered from having too easygoing a Master (the Earl of Sandwich) together with an incompetent and possibly dishonest Clerk, who acted as the Master's deputy as well as being the disbursing officer. Rather than having an active Master and an honest, efficient Clerk, two entirely new offices were created in the later 1660s, those of Comptroller and Surveyor, both at quite handsome salaries; this net addition to the costs of the office does, however, seem to have led to improved management and to the King getting better value for money.[12] The Office of Works, responsible for royal buildings, is of great interest for the history of English architecture. Still nominally under the Lord Chamberlain, in some ways it should be reckoned an independent department of state. One way of measuring the autonomy of sub-departments is according to whether they were funded direct from the Exchequer (or by assignment on particular revenues), as opposed to getting their money via either the Chamber or the Household; also whether they had an accounting officer who had to present his accounts direct to the Exchequer and have them formally 'declared' there. By this criterion, the Works, Robes (responsible for the King's personal wardrobe), and Great Wardrobe were relatively more independent, whereas the Stables, under a highly prestigious great officer of state, the Master of the Horse, was only funded directly in part, otherwise through both the Household and the Great Wardrobe. Although most branches of the Lord Steward's department were concerned with the supply of food, drink, fuel, lighting, and cleaning, they also included the portering staff and the Harbingers, who found lodgings when the court moved out of town.

[12] For the Great Wardrobe see Bucholz, *Officials of the Royal Household*, *pt. i*, pp. 62–4. For the easygoing Master see references elsewhere in this book to Edward Montagu, Earl of Sandwich; and for the inadequate Clerk those to Thomas Towns(h)end.

There was a structural difference between the two Households. The Chamber had a single hierarchy of posts: the Lord Chamberlain, with a personal secretary (who could be quite influential), the Vice-Chamberlain (who might be a privy councillor but had light, not to say minimal, duties), and the Treasurer with his own small accounting staff. By contrast the Household had a collective or collegiate structure. There was indeed a hierarchy there too: the Lord Steward, the Treasurer (almost a great officer of state but no longer the effective finance officer), the Comptroller, the Cofferer (the actual disbursing and accounting official), the first and second Clerks of Greencloth, and the first and second Clerks Comptroller. The Board of Greencloth (so named from the covering of the table at which it met) consisted of the Cofferer and the four Clerks, with the Treasurer or the Comptroller sometimes present and presiding. Thus more depended on the probity and efficiency of one man, the Treasurer, in the Chamber, than it did on the Cofferer, his opposite number below stairs. Given the men who held the Coffererership during these years that was just as well. The most gifted administrator in the Household and a key financial figure for the entire regime, Stephen Fox, began as senior Clerk Comptroller in 1660 and rose later to be senior Clerk of Greencloth. One of the few disappointments in his remarkable career was that he never became Cofferer, twice being passed over for mediocre court favourites.[13]

One branch of the Chamber which had no financial autonomy was of much more political consequence. The royal Bedchamber had been created by James I, to shelter himself from the excessively formal and English-dominated Privy Chamber. Its head, the first Gentleman, who normally also held the eponymous post of Groom of the Stole (= stool), claimed independence from the Lord Chamberlain. The other Gentlemen of the Bedchamber were peers, or heirs to peerages, who enjoyed special royal favour and often held some other

[13] Christopher Clay, *Public Finance and Private Wealth: The Career of Sir Stephen Fox, 1627–1716* (Oxford, 1978), a model biography, in every way worthy of its subject.

office as well. Below them were the Grooms and Pages of the Bedchamber who actually waited on the King and were his most immediate, intimate attendants. The first man appointed Groom of the Stole, the Marquis of Hertford, was already in his seventies; restored as Duke of Somerset in September 1660, he was dead before the end of October. His successor, Sir John Grenville, shortly to be created Earl of Bath, was to remain in post until superseded following the King's death. Son of a royalist general who had been killed in action, and himself a civil war veteran from his mid-teens, Bath had a strong regional power base in the far south-west, being Lord Steward of the Duchy of Cornwall, Lord Warden of the Stannaries (the courts in charge of tin mining), Lord Lieutenant of Cornwall, and Governor of Plymouth. He was generously rewarded in these various capacities, although his pensions were many years in arrears by the end of the reign. Although he became a privy councillor in 1663, Bath was never a major political figure at the highest level; the reason for this is not clear. However, the potential rivalry between the Bedchamber and the Lord Chamberlain boiled over in the early 1680s, when Bath came into conflict with Arlington (Lord Chamberlain since 1674). The specific issues involved control over entry to the royal apartments and hence direct access to the now prematurely ageing monarch, and the terms of appointment to Bedchamber offices. Although there was no actual bloodshed, it was all a little reminiscent of the last days of that ageing tyrant Henry VIII in the 1540s. The dispute was eventually referred to a committee of senior privy councillors, who found for Bath on the basis of formal precedent, but for Arlington on more general grounds: at least that is the way in which I read their report. Charles seems to have shirked an outright decision, perhaps sensibly not wishing to humiliate either of these long-serving trusties. If it is true that Arlington was denied access to the King's Bedchamber when Charles was fatally ill at the beginning of February 1685, it would seem that Bath had got the best of it; in a sense this was somewhat ironical for, whereas Bath lived and died a Church of England protestant, Arlington—like his royal master—took out a spiritual reinsurance policy and was received into the Roman Catholic Church on his deathbed.[14]

The Bedchamber Grooms were among the most generously rewarded of all the King's second-rank servants. The original appointees included a future Secretary of State (Henry Coventry) and a future Whig politician (Silius Titus); four of the twelve were to outlive the King himself. All of those then serving were replaced on James's accession. The original Pages of the Bedchamber were well favoured but did not come to very much; the future Lord Treasurer, Sidney Godolphin, incidentally was a Page of Honour in the royal Stables not of the Bedchamber. Its staff were important as channels of communication between other people and the King: doers as well as seekers of good turns. The importance of the Bedchamber is certainly underplayed in my first book, but at the same time it would be a mistake to generalize from its role in the 1610s and 1620s to the seventeenth century as a whole.

Some other Chamber staff may seem more properly to belong to the central executive than to the Household. The Sergeants at Arms were responsible for making arrests and holding political prisoners pending examination before the Council and/or trial in the courts. The Messengers were charged with taking royal and conciliar orders out to the relevant authorities in the counties and cities of England and Wales, and sometimes also of making arrests. Although under the orders of the Privy Council or else of the Secretaries of State, both were none the less on the payroll of the Chamber. By contrast the Keeper of the Privy Purse was in effect an additional member of the Bedchamber staff; he was unusual, not to say unique, insofar as he received

---

[14] For the clash between Arlington and Bath see *CSPD, Jan.–June 1683*, pp. 90, 91–2, 147, 152–3, 154, 165–6, 254, 284–5, 319–20. Although the (very high-powered) committee eventually reported, it is not clear that Charles ever took a decision. The exhumation here of earlier Bedchamber regulations is important for historians of the early Stuart court: see Neil Cuddy, 'The King's Chambers: The Bedchamber of James I in Administration and Politics, 1603–1625', Oxford D.Phil. thesis (1987). For Henry VIII see David Starkey, 'Intimacy and Innovation: The Rise of the Privy Chamber, 1485–1547', in Starkey *et al.*, *The English Court from the Wars of the Roses to the Civil War* (London, 1987), ch. 3 and other publications.

money direct from the Exchequer and other sources but did not have to present his accounts and get them approved, unlike all other royal disbursing officials. The first holder of this key post was Henry Bennet; on his becoming Secretary of State in 1662 he was succeeded by a rising young royal favourite, Sir Charles Berkeley, who was rapidly created first a Viscount and then Earl of Falmouth. When he was killed in battle during the Dutch War (1665) Falmouth was succeeded in his title by his own father, also Charles Berkeley, but in his office by Baptist May, a member of a prolific court family who had been a Page to James Duke of York; he was to remain in post until the next reign. If Berkeley might fairly be called a crony of the King, May is more aptly described as a toady.

The King's and the court's numerous medical personnel (of Physicians, Surgeons, and Apothecaries) were all on the Chamber establishment, as were the sporting and recreational staff, together with the theatrical staff (of the Revels office), the Ceremonies office for coping with foreign diplomats, and the Keeper of the royal Library. Among the most numerous and in aggregate most expensive of those on the Chamber's establishment (next to the Pensioners and the Yeomen) were the Huntsmen and Falconers and the court Musicians. Unlike his grandfather and his own brother James, Charles II was not in fact a passionate devotee of the chase (hunting or hawking); he was more interested in horse racing. The numbers and cost here arose from a combination of tradition and the King's dislike of saying No and disobliging people around him with whom he was on easy terms. The musical establishment reflected traditions of state (e.g. serried ranks of trumpeters) together with Charles's genuine love of music and, it would seem, his quite discerning taste. We often associate the Restoration court with the theatre, but the direct cost to the Crown arising from that was in practice very small.

Each member of the royal family had her or his own household establishment. These comprised James Duke of York (throughout the reign), Henry Duke of Gloucester (only until his premature death in late 1660), Henrietta Maria the Queen Mother (until her death in 1669), and Catherine of Braganza the Queen Consort (from 1662; she in turn became Queen Dowager in 1685). The King's cousin, Prince Rupert received a large pension to support himself from 1660 to his death in 1682, but did not really have a mini-royal household. James Duke of Monmouth, the King's oldest and for long his favourite son, and Charles's numerous other illegitimate children, besides his regular mistresses, all received pensions and other payments; their households, however, were private establishments, more like those of the non-royal nobility, although while he was in favour (until 1679) Monmouth's approached in scale a branch of the royal household. Because of her childlessness and relative lack of political influence, Queen Catherine's court provided a source of patronage in the way of appointments, for both the men and women who staffed it, but was not a significant political forum in its own right. The Duke of York's establishment was of altogether more consequence; as heir apparent, James attracted what in the next century would become known as the 'reversionary interest'. Having weathered the exclusion crisis of 1679–81 and then having seen their master's enemies decisively defeated by 1683–4, James's servants reaped their reward on his accession, although some, mainly the stronger Church of England protestants among them, left office before the King's ignominious overthrow and flight in 1688.

As we shall see, the household departments were the targets of various economy drives during the reign. Their overall importance was twofold: as a major royal spending commitment and as the foremost arena for patronage and political intrigue.[15]

---

[15] As is clear from Prof. Bucholz's Introduction to *Office-holders in Modern Britain*, xi, and indeed from previously published *Guides to the Public Records*, the Household is much more fully documented after 1660 than before 1642; but, except for internal appointments, such sources tell us nothing about what the late G. R. Elton meant by the court as a 'point of contact' (see his art. in *TRHS*, 5th ser. 26 (1976), 211–28) in relation to Tudor government.

IV. THE REVENUE DEPARTMENTS

Even if it was not as ancient as the king's household and his council, which in some form were as old as the monarchy itself, the royal exchequer's history can be traced back to the twelfth century. After the improvisations and experiments of the Long Parliament and the Commonwealth (1642–53), the traditional structure of financial administration had been partially restored under the Cromwellian Protectorate. In particular the Exchequer and the Duchy of Lancaster had been reconstituted in 1654. So here 1660 saw a great turnover in personnel, with the removal of most though not quite all of those who had been holding office under the republic, and the return of numerous royalists with claims on these offices. As an institution the Exchequer was simultaneously a court of common law, a department for taking the accounts of most other branches of government, and a bureau for receiving in and paying out money and tallies in lieu of cash. The distinction between the Upper Exchequer of Audit or Account and the Lower of Receipt, along with their respective structures and procedures, have been described too often to require repetition here.[16] Of the many officials and their even more numerous deputies and under clerks, those of most consequence, though not necessarily the most prestigious and best rewarded, were in the Upper Exchequer the seven Revenue Auditors and the two Auditors of

[16] See Elton, 'The Elizabethan Exchequer: War in the Receipt', in S. T. Bindoff, J. Hurstfield, and C. H. Williams (eds.), *Elizabethan Government and Society: Essays Presented to Sir John Neale* (London, 1961); Aylmer, *King's Servants*, ch. 2, sect. iv; ch. 4, sect. ii; id., 'Officers of the Exchequer, 1625–1642', in F. J. Fisher (ed.), *Essays in the Economic and Social History of Tudor and Stuart England* (Cambridge, 1961); C. D. Chandaman, *The English Public Revenue, 1660–1688* (Oxford, 1975), app. 1. 'The Revenue Accounts, Credit Techniques and Related Exchequer Procedures'; Sainty, *Officers of the Exchequer* (List and Index Society, spec. ser. 18 (1983)), contains valuable introductory notes as well as lists of appointments; M. S. Giuseppi, *Guide to the Public Records*, i (London, 1923), like earlier and later versions of this publication, has introductory sections on the Upper Exchequer and the Receipt; Lawrence Squibb, 'A Book of All the Several Officers of the Court of Exchequer', ed. W. H. Bryson, in *Camden Miscellany*, 26 (Camden 4th ser. 14 (1975)).

the Imprests, in the Receipt the Auditor and the four Tellers. While the great bulk of the king's revenues were accounted for and a large proportion of his moneys received in and paid out by the Exchequer, it was emphatically not like a modern finance ministry with the machinery for reviewing the crown's overall position and prospects, or for recommending and pursuing fiscal policies, although it was able to provide sets of figures on the basis of which such decisions might be taken.

For the nearest equivalent to a modern ministry of finance, we must turn to the Treasury. Until 1667 this scarcely existed as an institution. It consisted of the Lord Treasurer, the Under-Treasurer (also known as the Chancellor of the Exchequer), the Treasurer's Secretary, at most one or two Clerks, the four Messengers of the Receipt, and a Sergeant-at-Arms.[17] There are two modern histories of the Treasury: one detailed and accurate but strictly institutional in scope, the other with less detail for this period but stronger on the political and financial contexts.[18] Much changed with Lord Treasurer Southampton's death in May 1667 and the appointment of five Lords Commissioners to succeed him. It was the intention of the King and the Council that they should pursue a tougher, less generous and indulgent policy than had been followed before.

The Treasury had been in commission on previous occasions, in 1612–14, 1618–20, and 1635–6, also under the Cromwellian Protectors from 1654 to 1659. But under the Stuart kings these had been essentially stopgap measures or intervals between Lord Treasurers rather than marking any kind of change to a different system of management. There were indeed to be individual Lord Treasurers again, in the years 1672–9, 1685–7, 1702–10, and 1711–14; none the less the Treasury as an institution of state was effectively created with the Commission of

---

[17] Sainty, *Treasury Officials*. My only disagreement with Sainty is that I would include the four Messengers of the Receipt, who in spite of their name were in practice attached to the Treasury (ibid., 88).

[18] S. B. Baxter, *The Development of the Treasury, 1660–1702* (London, 1957); Henry Roseveare, *The Treasury: The Evolution of a British Institution* (London, 1969), esp. chs. 2 and 3; id., *The Treasury, 1660–1870: The Foundation of Control* (London, 1973). For the 1660s to early 1670s the latter is in some ways the more valuable of Roseveare's two books.

1667, although one of its historians, Henry Roseveare, has shown convincingly that even in 1665–6, when the Treasurer and Chancellor had both moved out of the plague-stricken capital to join the royal court in Oxford, the initiative in the mechanics of fiscal policy-making had been assumed de facto by someone whose only formal office was that of a Teller in the Receipt. This was one of the very ablest, if also least attractive of all Charles's servants, Sir George Downing, and it was a logical step for him to be made Secretary to the Commission in 1667.[19] Much was to depend on the Secretary in determining the smooth flow of business coming into and issuing out from the Board, and often the priorities accorded to different items; he was also crucial as a record-keeper of various series of minutes, orders, warrants, and letters. In this latter respect Downing scores very highly. His successor, when he moved to another branch of the revenue in 1671, the courtier and playwright Sir Robert Howard was a disaster; fortunately for the Treasury but unfortunately for the Exchequer, Howard moved laterally, succeeding a much more conscientious man Sir Robert Long as Auditor of the Receipt in 1673. Charles Bertie then came in as a client and relative by marriage of the new Treasurer, Thomas Osborne Lord Latimer, shortly to become Earl of Danby; he was certainly an improvement on Howard. His successor Henry Guy (1679–85 and 1691–5) is rated more highly than Bertie by Roseveare, although his record is in some respects more chequered. The full consummation of the early treasury bureaucracy was to be personified in the career of William Lowndes, who was a clerk from the mid-1670s, Chief Clerk in 1689, and Secretary from 1695 to his death in 1724. (He was therefore a servant of Charles II but only in a subordinate capacity.)

The actual revenue system was much more affected by the upheavals of the mid-century than was the formal structure of the institutions. The so-called 'feudal revenues' of the crown—wardship, livery, and purveyance—had been abolished by the Long Parliament in 1646, and this was ratified by statute in the

---

[19] Roseveare, *The Treasury, 1660–1870*, 22–6.

Restoration settlement of 1660–1. As compensation for this, the excise tax on drinks (initially only on beer, ale, cider, perry, mead, metheglin, and the soft drinks of the time—tea, coffee, chocolate, and sherbert) was made perpetual: half being voted to the Crown for ever and half to Charles for his lifetime. Although it was never again to cover as wide a range of commodities and consumables as had been included under the exigencies of civil war in the 1640s, the excise was later extended to home-produced spirits and to imported wines and spirits (in addition to the customs duties payable on these liquors). Tobacco, rather oddly, only paid customs but not excise until much later. The excise duties were managed by Commissioners in 1660–2, and then under various different tax farms on both a county and a national basis until 1683, when the tax came back under direct crown management, where it was to remain. There was a large staff at the head office in London but in the provinces there were only individual gaugers and sub-commissioners and/or farmers for the different cities and counties. The yield from the excise depended upon two basic variables: the general level of consumer spending—beer and cider being near necessities before clean water and other, more nutritious alternatives—and the honesty and efficiency of the revenue administration. The obvious attraction of tax farming was that the crown received an advance or deposit down payment plus a fixed annual rent. In practice, when times were bad (as during the Plague of 1665–6, the wars especially of 1664–7, and in the aftermath of the Great Fire of September 1666), the farmers were almost invariably allowed a rent reduction, or else could carry debts forward, whereas in good times the Crown got no more than the rent which had been agreed. Shorter leases thus tended to be in the public interest, while we can think of tax-farming as a privatization of the public revenues. Owing to favourable economic conditions and efficient management, the excise revenue was extremely buoyant during the last years of the reign and indeed also under James II. The senior posts of Auditor and Comptroller were held throughout Charles's reign by two interesting but very different individuals. As Auditor, the ex-parliamentarian Colonel John

Birch was something of a parliamentary pundit on financial matters; he had been criticizing government fiscal policies and management from as early as the first protectorate parliament in 1654. The Comptroller, the ex-neutral and then royalist, Elias Ashmole—astrologer, Freemason, herald at arms, and antiquarian scholar—was neither interested nor qualified in financial matters. Although called on from time to time by the Treasury, neither of them seems to have been involved in day-to-day management. Other senior officials, notably the Accountant-General, the Surveyors, and latterly the Receiver-General held the key places under the farmers or commissioners. The excise also had to carry a body of parliamentary and other sinecurists, the commissioners to hear appeals and to expedite arrears; they appear to have done remarkably little, but were present—it seems—as if to emphasize the parliamentary nature of the tax. An example of conflicting priorities within the royal government was to arise when the coffee-houses which had sprung up and rapidly multiplied in London and elsewhere were ordered to be closed as centres of idleness and subversion; the excise farmers complained vigorously that this would lead to a serious fall in their income from the duty on coffee. King and Council had to look for a compromise way out.[20] The overheads, namely the salaries bill and other allowable expenses, only amounted to a commendably modest fraction of the total yield from the excise. And by the eighteenth century it was to form the largest single branch of the public revenue and was the most administratively sophisticated.[21]

[20] See B. Lillywhite, *London Coffee Houses* (London, 1964); E. Ayton, *The Penny Universities* (London, 1956); *Old English Coffee Houses* (London, 1954); see refs in *CSPD, 1675–6*, pp. 465 (29 Dec.), pp. 496–7 (7 Jan.), pp. 500, 503 (8 Jan. 1675/6); and Tim Harris, *London Crowds in the Reign of Charles II: Propaganda and Politics from the Restoration until the Exclusion Crisis* (Cambridge, 1987), 28–9.
[21] Aylmer, 'From Office-holding to Civil Service: The Genesis of Modern Bureaucracy', TRHS, 5th ser. 50 (1980); J. S. Brewer, *The Sinews of Power: War, Money and the English State, 1688–1783* (London, 1989); also Patrick O'Brien and Philip A. Hunt 'The Rise of a Fiscal State in England, 1485–1815', *Hist. Res.*, 66 (1993), 129–76; and Michael J. Braddick, *The Nerves of State: Taxation and the Financing of the English State, 1558–1714* (Manchester, 1996).

The revenue from the customs duties had been at the centre of the constitutional disputes between the early Stuart kings and their 'country' critics in parliament. The early reforms of the Long Parliament (in 1641) had forced the crown to accept that these revenues should not be extended or increased except by statute. And the early legislation of Charles II's reign (1660–3) built on this foundation. There was a new Book of Rates, to set the level of duties and to list the types of goods which were taxable, besides some further codification of existing duties; the Commonwealth's Navigation Act was extended to cover exports as well as imports, and there were further measures to control 'plantation' (i.e. colonial) trade and to funnel it through the home country. As with the excise, the yield from the customs depended not only on the range and level of duties payable but also on the volume of trade and the quality of the fiscal administration. As with the excise too, a short spell of direct management by commissioners was followed by a longer period under farmers (1662–71). It was during the first Treasury Commission of the reign that the customs were taken out of farm and put back under crown management; this time the change proved permanent. And it was in fact as a result of this that Downing left the Treasury on being appointed as one of the Customs Commissioners. In spite of periodic, indeed at times constant investigations and purges of the revenue personnel, the net income accruing from the customs seems to have been more affected by external circumstances than by anything else, notably through the country's foreign relations. Thus the early years of peace (1661–4) were generally helpful; so later was the period when England was neutral while France and the Netherlands were still at war (1674–8); the mid- and later 1680s were beneficial for similar reasons, there being no general European war in progress. The granting of additional duties in 1670 and again for James in 1685 naturally increased the total yield.[22] One striking but by no means new feature of the customs was the extraordinary predominance of London in the country's overseas trade; over two-thirds of the customs revenue

---

[22] See particularly Chandaman, *English Public Revenue*, ch. 1 and app. 2.

was generated in the port of London and its down-river offshoots. Looking at this the other way round, it was much more difficult to get value for money from customs collection in the outports and their respective offshoots, known as members and creeks. Obviously the importance of the outports varied widely, with Hull, Newcastle, Bristol, and Exeter a long way ahead of the rest. The cost of overheads was unavoidably higher as a percentage of the yield with many scattered, mostly small-ish establishments than was the case with a single large one, close under the government's eye in the port of London and its members, of which Gravesend was the chief. The other, less familiar peculiarity of the customs administration, at least from after the reforms of 1671, was the existence of two tiers, almost two hierarchies of officials in each port. In 1660, and from a much earlier date than that, each port had a Customer, a Comptroller, and a Searcher, with some subordinate waiters and under-searchers; there was then added to this a Collector and a Surveyor with additional underlings. Since those styled 'comp-trollers' were traditionally intended to be a check on other officers in a department, this seems distinctly odd. And inevitably there were clashes between what were called the patent officers and the commission officers, the former in particular asserting that the work would be done more efficiently as well as more economically if they were left in sole charge. The Commissioners and the Lord Treasurer rejected this claim, and there the matter appears to have rested, with the result that the patent officers became sinecurists by the early eighteenth century, their deputies performing such duties as there were to be carried out.[23]

The third largest branch of the king's ordinary revenue was unique to the years 1662–89. This was the famous Hearth Tax;

[23] For the 1671 establishment see BL Sloane MS 1,425; for the patent officers' complaints see BL Add. MS 28,078, fos. 133–5; there is another version in Egerton MS 3,351, fos. 10v–11r, 16v–17r. See PRO, SP29/380/54 (*CSPD, 1675–6*, p. 39), an (anonymous) essay on the management of the Customs. For the original 1660–1 establishment see PRO, T51/8, continued for 1661–2 appointments in T51/9–10. For the position at the end of the century see E. E. Hoon, *The Organisation of the English Customs System, 1696–1786* (New York, 1938).

often known as the 'chimney money' it was in fact assessed on the number of fireplaces and stoves in people's houses and other premises, not on the number of chimneys protruding from them. It was granted to the king specifically to meet the short-fall between the gross revenue of £1.2 million which had been settled on him in 1660–1 and the actual yield of his existing revenues which was reckoned at less than three-quarters of this. Even at its height under James II the Hearth Tax did not bring in more than £250,000 a year, and for most of Charles's reign it was yielding much less than that. Considering the amount of controversy, indeed odium, which it generated, not surprisingly the chimney money was abolished as part of the Revolution Settlement (in 1689). The story of its management is a complex one which can only be summarized at the risk of inaccuracy. From 1662 to 1664 it was the responsibility of the sheriffs of counties and cities (who had had the same, unpleasing burden put on them with Ship Money back in the 1630s, as the old gang—Clarendon, Southampton, and co.—would have well remembered). From 1664 to 1665 and in 1666 it was under direct management by royal officials; from 1666 to 1669 it was leased to tax farmers; from 1669 to 1674 it went back under direct management; from 1674 to 1679 it was farmed again; from 1679 to 1684 it was under a hybrid form of management which amounted in substance to farming; from 1684 to 1688 it was under direct collection, the managers then being the Excise Commissioners, except for an anomalous three weeks at the very beginning of James's reign. Though many people inevitably had a hand in the Hearth Tax, no single major administrative figure or otherwise outstandingly interesting individual can be identified with it.[24]

Although the crown's landed estate was restored in 1660–1, and for the most part without compensation being paid to those who had acquired these lands under the Commonwealth,

---

[24] Chandaman, *English Public Revenue*, ch. 3 and app. 2, sect. 3. C. A. F. Meekings of the Public Record Office edited the Hearth Tax returns for various counties, but unfortunately never wrote the general history of it which he had planned. For the three weeks' separation in Feb. 1685 see Chandaman, ibid., 74 n. 4 and 105 n. 3.

income from land was never a major element in the total royal revenue. This is true even if we include what came from the two royal Duchies of Lancaster and Cornwall. The two Duchies existed both as land management agencies and as jurisdictions or courts of law; Lancaster was the more prestigious, its Chancellor being almost a great officer of state, but Cornwall was the more financially buoyant because of the tin mines.[25] The sale of the fee-farm rents, a form of capital liquidation, in the early 1670s, temporarily boosted the income from land, but then of course left it still further reduced. The administrative structure of around forty Receivers-General for the counties, each answerable to one of the seven revenue Auditors of the Upper Exchequer, survived unchanged but would have been hard to justify in terms of cost effectiveness. The senior of these seven, Sir Edmund Sawyer, had been in trouble with parliament back in the 1620s and was one of the oldest serving officials by the 1670s. Clerical Tenths and First Fruits and receipts from fines, forfeitures, and compositions in the law courts were all traditional branches of the revenue which were handled in similar ways at the Exchequer, but were of little consequence in relation to total income. Some small branches of the revenue were managed by their own separate establishments outside the Exchequer. For example, the Alienations Office in theory acted by deputation from the Treasury; it consisted of three Deputies or Commissioners, a Receiver-General, a Chancery Master, and a clerical staff—an absurdly large and expensive establishment to bring in at most a few £100s a year, its income having been much reduced by the abolition of tenancies-in-chief and the feudal duties.[26] The Clerk of the Hanaper, an officer of the court of Chancery, was responsible for paying in the net profits of the Great Seal, for which he was in effect the receiver; the money arising from fines (procedural rather than punitive), from the use of green-wax sealings in the courts, were farmed out but amounted to

[25] The latter is omitted by Chandaman, apparently because its accounts did not pass through the Exchequer.
[26] The clearest account is in *Guide to the Public Records*, i. 258–9. One of the commissionerships was semi-hereditary in the Courthope family of Sussex.

little. Penal fines imposed in the courts were the most substantial of these various minor revenues.[27]

Another fiscal innovation of the 1670s is interesting for the direction in which it pointed, rather than important for what it achieved. The act 'for laying impositions upon proceedings at law', commonly known as the Law Duty, was a tax on legal documents and proceedings, the forerunner of the later Stamp Taxes. It was farmed for most of its duration (1671–80), but collection was the responsibility of particular, named officials in each court, who answered to a central office, controlled by the farmers except briefly in 1671–2 and 1675–6. The Law Duty is significant as an attempt to tax lawyers and their clients; the surviving records of its collection are of interest in providing information, otherwise hard to come by, about the internal structure of the courts.[28]

For the granting of parliamentary taxes on property and persons this was a time of experiment and variety besides repetition of the familiar. The Crown's need for such extraordinary revenues, which since 1641 could only be by consent of parliament, arose directly from the circumstances of the Restoration itself and then from the country's involvement in foreign war. The first and prime necessity was to pay off the ex-Cromwellian army as a condition of its peaceful demobilization and its members' return to civilian life; only second to this was the need to reduce the debt on naval expenditure, including unpaid seamen's wages, which had grown shockingly large since the latter years of the Protectorate. This explains the various taxes voted during the early years of the reign. The Dutch Wars of 1664–7 and 1672–4 necessitated further grants, as did the preparations for the pretended war against France in 1677–8. The kinds of tax which were voted included the traditional subsidy, constituting a rate in the pound on realty and personalty; resort was also had to the one-time parliamentarian assessment of the 1640s and 1650s, a fixed amount laid upon each

---

[27] Ibid., i. 7–8; Chandaman, *English Public Revenue*, 126, 128.
[28] Edward Hughes, 'The English Stamp Duties, 1664–1764', *Eng. Hist. Rev.*, 56 (1941) remains the best account; Chandaman, *English Public Revenue*, 121–4, demonstrates its ineffectuality in fiscal terms.

county and city, together with poll taxes graded according to the rank and wealth of individuals. All these grants involved the appointment of commissioners to oversee collection in each county, which was the responsibility of a receiver, usually paid so much in the pound raised rather than by salary; until 1671 the county commissioners were appointed by parliament in the text of the respective statutes, after that by the king, but with the tacit agreement of parliament. In 1667–70 an Exchange Office was set up, to obviate the need for large quantities of coin being transported from all over the country to London. This body was answerable directly to the Treasury, not the Exchequer; it overlapped in personnel with Agents who were appointed to oversee and hasten the nationwide collection and payment of the Hearth Tax; this in turn led to the development of a Tax Office with similar responsibilities for parliamentary grants, exclusively so from 1677. It is not a coincidence that two of the original Agents were ex-state's servants of the 1650s, one probably being a client of Lord Ashley, Chancellor of the Exchequer from 1661 to 1672; continuity was to be provided by a younger man, an obscure individual from Nottinghamshire, Bartholomew Fillingham, who was involved in tax collection as early as 1662–3 and served as one of the Agents from the early 1670s to the eve of his death in 1697. The evolution of the Tax Office as a trouble-shooting agency under the Treasury awaits its historian, but is yet another indicator of the Exchequer's inadequacy for purposes of fiscal management.[29]

OTHER DEPARTMENTS OF STATE

The institutions needed to provide for the armed forces of the crown were, as we should expect, much the most important of

---

[29] Baxter, *Treasury*, 26–9; Chandaman, *English Public Revenue*, 157, table 2; app. 2, sect. 5, pp. 326–9, 330, graph 6. If anything, Prof. Chandaman underestimated the significance of the Tax Office. For an alternative account to that given here see W. R. Ward, 'The Office of Taxes, 1665–1798', *Bull. IHR*, 25 (1952), 204–12.

these other departments. It seems logical to look at them in sequence according to their closeness, administratively speaking, to the king and the central executive.

V. THE POST OFFICE

The Post Office, sometimes also known as the Letter Office, was so closely under the authority of the Secretaries of State that it might almost equally well have been discussed earlier along with their other staffs. Since it was assumed that private correspondence was liable to be tampered with, in the real or supposed interests of the Crown, it is not surprising that there were close links between the Post Office and the world of intelligence and counter-espionage. In terms of management and finance, however, it was more like a semi-privatized agency. The senior Secretary of State was Post Master General, having a deputy Postmaster in actual charge under him, answerable for both the home and foreign letter services, with another subordinate in immediate charge of the London letter office and for the network of provincial postmasters or deputies, together with the packet-boat captains for the services to the continent from Dover and Harwich and to Ireland, normally from Holyhead. Unhappily for clear description, this is an oversimplification. The King's brother, the Duke of York had pension rights assigned on the postal revenues and eventually himself became Post Master General with Arlington as his deputy. So at times we have to identify deputies' deputies' deputies to find the people actually running things from day to day. At the Restoration the republican and ex-Leveller John Wildman was very briefly in charge; he was speedily removed and in fact spent much of the 1660s in prison, under what we should now call preventive detention: never put on trial then or later, Wildman was one of the great survivors in seventeenth-century England. He was replaced by Colonel Henry Bishop, an ex-royalist spy whom some contemporaries and some historians have believed was in fact a Cromwellian double agent.[30] Bishop farmed the

---

[30] P. R. Newman, *Royalist Officers in England and Wales, 1642–1660: A*

post office revenues for £21,500 a year from 1660 to 1663, and is credited with the invention of the (franked) postmark. The senior clerk of the London office, James Hickes, was probably responsible for the daily—and nightly—routine in the office. But when Bishop sold the farm to the royal favourite and Bedchamberman, Captain Daniel O'Neal in 1663, yet another ex-cavalier army officer, Colonel Philip Frowde, came in at some level between him and Hickes. For three years after O'Neal's death in 1664, his widow the Countess of Chesterfield (who had been made a peeress in her own right for financial help to the King in exile) received the financial benefits as if she were Post Mistress General.[31] A reversionary grant to Arlington and John Lord Berkeley of Stratton then took effect, control at the intermediate level apparently being exercised by the Secretary's brother Sir John Bennet (who ended his days as Lord Ossulston) together with Sir Philip Frowde, as the Colonel had by then become; but in practice the office was soon being managed by yet another deputy to Arlington, an otherwise unknown man, Andrew Ellis. It was his death in 1672 which led to the appointment of another ex-royalist army officer and Cavalier conspirator, Colonel Roger Whitley of Denbighshire and Chester, who effectively ran the Post Office for the next five years. Thanks to the fortunate survival of his letter-books (of outgoing correspondence with local postmasters and others), it is possible to obtain a much fuller and clearer picture of how the system actually worked than for any other period before the

---

Biographical Dictionary (New York and London, 1981), no. 122, suggests that he was a double agent; David Underdown, *Royalist Conspiracy in England, 1649–1660* (New Haven, Conn., 1960), 176, concluded that he was not. Be this as it may, Bishop lived for another thirty years but never held office again.

[31] This illustrates how family and marriage connections could interact with administrative arrangements. Her first husband, Henry Lord Stanhope (d. 1634) had predeceased his father (d. 1656), who was therefore succeeded in the Earldom of Chesterfield by her son Philip; her second husband, a Dutch nobleman, died early in 1660, and in 1662/3 she married O'Neal (himself the son and heir of an Old Irish landowner from county Down, and a convert from Rome to the Church of England). See *DNB*, under her second husband's surname, misspelt Kirkhoven instead of Kerckhoven, and Daniel O'Neill [*sic*]; *Hist. Parl.*, iii. 172–4; and above all an excellent series of articles by Donal F. Cregan in *Studia Hibernica*, iii–v (1963–5).

eighteenth century. In 1677 the Arlington–Berkeley grant terminated, and the Duke of York, in spite of his disqualification from office under the Test Act of 1673, assumed supreme control. He did not renew Whitley's appointment, putting in Frowde's son, Philip the younger, and one of his own servants, Thomas Gardiner, who seem to have remained in charge until the Revolution, apart from the sub-farm of the London 'penny post' to William Docwra in 1680–2 and then his appointment as a separate London Postmaster from 1682 to 1689. The only element of continuity during all these changes at the upper and middle levels was provided by the long-suffering James Hickes (never promoted and, to judge from his letters, always feeling put upon), whose rank or standing seems analogous to a chief petty officer in the modern Royal Navy, perhaps to an RSM in the Army, or to a Higher Executive Officer in the modern civil service. Turning to the financial aspect, the king's and other genuinely official correspondence were carried free, with allowance being made to the farmer or manager for this; the postal revenue arose from the carriage of private mails, the charges varying according to size, weight, and distance. We shall return to Whitley and some of the others mentioned here. Meanwhile it seems remarkable that such an institution worked as well as, on the whole, it seems to have done.[32]

VI. THE MINT

In any national (or federal) state, control over the currency is among the most jealously guarded of all prerogatives. Preserving the quality and thereby the value of the coinage is one of the tests by which rulers and regimes have often been

---

[32] J. C. Hemmeon, *The History of the British Post Office* (Cambridge, Mass., 1912), 25–7; Howard Robinson, *The British Post Office: A History* (Princeton, NJ, 1948), chs. 5 and 6; Brian Austen, *English Provincial Posts, 1633–1840: A Study Based on Kent Examples, 1633–1840* (London and Chichester, 1978), chs. 2–3 and app. 1; Jean Farrugia, *A Guide to Post Office Archives* (London, [1986–7]); J. W. M. Stone (ed.), *The Inland Posts (1392–1672): A Calendar of Historical Documents with Appendices* (London, 1987). See below, Ch. 4 sect. xiii for more on Whitley.

judged, even though most modern economists see more than solely monetary explanations for inflation and deflation. By this test Charles II and his advisers come out quite well, if more perhaps by good luck than anything else. After some initial fumbling and having to accept that not all existing coins of the republic could be called in and replaced overnight, the surviving pre-Civil War staff of the royal Mint were restored to their positions. Of the two Wardens, the most senior officials, one had been born in the 1590s, the other in 1603; the surviving Master, next most senior to them, was already into his seventies. His deputy, who soon succeeded to the Mastership, was the person effectively in charge for much of the reign (1662–80); Henry Slingsby, the younger son of a Yorkshire gentry family, was eventually disgraced on being found to owe the Crown large sums and was replaced by a troika of commissioners and later by a new Master, though not until the next reign. The most recent and authoritative history of the Mint suggests that the decline of the Wardenship into being a mere sinecure was only reversed by the appointment of Isaac Newton in 1697. Still, perhaps due in part to the Treasury's vigilance, there was no serious deterioration in the coinage or fall in the value of money during the reign; for demographic and economic, not monetary, reasons some prices were if anything tending downwards in the later, by contrast with the earlier seventeenth century. Much attention was devoted, even by the King himself and the Privy Council, to the chronic, seemingly intractable shortage of small change, and the question of whether halfpennies and farthings should be made of copper or of tin.[33]

---

[33] Sir John Craig, *The Mint: A History of the London Mint from AD287 to 1948* (Cambridge, 1953), chs. 9 and 10, has been largely superseded by C. E. Challis (ed.), *A New History of the Royal Mint* (Cambridge, 1992), pt. 3 and app. 2, by the editor himself. There are some additional references in the *Calendars of Treasury Books* for the 1670s–1680s, which amplify Challis's account on the administrative as opposed to the monetary side, where I defer wholly to him.

VII. THE TOWER

Since the Mint, as well as the royal Ordnance Office, was phys-
ically located in the Tower of London, it is sensible to look there
next. It was at once a state prison, a fortress, the site of two
departments of state, and the home of both the royal armoury
and the crown jewels, and of some government records (the
other 'record offices' were in Chancery Lane and Westminster
Hall). Its executive head was the Lieutenant. The holder of this
office from 1660 to 1679, Sir John Robinson, had impeccably
Anglican and royalist credentials but his capacity remains more
in doubt. We might think that he was lucky to survive 'Colonel'
Thomas Blood's audacious theft of the crown jewels (or at least
part of the regalia) in 1671; but the King turned this bizarre
episode into a kind of sick joke, thereby strengthening the case
for supposing that Blood was in fact already a double agent in
the government's service, indeed quite possibly before his
equally outrageous kidnapping of the Duke of Ormonde the
previous year.[34] Robinson survived until he became a political
victim of the Popish Plot–Exclusion crisis and was sacrificed by
the King in 1679. The subordinate staff of Porters and Warders
were financially dependent in part on fees and gratuities from
prisoners, with whom they therefore had a kind of symbiotic
relationship.[35]

VIII. OTHER PRISONS

We think of prisons primarily as places where people are sent as
a punishment after being convicted of serious criminal offences,
but in the seventeenth century this was only true to a very
limited extent. Most occupants of prisons were either insolvent

[34] Alan Marshall, 'Colonel Thomas Blood and the Restoration Political
Scene', *Hist. J.*, 32 (1982), 561–82, and Dr Marshall's book already cited.
[35] Both the *Hist. Parl.*, iii. 340–3 and the *DNB: Missing Persons*, ed. C. S.
Nicholls (Oxford, 1993) seek to rehabilitate him from Pepys's strictures. For
the numbers and duties of the Tower officers in 1677 see *CSPD, 1677–8*, pp.
333–4 (PRO, SP29/396/74 adds little to what is in the *Calendar*).

debtors (in the Fleet or the Marshalsea), unbailed defendants pending trial, prisoners of state detained without trial, or convicted felons awaiting either execution or transportation (and occasionally pardon).[36] The Wardens or Keepers of the London prisons were predictably unpopular; perhaps the most notorious was Sir John Lenthall, Marshal of the Marshalsea, but even he was able to pass his office on to his son or grandson.[37] Prisons other than the Tower were more like semi-privatized agencies than government departments.

IX. THE ORDNANCE OFFICE

The formal structure of this office had changed relatively little since early Stuart times. The Armoury, previously a separate sub-department, in charge of hand-to-hand weapons and ceremonial arms and armour, was absorbed into the Ordnance during the 1660s. More significant was its continued responsibility for naval guns and munitions as well as for land-based artillery and handguns (muskets, pistols, etc.) for both land and sea service. As the excellent modern monograph on it demonstrates, the scale of the office's activities and hence its importance fluctuated according to the country's situation, peaking in time of war. The Mastership of the Ordnance was placed in commission from 1664 to 1670 and again in 1679–82; whether this should be seen as part of a drive for greater efficiency or as owing to royal indecisiveness about whom to appoint is not immediately clear. The Lieutenant, who ranked next to the Master and was often the effective head of the office, ceased to be also its accounting officer with the creation of a separate

---

[36] Until the Transportation Act of George I's reign, this took place by prerogative orders from the king to the judges. The state papers for Charles's reign contain many instances, but I doubt whether it would be possible to arrive at a reliable total of those so reprieved and shipped to the plantations.

[37] The *DNB* appears to telescope the two Sir John Lenthalls. The prison keeper and ex-Speaker's brother died in 1668 (Aylmer, *State's Servants*, 139, 163); for William Lenthall, Marshal 1669–87 and 90–7, see *Hist. Parl.*, ii, 733–4, although *Visitations of Berkshire*, ii (Harleian Soc., 57 (1908)), 169–70, shows him as the son, not the grandson of Sir John.

Paymastership—an instance, as we have seen with the Great Wardrobe, where an enlargement of the establishment seems likely to have led to greater efficiency. Relations between the Ordnance and the Navy were seldom easy and often fraught, but the career of George Legge (who became Lord Dartmouth) straddled the two. According to Dr Tomlinson, Dartmouth's reforms embodied in his Instructions for the Office issued in 1683, should be seen as regulating and codifying existing practices rather than as innovatory.[38] While numbers are not everything, Tomlinson's figures for the totals of officers at all levels on the payroll reflect these fluctuations: in 1667 about 175; 1679–81 c.237; 1683 c.60; 1692 c.268; 1704 nearly 450.[39]

While English regiments fought on the continent of Europe, attached to both the French and the Dutch armies, the only land wars in which the English crown was directly involved on any scale were the campaigns in and around Tangier against the Moroccans. The Navy, by contrast, was fighting major wars in home waters in 1665–7 and 1672–4, and was engaged in more distant parts of the world for much more of the time than that. This difference is naturally reflected in the respective histories of the two services.

X. THE ARMY: GUARDS AND GARRISONS

The process by which England gradually came to have a peacetime standing army is an important part of later seventeenth-century political history. After the successful demobilization of 1660–1, the military establishment which remained was initially very modest. Although the threat of invasion or at least of coastal raids saw temporary expansion in the mid–1660s, after the conclusion of peace in 1667 the army consisted of the King's (mounted) Life Guards, his regiment of horse, and two regiments of foot (his own and the Lord General's). There were in

[38] Howard Tomlinson, *Guns and Government: The Ordnance Office under the Later Stuarts* (London, 1979).
[39] Ibid., 14–15, 16–17, 218, 220.

addition twenty-two garrisons, almost all (except Windsor and York) being around the coast or else on off-shore islands. Including general officers, those of regiments serving abroad, and contingencies, the total establishment was reckoned at £208,631 a year.[40] The administrative structure was comparably modest, consisting of the Lord General's Secretary who became known, however anomalously, as the Secretary-at-War, the Muster-Master-General in charge of recruiting, and most important of all the Paymaster, which was the post held by the great Stephen Fox from 1661 to 1676, and again by proxy in 1679–80. Between the death of William Clarke in 1666 and the appointment of another very distinguished administrator, William Blathwayt, in 1683, the Secretaryship at War was held by a near nonentity who has left virtually no mark at all on the history of his time. The way in which the guards and garrisons were financed has been so fully and clearly explained by Fox's biographer that more need not be said here. On the other hand, the patronage involved in military appointments, besides the purchase of commissions, was of increasing importance as the army grew larger in the 1670s and 1680s.[41]

XI. THE NAVY

Historians are generally agreed that this was a significant period in the history of the Navy, or perhaps we should say in the naval history of England. This is not the time or place to attempt a retelling of that story, which in any case is now in surer hands than mine.[42] There is, however, room for some modest revision of the administrative aspects of this history. Two separate departments of state were involved. The High Court of

---

[40] PRO, SP29/218/33. This excludes the Tangier garrison and the Army in Ireland, besides any small units in other colonies.

[41] John Childs, *The Army of Charles II* (London, Toronto, and Buffalo, 1976), ch. 3, sect. 1 and ch. 5, for finance and administration; app. A sets out the growth in the number of regiments.

[42] The second volume of N. A. M. Rodger's *Naval History of Britain*, covering 1649–1815, may well appear before this book is published.

Admiralty was ancient as a judicial body, but the Admiralty was of more recent origin as the supreme policy-making body under the monarch for all matters maritime. As such, it was tiny, consisting from the Restoration of James Duke of York as Lord Admiral, Sir William Coventry, the youngest son of Charles I's Lord Keeper, as his Secretary, and a single Clerk. In a manner which is rather comparable to the development of the Treasury, growth was accelerated when the Admiralty was put into commission on James's forced retirement as an avowed Roman Catholic in 1673. Besides the twelve Lords Commissioners (of whom Prince Rupert was named first though it is not clear that he presided), and their new Secretary, Samuel Pepys, there were now two clerks, a messenger and a legal counsel, in addition to the Judge Advocate of the Fleet, his deputy and other officers of the Court of Admiralty.[43] The Lord Admiral had a historic right to serve as commander-in-chief at sea, especially in wartime, and the change to commissioners possibly hastened the development of a regular hierarchy of seagoing admirals, the last Lord Admiral (not a seagoing one) being Queen Anne's husband Prince George of Denmark in the early 1700s.

Administration was the business of the Navy Board or Office, a Tudor creation which was to be abolished and its staff amalgamated with those of the Admiralty in 1832. It is almost impossibly difficult not to see the Navy Office of the 1660s through the eyes of its most junior principal officer, the Clerk of the Acts; and in many ways it would be perverse not to do so. Of the others, the Treasurer was not a member of the Board and was often somewhat remote from naval affairs. Given the utter inadequacy of Sir George Carteret, who held the office from 1661 to 16671, this was just as well, though his presence certainly contributed to the navy's financial difficulties. Of the other principal officers, Sir Robert Slingsby, appointed Comptroller in 1660, only held the post for fourteen months before his death; his successor Sir John Mennes had been a gallant royalist naval commander in the Civil War; although only in his early sixties he is portrayed by

---

[43] Sainty, *Admiralty Officials, 1660–1870*; Rodger, *The Admiralty* (Lavenham, 1979).

the diarist as distinctly failing, if not sinking, into senility. Sir William Batten, the Surveyor, and Sir William Penn, the more active of the two remaining commissioners 'without portfolio', were Pepys's particular bêtes noires, the 'two Sir Williams' of the Diary; the other Commissioner extraordinary, Lord Berkeley of Stratton, was distinctly less active. Both Sir Williams had a parliamentarian (in Penn's case also a Cromwellian) background, and both had certainly been capable officers. So perhaps we should allow for an element of caricature by the diarist, who so cordially disliked them. The link with the Admiralty was strengthened when Coventry became an extra Commissioner in 1662, and Pepys certainly saw him as setting a standard for the rest of them, if his admiration was at first perhaps a little uncritical. Lord Brouncker who was a Commissioner from 1664 to 1680 was quite unqualified in naval matters; he is best known as the first President of the Royal Society, a position which Pepys, who detested him, was himself to hold much later in the century. On Batten's death in 1667 he was succeeded in the Surveyorship by another professional, 'Colonel' Thomas Middleton, previously resident Commissioner at Portsmouth. Other Commissioners were added in 1665 and 1669. The number of clerks also began to increase during the later 1660s and the 1670s. It is difficult to know how far the Navy Board's positive achievements in these early years should be ascribed to Pepys, with the backing of Coventry, in spite of the allegedly senile Mennes, the two corrupt and idle Sir Williams and the odious Brouncker. While successive diary entries for 1662–3 show Pepys resolving to master every aspect of the business of the office, in order to increase his own influence as well as to serve the King more effectively, it seems intrinsically unlikely that he could have done it all single-handed. As his modern biographers have pointed out, he was clearly much influenced by William Coventry, who put Pepys on his mettle and persuaded him to take himself seriously as an administrator.[44]

---

[44] Arthur Bryant, *Samuel Pepys: The Man in the Making* (London, 1933 and 1947) and more particularly, Richard Ollard, *Samuel Pepys: A Biography* (London, 1974 and 1977).

If the navy was run from Tower Hill, and from the Admiralty in Whitehall, the actual work of fitting out, repairing, supplying, and manning of the ships was largely undertaken in the four principal royal dockyards: Deptford, Woolwich, Chatham, and Portsmouth. The senior established officials in each were the Master Shipwright, the Master Attendant (a kind of Captain-in-charge), the Clerk of the Cheque, and the Storekeeper. There were in addition Navy Commissioners who were not members of the Board in London but either had a roving commission or more often were responsible for overseeing a particular yard. The correspondence of these men with either the Clerk of the Acts individually or with the Board collectively provides a marvellous—and relatively under-used—source for insight into the real workings of the system. This is true of the returned colonial Thomas Middleton at Portsmouth in 1664–7, and a little later of Anthony Deane and John Tippetts at various of the yards. When there was no resident Commissioner, the senior dockyard officials had correspondingly more day-to-day autonomy and hence more responsibility for whether matters went well or badly. This can be seen at Portsmouth after Middleton left to become Surveyor, and temporarily at Chatham after Commissioner Peter Pett's disgrace in 1667. Deane, arguably the foremost ship designer since the first Phineas Pett in the early seventeenth century, who has the added distinction of having taught Pepys how to use a slide rule, served as Master Shipwright at both Harwich and Portsmouth before in turn becoming a Commissioner in 1672.[45] The establishments at Harwich, Sheerness, and Plymouth were smaller and definitely secondary to the big four. What happened there and in the Victualling Office in East London was crucial to the navy's well-being and to how it performed at sea. Naval victualling was farmed until 1683, and for the first half of the reign was in the hands of Sir Denis Gauden who had been prin-

---

[45] For accounts of Deane's remarkable career see *DNB*; A. W. Johns, 'Sir Anthony Deane', *Mariner's Mirror*, 11 (1925), 164–93; *Hist. Parl.*, ii. 200–1; *Pepys Diary*, x, *Companion*. If he was indeed a relative of the Commonwealth Admiral, Richard Deane (killed in battle, 1653) then—like many others—he too may have had a puritan-republican past to live down.

cipal victualler to both the navy and the army in the 1650s. From 1667 one of the regular Commissioners was Comptroller of Victualling Accounts, though this by no means overcame the evils of rotten and inadequate food and drink. Although Commissioner Pett was made the scapegoat for the Medway disaster of June 1667, failures at sea in the two Dutch Wars were only in part due to administrative weaknesses. As for the Medway, the question was (and is) whether Pett could and should have constructed an impregnable boom across the river somewhere below Chatham, instead of relying on the chain which the Dutch ships succeeded in breaking. This apart, the general level of corruption, much of it admittedly only petty pilfering, catalogued by Middleton at Portsmouth and by Pepys, Tippetts, and others at Chatham, was endemic in a system where officials and workmen were inadequately paid and were allowed to take perquisites instead of having decent and punctual wages. How far things had improved in these respects by the end of the reign is something to which we shall return.[46]

XII. THE OFFICE OF ARMS

This body, also known as the Heralds' College, has long laid claims to be an independent corporation under the Earl Marshal, not a government department. Fortunately we need not enter here into the controversy about its present-day status. Under Charles II the office of Earl Marshal was held by various peers of the Howard family, that is those who were neither insane nor Roman Catholic, and at other times by Commissioners. Apart from the Earl Marshal's role at royal

[46] For the Navy Office and its staff see J. M. Collinge, *Navy Board Officials, 1660–1832* (London, 1978). Unfortunately Dr Collinge decided to exclude the Treasurer and his staff and the Commissioners in the ports and yards, on the grounds that they rarely attended the Board (see p. 20 n. 1); Jonathan M. Coad, *The Royal Dockyards, 1690–1850* (Aldershot and Brookfield, Vt., 1989), although fully documented and lavishly illustrated, is not concerned with this period. The correspondence of Middleton and other 'out of town' Commissioners is in the State Papers Domestic down to 1673, thereafter scattered in PRO, ADM 106 (see below, Ch. 4, sect. vi).

coronations, weddings, and funerals and at trials of peers, the College was responsible for registering the pedigrees and coat armour of armigerous families, disclaiming those not so entitled, and overseeing funeral escutcheons. It also presented cases arising from disputes about precedence, coats of arms, and so forth before the ancient Court of Chivalry.[47] Since heraldic visitations of the counties were resumed in the 1660s and were to continue until the eve of the Revolution, the Office of Arms was an active agency of government under Charles and James II. Its staff consisted of the three Kings of Arms, six Heralds, and four Pursuivants in ordinary, sometimes with a few additional 'extra-ordinaries'. These posts were all crown appointments whose holders received annual fees from the Exchequer. It is therefore right and proper for them to be included here. Moreover, the lists of the county visitations are a valuable source for the study of family descents and other connections among the armigerous gentry. The scholarly traditions of the College were ably maintained by two of the Kings of Arms, who were historians of the mid-century troubles; one of them, Sir William Dugdale, also being among the leading medieval scholars of his time, the other, Sir Edward Walker, a more narrowly political author. Elias Ashmole, Windsor Herald, became the historian of the Order of the Garter, an undertaking surely nearer to his heart than his work as Comptroller of the Excise. The sole surviving herald from Cromwellian times, Edward Bysshe, was restored as Norroy-King-of-Arms and permitted to serve out his time.[48]

XIII. OUTLYERS: IRELAND AND THE PLANTATIONS

What has been put in and left out here will inevitably be more

[47] For which see G. D. Squibb, *The High Court of Chivalry* (Oxford, 1955).
[48] Besides Squibb see A. R. Wagner, *Collections and Records of the College of Arms* (1951); id., *Heralds and Heraldry*, 2nd edn. (Oxford, 1956). For assessments of Dugdale and Walker as contemporary historians see Roger Macgillivray, *Restoration Historians and the English Civil War* (The Hague, 1974); for Dugdale's overall scholarly achievement, D. C. Douglas, *English Scholars, 1660–1730* (London, 1938, 1951, and more recent paperback reprints) has not in my opinion been superseded.

controversial. It may seem arbitrary that the viceregal court and central administration in Ireland should be included in this study, whereas the government of Scotland is excluded. This is not simply because I am more ignorant of Scottish than of Irish history (although that is indeed the case). Scotland was a genuinely separate kingdom, governed and administered by Scots, even though the Scottish Secretary of State, John Maitland Earl (later Duke) of Lauderdale, was a major figure on the English political scene. By contrast, since the completion of the English conquest of Ireland under the Tudors and the extension of English settlement there, that country had been ruled as if it were a subordinate province, in spite of the King of England having (since Henry VIII) a separate title as King of Ireland. It had the name but not the status of a kingdom. The Lord Lieutenancy, or its less honorific alternative the Lord Deputyship, was one of the most prestigious, if also most hazardous offices at the King's disposal. After the abortive offer of the viceroyalty to George Monck at the Restoration, with the ex-parliamentarian Lord Robartes as his Deputy, there was a short period of rule by Lords Justices (equivalent to the post being put into commission). The Lieutenancy was then settled on the Anglo-Irish but protestant magnate the Marquis of Ormonde (soon elevated to a Dukedom), who held it from 1662 to 1669 and again from 1677 to the end of the reign. In between these two periods under Ormonde, whose removal reflected the shifting balance of political power in England rather than any substantial change of policy in Ireland, came three other viceroys: two, the rather gloomy (perhaps depressive) Robartes and the lightweight ex-cavalier Lord Berkeley, did not make much of a showing; then came the young Earl of Essex, son of a cavalier martyr of 1649, but who was himself to end as a suicide (or murder victim, as some historians still believe) in the Tower, as an alleged Whig conspirator against the King years later (in 1683). Essex had the potential and the inclinations to be an administrative reformer, but achieved little. The viceroy was assisted by a Privy Council but, even more than in England, this was far too large a body to be of any use, and in practice he relied on a few great officers of state and other councillors plus his own staff. The other great offices were much as in England: Lord Chancellor, Lord Treasurer, Chancellor of the Exchequer, Secretaries of State, crown law officers, chief justices, and so on. There was one important exception to this; the post of Vice- (or Under) Treasurer was not combined with the Chancellorship of the Exchequer as in England; its holder, also known as the Treasurer-at-Wars—a reminder of the country's bloody past— was for much of the time the key financial office-holder, though the Irish revenues were alternatively farmed, managed with a farm, and finally put under direct management by Commissioners. No Irish parliament met between the later 1660s and the late 1680s, and there was no direct parliamentary taxation in Ireland for most of the reign.

Royal policy in Ireland was dominated by concerns about security, with at least on paper a larger army than in England. The next greatest preoccupation was the land question: who was to get what back and keep what, after the upheavals and vast changes of ownership which had followed the English reconquest in 1650–3 and then the fall of the Republic and the Restoration in 1659–60. Religious and ethnic differences were of course present too, but for much of the time below the surface, or taking the form of conflicts over titles to land. As in the government of Ireland before the Civil War, in Strafford's time and earlier, it is possible to classify individuals according to whether they were new and very recent arrivals from England or belonged to families long resident in Ireland, and if the latter whether 'Old English' or Irish, protestant or catholic; as before, the Anglo-Irish straddled the religious divide. During Charles II's reign, the traditional regional divisions, corresponding to two of the four ancient Irish provinces, of Munster and Connaught, under subordinate Lord Presidents, were phased out. Without going into further detail here, the government and the army were fertile fields for the exercise of patronage, either direct from England or at one remove through the viceroy and his circle.

Some of this was replicated on a far smaller scale in those parts of the early English colonial empire which were under direct royal control, not in the hands of chartered companies or proprietors. These comprised Virginia (since 1624), Jamaica (conquered under Cromwell in 1655 but not returned to Spain by Charles II), Barbados and the Leeward Islands (from which the various proprietors or claimants were effectively bought out by the mid-1660s), and—as part of the King's marriage dowry from the Crown of Portugal—Bombay (which was very soon transferred, to be governed, guarded, and financed by the East India Company) and Tangier, also acquired from Portugal (until it was abandoned to the neighbouring Moroccans in 1684). Massachusetts only became a crown colony after the loss of its original charter in 1683; New York (taken from the Dutch in 1664, lost to them again in 1672, and finally regained in 1674) only with the accession of its royal proprietor to the throne in 1685. Of the royal or crown colonies, Virginia was easily the foremost in status, wealth, and population. Naturally the government of these territories did not compare in size or cost with that of Ireland; nevertheless many of the senior office-holders were new arrivals from England, not established settlers, and their respective administrations can properly be thought of as extensions of the royal government at home, although more on the scale of an English city or county than of a province, let alone a kingdom.

There was no single minister or department of state responsible for the Crown's overseas possessions, nor for foreign and colonial trade. In fact this was still substantially true down to the eve of American Independence a hundred years later. Executive orders to colonial governors normally came from a Secretary of State; on the other hand management of the colonial customs service became increasingly the business of the Treasury, either directly or through the Customs Commissioners. By the end of the reign this was in the capable and energetic hands of William Blathwayt, assisted at the American end by the equally energetic, if unpopular, Edward Randolph. Very much in continuation of the 1640s and 1650s, this period saw a bewildering succession of councils, commissions, and committees for trade, foreign plantations, or both. The Trade and Plantations Commission of 1672–4 is distinguished by having had two successive Secretaries of quite exceptional talent. Dr Benjamin Worsley, a well-known figure from the 1650s, was appointed in 1672, but left office the following year, being one of the very few Protestant nonconformists forced out by the 1673 Test Act, through not being prepared to receive Anglican communion or subscribe to the other requirements which were imposed. His successor was John Locke, who had already been hoisted out of relative academic obscurity by his patron, the Earl of Shaftesbury, but was destined to lose office again when the Commission was dissolved a year after the Earl had himself been removed from his place as Lord Chancellor (and chairman of the Commission). From 1675 until the establishment of the Board of Trade in the later 1690s, the Lords of Trade and Plantations were little more than a standing committee of the Privy Council. None of these bodies had much in the way of executive powers, and indeed enjoyed only varying influence in their advisory capacities. Yet their very existence indicates the attention being paid to matters commercial and imperial by the governing elite; the elaboration and enforcement of the so-called Navigation Acts, also known as the 'trade laws', provides the clearest evidence of this.[49]

Plans for closer union with Scotland came to nothing, its forcible union with England (1652–60) having automatically lapsed at the Restoration. The links at the very top were to be underlined by the role in turn of the King's son, Monmouth, as commander-in-chief, to put down a local rebellion, and then of his brother, as something nearer to a viceroy, though in substance not in name, during the last years of the reign.

---

[49] The elderly monograph by C. M. Andrews, *British Committees, Commissions and Councils of Trade and Plantations, 1622–1675* (Baltimore, 1908; repr. New York, 1970) should still be consulted; see also R. P. Bieber, *The Lords of Trade and Plantations, 1675–1696* (Allentown, Pa., 1919). For Worsley see Aylmer, *State's Servants*, 270–2, 416–17; and Charles Webster, *The Great Instauration: Science, Medicine and Reform, 1626–1660* (London, 1975), *passim,* and *From Paracelsus to Newton: Magic and the Making of Modern Science* (Cambridge 1982), 32 and 45 nn. 43–4; for Locke see Maurice Cranston, *John Locke* (London and New York, 1957, and later reprints); K. H. D. Haley, *The First Earl of Shaftesbury* (Oxford, 1968), ch. 12; E. S. de Beer (ed.), *The Correspondence of John Locke* (8 vols., Oxford, 1976–89) is a remarkable feat of editing but adds little for this aspect of Locke's career. For Blathwayt and Randolph see refs in Ch. 4 below.

Moreover, one of Charles's very latest appointments was that of the existing Scottish Secretary (Lauderdale's successor), the Earl of Middleton, to be one of the Secretaries of State in England. There was a thin sprinkling of Scots in the royal Privy and Bedchambers but nothing comparable to the situation under the early Stuart kings. Whatever view is taken of the Union of 1707, the government of Scotland remained distinct until then, and the overlap in personnel was very slight.

XIV. LAW AND THE COURTS

In this area of government the upheavals of the mid-century were more obvious and direct in their effects, that is where there were any at all. The Act of 1641 which had abolished the Court of Star Chamber, along with other conciliar jurisdiction, was not repealed. Nor was that which abolished the Court of High Commission, although James II was to try to reintroduce it under another name. The Council of the North, with its equity court at York, was not resurrected, although there were intermittent rumours that the most erratic and unreliable of all Charles II's leading favourites and ministers, George Villiers, second Duke of Buckingham, aspired to become Lord President of the North. Precisely why the Council for Wales and the Marches, with its court at Ludlow, was revived is a little more puzzling. The court at York had been closely identified with its last but one Lord President, the greatest but most feared and hated of all Charles I's ministers, Thomas Wentworth Earl of Strafford; and it was therefore singled out for condemnation by the Long Parliament. The court at Ludlow may actually have been less popular with regional litigants but had no comparable political associations.[50]

---

[50] For York see HMC, *Seventh Report*, app., House of Lords MSS, 147, 154; *Lords Journals*, xi. 293; for Wales see Penry Williams, 'The Attack on the Council in the Marches, 1603–1642', *Trans. Hon. Soc. Cymmrodorion, for 1961*, pt. I, pp. 1–22, and id., 'The Activity of the Council in the Marches under the Early Stuarts', *Welsh Hist. Rev.*, 1 (1961), 133–60. I am not aware of any attempt to carry the story forward from 1660 to 1688, but see below, Ch. 4, sect. xii, on Henry Somerset, First Duke of Beaufort.

The Court of Wards and Liveries had first been abolished by parliamentary ordinance in 1646, a form of legislation not recognized by royalists. Its demise was made legally definitive by statute as part of the Restoration revenue settlement in 1660–1. The non-fiscal business of the Court, to do with the property rights and interests of widows, orphans, and lunatics among the landed classes, seems to have been de facto transferred to the Court of Chancery.[51]

The ecclesiastical courts, other than High Commission, were reconstituted in 1660–2, but they were only royal institutions as it were at one remove, and thus do not come within our scope here. There was one exception to this. The Prerogative Court of Canterbury, in charge of wills and probates, had been laicized and had its jurisdiction extended to cover all testamentary business in the whole country during the 1650s. From 1661 its jurisdiction was again restricted to the province of Canterbury, besides being reduced by the restored diocesan and archdeaconry courts, and once more became technically ecclesiastical, although its senior judge was a direct royal appointee.[52]

The changes of 1641 and after had more effect on the equity courts, or—to be more precise—the equity jurisdictions of the surviving courts, than on the common law. Chancery was the principal equity court, and from the time of the Interregnum there were fewer alternatives to its jurisdiction; this remained so after the Restoration. The only judges able to give final decisions were the Lord Chancellor (or Lord Keeper) and his deputy, the Master of the Rolls. The other eleven Masters in ordinary acted as intermediate or subordinate judges, processing cases as they wended their ways through the court, but not deciding on them. All legal business coming to the court had to be channelled through one or other of the Six Clerks, each of whom had deputies and a large staff of

---

[51] H. E. Bell, *An Introduction to the History and Records of the Court of Wards and Liveries* (Cambridge, 1953); for Chancery see the next section; for this point see W. Holdsworth, *History of English Law*, vi, 2nd edn. (London, 1937), 648.
[52] Aylmer, *State's Servants*, 33; C. J. Kitching, 'Probate during the Civil War and Interregnum', *J. Soc. Archivists*, 5, pts. 5–6 (1976), 283–93, 346–56.

under clerks. A serious attempt to reform Chancery had been made under the Protectorate, but had collapsed by 1658–9. In his capacity as Lord Chancellor, Edward Hyde Earl of Clarendon made one or two attempts at reform but appears to have achieved little. Not until the appointment of Heneage Finch, created Earl of Nottingham, who was Lord Keeper in 1673–5 and then Lord Chancellor from 1675 to his death in 1680, was there a professional lawyer who had positive ideas about the reform of equity, combined with the political influence needed to put these into effect. Every successive Lord Chancellor or Lord Keeper issued orders, jointly with Grimston, the Master of the Rolls, for the better regulation of the court, with such monotonous frequency that we can only doubt whether these had any result at all. Whether or not because of Nottingham's changes in the way equity operated for certain types of case, the volume of incoming business seems to have been at an all-time peak in the mid-1680s and to have declined again thereafter.[53]

The only real challenge to Chancery's jurisdiction came from the equity side of the Court of Exchequer. This had been in existence since Elizabethan times, if not earlier, but from 1649 the rule that litigants there must be either accountants or debtors of the State became an accepted legal fiction, and one which could not be challenged. This continued after the Restoration; whether it should be seen as a rare fruit of the republican movement for law reform, or simply as an autonomous development within the legal system is unclear. More important, this jurisdiction, channelled through the King's Remembrancer's office,

---

[53] George William Sanders, *Orders of the High Court of Chancery and Statutes of the Realm Relating to Chancery, from the Earliest Period to the Present Time*, I, pts. i and ii (London, 1845), 296–313, 314–16, 318–20, 322–3, 324, 328–32, 333, 340–1, 342–4, 345, *et seq.*, 357, *et seq.*, app. pp. 1050–77 (a mine of information, not so far as I know superseded); D. E. C. Yale (ed.), *Lord Nottingham's Chancery Cases*, i and ii (Selden Soc., 73 and 79 (1957, 1961)), with long and valuable introductions, if hard going for non-lawyers like myself; Henry Horwitz, *A Guide to Chancery Equity Records and Procedures, 1600–1800* (PRO, Kew, 1995 and 1998), also Horwitz and Charles Moreton (comp.), *Samples of Chancery Pleadings and Suits: 1627, 1685, 1735, and 1785.* (List and Index Soc., 257 (1995)) are extremely helpful.

grew significantly in scale and popularity, evidently offering a quicker and cheaper alternative to that of Chancery.[54]

The common law courts—King's Bench, Common Pleas, and Exchequer—would seem to have been less affected by the upheavals of the mid-century than almost any other part of the central government. Not enough work has been done on the records of these courts to say with confidence whether or not the main pre-Civil War trend continued, namely that the pleas (or private actions) side of King's Bench and of the Exchequer of Pleas were gaining business at the expense of Common Pleas. It is, however, generally agreed that the total volume of common-law litigation was declining. Logically, therefore, we might expect competition between rival courts to have intensified; but insofar as the size of the legal profession, at least the number of barristers, was also shrinking, this might have cancelled out. Below the judges the most senior officials in King's Bench were the Coroner, or Attorney, sometimes known as the Clerk of the Crown, and on the private or pleas side the Chief Clerk, whose office was one of the most lucrative in the entire administration. In Common Pleas, those next in seniority were the three Prothonotaries, the Chirographer and the Custos Brevium. In the Exchequer, below the Barons, came the Prothonotary, or Clerk of the Pleas and his deputy, the Master of the Pleas office.[55]

---

[54] W. H. Bryson, *The Equity Side of the Exchequer: Its Jurisdiction, Administration, Procedures and Records* (Cambridge, 1975), a valuable monograph. Prof. Horwitz is preparing another PRO Handbook on Exchequer equity proceedings and records. For helpful suggestions I am also grateful to Prof. Margaret Hunt and other participants in the symposium on credit, held in Oxford in September 2000, and organized by Nicholas Mayhew, Keeper of the coin collections in the Ashmolean Museum.

[55] See *Guide to the Public Records*, i, introductory sections on each of these courts. I am very grateful to Prof. J. H. Baker, QC, for his help with the holders of these offices. On the profession see W. R. Prest, *The Rise of the Barristers. A Social History of the English Bar, 1590–1640* (Oxford, 1986), and David Lemmings, *The Inns of Court and the English Bar, 1680–1730* (Oxford, 1990). Apart from Baker's fascinating article on Sir Thomas Robinson (Chief Prothonotary), in *Bodleian Library Record*, 10 (1978), 27–40, I know of nothing to bridge the chronological gap between Prest and Lemmings, though there are scattered references in various volumes of Holdsworth's monumental *History of English Law*. J. H. Baker, *The Order of*

The common-law judges, particularly the two Chief Justices, were in the fullest sense political appointees. Those accused of crimes against the state were normally tried in King's Bench. If the offences alleged against them were strictly financial, to do with the royal revenues, their case would be heard in the Exchequer. The extent to which the Stuart kings were held to have manipulated judicial appointments for political purposes was to be reflected in the post-Revolution change in their tenure; until very recent times this operated in such a way as to make them for practical purposes irremovable. The twelve judges of the three courts and (if they could not all act, owing to illness, etc.) the most senior of the King's Sergeants at Law, also provided a vital link between English central and local government, in conducting the half-yearly assizes, two of them taking each of the six groups of counties (or circuits) into which the country was divided for this purpose. The county of Chester (a royal palatinate) was included in one of the four 'Great Sessions', the circuits into which Wales was divided, and was thus outside the English assize system. The crown law officers, that is the Attorney- and the Solicitor-General, were closely related to the chief justices as legal and constitutional advisers to the king and privy council. Rather confusingly some individual courts also had an official called an Attorney, as a kind of crown prosecutor, while the major financial and revenue departments also had their own Solicitors. The post of Treasury Solicitor can be traced at least as far back as the 1650s and was reinstituted from 1661, yet even by the end of the reign it had not attained anything like its later importance. By the 1670s both the Customs and the Excise had their own Solicitors; their functions, however, are often hard to distinguish from those of the Tax Agents, although they would obviously have needed to have some legal training and experience, which not all the agents possessed. The rank of King's Counsel existed but was not yet a regular, recognized step up in the legal profession so much as an occasional mark of royal favour. For example, there

Sergeants of Law: A Chronicle of Creations, with Related Texts and a Historical Introduction (Selden Soc., suppl. ser., 5 (London, 1984)) is definitive on this elite group within the profession of common-law pleaders.

seem to have been about five such in the later 1660s and only about twelve in the later 1670s.[56]

The other law courts have a miscellaneous appearance but should not be overlooked. The High Court of Admiralty was concerned with prize cases and other maritime disputes. It was a court of civil law, in that the basis of its jurisdiction was more like that of the ecclesiastical courts and that of Chivalry. With the naval wars of the 1660s and 1670s and the growth of over-seas trade we might have expected that the volume of business in the Admiralty would have been increasing, but in fact cases concerning ships, their cargoes, and merchants' assets were also being dealt with in Chancery and probably in Common Pleas as well, although it had actually been a jurisdictional dispute with King's Bench which had led to the Admiralty's powers being defined, and to some extent restricted, earlier in the century (1630–2). Again under Charles II, following Interregnum prece-dents, disputes about prize vessels and cargoes were entrusted to special commissioners during the two Dutch wars.[57]

The two royal Duchies of Lancaster and Cornwall had their own courts. Of these the Court of Duchy Chamber had been successively restricted, abolished, and re-established under the Long Parliament, the Commonwealth, and the Protectorate. The volume of business which was transacted in it is hard to assess.[58] Likewise with the Court of the Stannaries, where the King's profits arose from the controls over tin mining in Cornwall and Devon rather than from conventional land revenues as with the Duchy of Lancaster.

The Palace Court which had replaced the Courts of the Verge

---

[56] Sainty, *A List of the English Law Officers, King's Counsel and Holders of Patents of Precedence* (Selden Soc., suppl. ser., 7 (1987)) and id., *The Judges of England, 1272–1990: A List of Judges of the Superior Courts* (ibid., 10 (1993)) have put the identification of these posts and their holders on a wholly more reliable footing than ever before, but I know of nothing which deals specifically with departmental Solicitors.

[57] Giuseppi, *Guide*, i. 283–90; Aylmer, *King's Servants* (2nd edn., 1974), 53–4, and id., *State's Servants*, 33.

[58] Robert Somerville, *Office-holders in the Duchy and County Palatine of Lancaster from 1603* (London and Chichester, 1972). I am extremely grateful to the late Sir Robert Somerville, KCVO, for much help and friendly advice over the years concerning the Duchy and other matters.

and of the Marshalsea in 1630 was reconstituted in 1664. In effect it was the jurisdictional arm of the royal household, though serious disorder in the royal presence usually went straight to higher authority.[59] Finally, peers had to be tried by their peers, that is by a specially constituted court, normally assembled by the Earl Marshal or his deputies and presided over by the Lord Steward or his deputies. This came near to being a form of parliamentary jurisdiction, but is to be distinguished from the House of Lords sitting in judicial capacity, as it did in actions of impeachment where the Commons were the prosecutors.[60]

XV. PARLIAMENT

To write about English central government and to leave out parliament would be, if not to play *Hamlet* without the Prince, then at least perhaps to stage *Macbeth* without Duncan or Macduff.

The executive functions which the Long Parliament had exercised from 1641 to 1653 and again in 1659–60 had automatically lapsed when this body dissolved itself two months before the Restoration. Yet, as we have seen, that event was not a total reaction, even although the King's return was substantially unconditional. There was to be a parliamentary session or at any rate a meeting of parliament in every calendar year but three until the last four years of Charles's reign. That is to elide or pass over the remarkable fact that a single parliament lasted for eighteen of these years (1661–79) with numerous adjournments and prorogations. In what sense, if any, this made parliament a more regular part of the country's government is much harder to define. Fortunately this is not a constitutional history of Charles II's reign, so I feel justified in sidestepping that question, or anyway in approaching it obliquely.[61] The Convention

---

[59] Giuseppi, *Guide*, i, 217, 278.

[60] Maurice F. Bond, *Guide to the Records of Parliament* (HLRO, 1971), 111–14.

[61] David L. Smith, *The Stuart Parliaments, 1603–1689* (London, 1999) is now the best book on this, suitable alike for fellow historians, students, and interested general readers.

Parliament of 1660, so called because it was not summoned by royal writ, was responsible for reinstituting government by King, Lords, and Commons, and for arranging the monarch's return. It also made quite strenuous attempts to settle other unfinished business, being on the whole more successful with finance than with religion. The so-called 'Cavalier Parliament', elected the next year, is often described as having been more royalist than the King; more Anglican in religion than him it certainly was. It had to abrogate and reverse an Act of early 1642 in order to restore the bishops to their seats in the Lords. The apogee of ultra-royalism was perhaps reached in 1664, with the completion of the measures—half unfairly known as the Clarendon Code—against Dissenters (mainly Puritan and Quaker), a new Triennial Act emasculating that of 1641, and the voting of a huge sum to be raised by direct taxation in preparation for the prospective naval war against the Dutch. It was the failure to use these very generous financial provisions effectively and to gain a decisive victory, culminating in the disgrace of the Dutch attack on the fleet in the Medway of June 1667, which led to the Commons' first re-encroachment on the executive side of government and on the boundaries of the royal prerogative. Realizing the strength of feeling about the alleged misuse of public funds, Charles tried to pre-empt the situation by appointing a royal commission of six peers and twelve MPs to investigate the accounts of the kingdom and report back to him and the Privy Council. It soon became clear that this was wholly unacceptable to the Commons. He then executed a tactical retreat and allowed instead the appointment by statute for three years of a quite different commission, consisting of one peer, three MPs, and five other substantial independent figures. This body may fairly be called the first public accounts committee in modern parliamentary history, although it was to have no successor until the early 1690s, and the standing accounts committee of today does not have nearly so long an ancestry as that. Whether this Commission's investigations and the report which they submitted made much difference to the use, or the misuse of public money, does not allow of an easy answer. If one follows their activities as these affected the navy, through

Pepys's diary and correspondence, it becomes abundantly clear that office-holders with financial responsibilities must have been kept on their toes, and at the very least have been more cautious in consequence. Yet any idea that corruption, malversation, and other scandals all came to a sudden end, or were even much reduced after the Commission's work in 1668–70, must be set aside. The King seems most of all to have resented confrontations with an apparently fearless one-time Admiralty and Navy Commissioner from the great days of the first Dutch War in the early 1650s, when he attended meetings of the Commission.[62]

The role of the Speaker belongs to political more than administrative history. Technically chosen by the Commons collectively and then presented to the king, the choice of Speaker shows Charles and his ministers consistently interfering in various ways; they were absolutely determined never to suffer a repetition of having someone like William Lenthall in the Long Parliament. The corollary was that successive Speakers of whom the Crown did approve were rewarded with other offices, pensions, or both.[63] By contrast the staff of the parliament office were strictly royal appointees. As is still in theory the case today, the Clerk of the Parliaments (who was actually Clerk to the House of Lords) was senior to the Clerk of the Commons. The former office was held continuously by one man, John Browne, until he died in his eighties after the Revolution, the latter post by two, William Goldsborough senior and junior from 1661 to 1684; so, except for the granting of reversions most of which never took effect, there was little scope for patronage here. The total size of the office staff is harder to determine. Besides various subordinate clerks for

---

[62] To distinguish the two commissions, see *Lords Journals*, xii., 54, 57; PRO, SO3/11, p. 83; *CSPD, 1667–1668*, p. 90; *Statutes of the Realm*, v. 624–7. There are numerous references in Latham and Matthews, *Pepys Diary*, viii and ix. For the main report and annexed documents see HMC, *Eighth Report*, app., House of Lords MSS., pp. 128–33. For the chairman Lord Brereton see *Complete Peerage*, ii. 300–1; *Hist. Parl.*, i. 715–16; for the ex-republican George Thompson see *DNB*; Latham and Matthews, *Pepys Diary*, num. refs.; will, PCC 15 Vere, 1690.

[63] *Hist. Parl.*, i. 88, and entries in vols. ii and iii for Grimston, Turnor, Charlton, Seymour, and Sawyer (all also in *DNB*).

both Houses, there were doorkeepers, yeomen ushers, sergeants, and marshals in attendance when parliament was sitting. What they lived on between sessions is far from clear.[64]

Local government as such is not our concern. It is, however, important to remember the number of central offices stationed in the localities. For the organization and operation of the customs, the excise, the hearth tax, the land revenues, the post office, and the naval dockyards this should already have become clear; likewise with the role of the common law judges on their assize circuits. In spite of the numerical expansion of the revenue and defence departments, and the growing power of the Treasury, England remained a centralized but at the same time a lightly governed state. The permanent demise of the prerogative courts and of non-parliamentary direct taxation amounted to a political legacy with weighty administrative implications.

XI. CHRONOLOGY

Some kind of chronological framework is needed for what has so far been a largely synchronic description and analysis. It is useful to take the conventional political divisions of the reign in order to see how far these require to be supplemented or modified for our purposes. The normal view is something like this:

1660: Restoration of
    Charles II
1661–79: Cavalier Parliament   *1663: economies in*
                                Household and pensions
1664–7: second Anglo-Dutch   *1666: Downing's system of*
    War   *assignment*
1667: fall of Clarendon   *1667–72: first Treasury*
                                     Commission

---

[64] DNB: *Missing Persons* (Oxford, 1993), for Browne; Sainty, *The Parliament Office in the 17th and 18th Centuries* (HLRO, 1977); W. R. McKay, *Clerks in the House of Commons, 1363–1989* (HLRO, 1989). Petitions for payment in *CTB* and in HMC, *House of Lords MSS* are better than nothing for identifying other staff.

1668 Triple Alliance	*1671: end of customs farming*
1670: Treaties of Dover	*1671–2: Stop of the Exchequer*
1672–4: third Dutch War	
1672: Declaration of Indulgence	
1673: Test Act	
1673–9: Danby's ministry	
1679–81: Popish Plot– Exclusion crisis	*1679–84: second Treasury Commission*
1683: Rye House Plot	*1683: end of excise farming*
1685: accession of James II.	

Without contradicting any of this, we may reasonably add a further parallel column, as indicated above right; other dates or indicators may have to be brought in as we proceed through different aspects of our subject.

XVII. THE ROLE OF THE MONARCH

Another way of thinking about the connection between administration and politics is to ask what could and could not happen without the participation, or at least the approval—explicit or otherwise—of the king and the Council or one of its committees. Large parts of the legal and revenue systems and parts of the work of other departments could be carried on at a routine level, if not quite automatically then without any action by the king or his advisers. Changes of policy, new appointments, revised diplomatic, ecclesiastical, financial, military, or naval commitments and initiatives would all invariably involve the king unless he had specifically delegated authority to others. As an example, less tangential to our main concerns here than it may seem, the problems associated with the Irish revenue system, whether it should be farmed, managed, or put under a direct commission, in whose hands and on what terms, was a frequent, at times indeed a constant, almost a chronic preoccupation at the highest level. This was partly because a key figure during the 1670s, Richard Jones, Lord Ranelagh, was an immensely plausible character, a crony of the King and Lord Treasurer Danby. As late as March 1682 there was a bitter exchange, harking back to the conflicts of an earlier generation. As his friend, and ex-client, Lord Longford wrote to Ormonde:

My Lord Ranelagh in the Treasury Chamber before the King reproached Mr. Roberts for his being auditor to Cromwell, to which Roberts replied that if it were fit for him in that assembly to make his lordship an answer, he could tell him that he was beholding to the famous Milton, for all his learning, he being his tutor.[65]

The problem of Irish government finance also arose in part from the aftermath of the exceedingly complicated post-Restoration land settlement in Ireland and the vested interests of the various parties. This in turn helps to explain the fact of no parliament having been called in Ireland after 1666, and the Crown's consequent dependence on indirect taxation in that kingdom. According to one recent study, it was also due to the foremost viceroy of the reign, the Duke of Ormonde, having been something of a duffer in matters of finance. My own inclination is to see him as more like his royal master, exemplifying the old adage: 'why keep a dog, let alone a pack of hounds, in order to bark yourself?'[66]

Dynastic and foreign policy were traditionally the strict preserves of the royal prerogative, where the monarch consulted whom he or she wished, but then took the decisions. Religion had come, over the course of the previous reigns, to be more the province of the Crown in Parliament. Hence the revolutionary implications of the parliamentary campaigns to exclude James from the succession, pursued in opposition to the King's express wishes. Compared to Elizabeth I, Charles II certainly took more

---

[65] HMC, *Ormonde Papers at Kilkenny*, NS, 6 (London, 1911), 335; Edward Roberts was by then back in a senior revenue post, having had a spell in the wilderness after 1660.

[66] Sean Egan, 'Finance and the Government of Ireland, 1660–85', Trinity College, Dublin Ph.D. thesis (1983); Aylmer, 'The First Duke of Ormond as Patron and Administrator', in Toby Barnard and Jane Fenlon (eds.), *The Dukes of Ormonde, 1610–1745* (Woodbridge, 2000), ch. 5, pp. 115–36.

interest in the navy and in some aspects of finance; compared to Charles I he fussed less about order, decorum, and ceremonial. His style and his private life were so different from those of his father that a direct comparison is scarcely meaningful. He did not busy himself with the details of government as much as his brother was to do during his short reign. Charles's nephew, William III, was perhaps the last monarch to be, in the fullest sense, head of government as well as formal head of state. Charles II was more quickly bored and more easily distracted (whether by women or sporting pastimes or other social diversions) than were the most effective personal rulers of early-modern times. None the less a great deal of business did at least pass before his eyes, much of it requiring his signature; and, except when he was ill, he normally presided at meetings of the Council, whether at Whitehall, Hampton Court, or Windsor (there were no sittings at Newmarket). Occasionally he took direct, personal charge, as with the 1683 security investigations, when he told the turncoat ex-Whig magistrate Edmund Warcup that he 'loved to discover plots, but *not* to create any. . .'.[67] Because of his own temperament and inclinations, Charles needed ministers and other servants whom he could trust, whose judgement he respected and who would themselves be energetic concerning precisely those aspects of business with which he himself either could not or would not be bothered. The greatest hostage which he ever gave to fortune was unquestionably the Secret Treaty of Dover (1670). Charles was not, on the whole, I would suggest, a very reflective or introspective person. But did he never think about the potentially explosive contents of that document, of which one copy was in the possession of the French Crown, the other in the Clifford family home at Ugbrooke in Devonshire? This seemingly reckless act was carried through with the help of the King's sister, not under the influence of a mistress or favourite. The more normal task of his ministers and other attendants was to persuade or cajole him

[67] K. Feiling and F. R. D. Needham, 'The Journal of Edmund Warcup, 1676–84', *Eng. Hist. Rev.*, 40 (1925) 235–60 (quot., p. 245); *DNB: Missing Persons*, where the excellent article by the late Kenneth Haley is a little kinder to its subject than I should be.

into reading warrants, letters, and other papers and, where necessary, adding his signature. A recurring theme of this book will be to assess how successful Charles was in his choice of servants, how far he was simply fortunate in a number of those by whom he was served.[68]

[68] Biographies of Charles II are legion. Among the best of recent years are those by Antonia Fraser, Ronald Hutton, and J. R. Jones. I have found John Miller, *Charles II* (London, 1991), the most helpful for my purposes.

3. Terms and Conditions of Service

WHAT KIND OF administrative system England would have had in the later seventeenth century if the Republic had survived is, like other 'might-have-beens' in history, an unanswerable question. This was not to be; and that perhaps is that. It is, however, reasonable, and I hope of some interest, to ask ourselves how different things were after 1660 compared with what they had been before 1640–2. Did the upheavals of civil war, regicide, republic, and restoration leave any positive legacies, or merely generate a reaction, an urge to get back, to revive as well as to restore? Common sense suggests that the answer is likely to be, a bit of both. But this needs to be put to the proof in rather more detail. We shall look at some of the individuals and the kind of people who were crown servants, in greater detail, in the next chapter, but first we must consider the ways in which they were appointed and the conditions under which they served.

I. APPOINTMENT AND ENTRY TO OFFICE

Just as Charles II's restoration in 1660 was different politically from a normal succession to the throne, so it was also with regard to office-holding. We have already seen some of the reasons why individuals were appointed to the great offices of state and to the privy council in 1660 and the years immediately following. Something of the same variety of reasons for appointments, reappointment, confirmation in post, and promotion can be found in the middling levels of the royal court and the other branches of central government.

A few fortunate survivors from the time of Charles I whose offices had ceased to exist under the Long Parliament or the Commonwealth were simply able to take them up again where they had left off. This was most obviously the case in the royal household, though relatively few such post-holders from before the royalist defeat survived for more than a few years. Nicholas Lanier had become Master of the King's Music back at the very beginning of Charles I's reign; he resumed this position under Charles II but died in 1666.[1] Sir Edward Griffin had succeeded his father-in-law Sir William Uvedale as Treasurer of the Chamber in 1642, took it up again in 1660, and was able to hand it on to his own son in 1679.[2] Sir Henry Herbert resumed his position as Master of the Revels, held since 1623, but was less effectively in charge of the London theatres and the drama generally because of conflicting grants made by the King to William Davenant, Dryden's predecessor as Poet Laureate, and to various members of another ubiquitous courtly family, the Killigrews.[3] Below stairs the position was not so different. William Ashburnham resumed his place as Cofferer.[4] One of the Kitchen Clerks, Leonard Pinckney, returned to the office to which he had been appointed in 1646.[5] Perhaps the most astonishing case of someone resuming an office and then outlasting the King's reign was not in the household. John Browne, who was Clerk of the Parliaments from 1638 until the abolition of the House of Lords in 1649, took up his place again in 1660 and held it until his death in 1691.[6]

Then there were those who had been in the service of Charles

---

[1]   See Andrew Ashbee and David Lasockis, *A Biographical Dictionary of English Court Musicians, 1485–1714* (2 vols., Aldershot, 1998), 689–93.

[2]   Aylmer, *King's Servants*, 83, 391–2.

[3]   *DNB*; Keeler, *The Long Parliament*, 211; *Hist. Parl.*, ii. 531–2; PRO, PROB 11/342, q. 59, his will in which he laments his reduced circumstances and the large debts owed him by both kings.

[4]   *DNB* (quite inadequate); Keeler, *The Long Parliament*, 89–90; *Hist. Parl.*, i. 554 (good); PRO, LS 13/252–3.

[5]   E. S. de Beer (ed.), *The Diary of John Evelyn* (6 vols., Oxford, 1955), iii. 330; PRO, LS 13/252–3.

[6]   *DNB: Missing Persons.* He did not need a royal pardon for having served as a parliamentarian from 1642 to 1649 (HMC, *House of Lords MSS*, xi, *Addenda*, 1514–1714, p. 478).

I or of his successor in exile, sometimes in junior positions, but who had overwhelming claims to promotion. A classic case was that of Stephen Fox, who had been paymaster and general financial factotum for the royal household in exile, and who became the senior of the two Clerks Comptrollers in 1660. Rather different was the case of those who had been in office under the republic but who managed to retain their positions. Clement Kinnersley, Yeoman of the Removing Wardrobes (d. 1662) was one such; another, better known, was Sir George Downing, Teller in the Exchequer of Receipt from 1656 to his death in 1684, an able and dextrous side-changer.[7] The royalist academic John Cooke had been a fellow of Trinity College, Cambridge, and was expelled in 1644–5, but he managed to become secretary to Sir William Lockhart, Cromwell's ambassador to France and commander of the English forces in Flanders (1658–60); he then served as an under-secretary to successive Secretaries of State from 1660–1688 and was also Latin Secretary from 1682 until his death in 1691.[8] Complete continuity across the great political divide of 1660 is most evident in the law courts, not for the most part at the top level among the judges, though there were one or two instances even there;[9] but much more so one rung down the ladder. Such survivors included some of the longest-serving Masters and Six Clerks in Chancery, the Prothonotaries in Common Pleas, the Custos Brevium in King's Bench (which had been styled Upper Bench from 1649 to 1660), besides other, more subordinate clerks in these courts and (from 1654) in the restored

---

[7] It would be pedantic to provide references for each mention of such well-known figures as Downing and Fox. For Kinnersley see PRO, LC 7/1; PROB 11/309, q. 108 (claiming that he was owed arrears by Charles I); and innum. refs. in *CSPD, 1630s–1650s*.

[8] John Venn and J. A. Venn (eds.), *Alumni Cantabrigienses* (10 vols., Cambridge, 1922–54), I. i. 385; W. W. Rouse Ball and J. A. Venn, *Admissions to Trinity College, Cambridge*, i, 1546–1700 (Cambridge, 1913), 329; H. M. Innes, *Fellows of Trinity College, Cambridge* (Cambridge, 1941), 32; John Twigg, *The University of Cambridge and the English Revolution* (Woodbridge, 1990), app. 4, p. 296; J. C. Sainty, *Office-holders in Modern Britain*, ii, *Officials of the Secretaries of State, 1660–1782* (London, 1973), 27, 47, 72.

[9] See *DNB* and Sainty, *The Judges of England, 1272–1990* (Selden Soc., suppl. ser., 10 (1993)) for Matthew Hale and Hugh Wyndham.

Exchequer. Amongst these lawyers and others, it seems almost as if the great upheavals of their time had simply passed them by, though naturally some had been affected by the suspension and virtual abolition of the Exchequer under the Long Parliament and then the Commonwealth, and in a different way by the temporary reform and reconstruction of Chancery under the Protectorate (in the years 1655–8).

There were numerous royalists who had reversionary grants from before 1646, or else made by Charles II in exile. And there were many others with less binding promises or assurances of future appointments. To judge from the petitions which have survived from the early 1660s, more of these characters were disappointed of their hopes, although some obtained alternative places. Thus it was pointless for George Duke to claim that he had a reversion to the Clerkship of Star Chamber when that court had been abolished in 1641 and was not going to be resurrected, but he did become Secretary to the Council of Trade from 1660 until 1667 or 8.[10] The same applied with the one-time officers of the Court of Wards and Liveries, but in their case a detailed scheme of monetary compensation was proposed in the House of Commons, comparable to that which the Long Parliament had agreed on for the officers of their Court which was abolished by ordinance in 1646. It seems unlikely that all the royalist ex-office-holders, who were still alive, actually received the sums recommended, any more than their parliamentarian opposite numbers had done fifteen years before; we may, however, safely concur with the historian of that Court in not weeping too many tears over people who had done so well out of exploiting the misfortunes of other families.[11]

A remarkable case of corporate survival is provided by the Customs Farmers of 1640–1. They were all still alive to be reappointed as Commissioners in 1660, most of them living long enough to become Farmers again in 1662, and three of them

---

[10] *CSPD, 1660–1*, pp. 287–8; Sainty, *Office-holders in Modern Britain*, iii, *Officials of Boards of Trade, 1660–1870* (London, 1974), 19, 95.

[11] *Commons Journals*, viii. 219–20; H. E. Bell, *An Introduction to the History and Records of the Court of Wards and Liveries* (Cambridge, 1953), 160–2.

also holding among the most lucrative salaried posts in the London customs service, the duties almost certainly being performed by deputies. Cadwallader Jones, who had been Receiver-General of the royalist controlled customs during the Civil War, seems to have been regarded with slight suspicion or at least disfavour, and was rewarded only by being made Customer and Collector at the minor (but strategically sensitive) port of Sandwich. In the excise there could, by definition, be no claimants from earlier than 1643, and—apart from the singular figure of Elias Ashmole—I have not identified anyone from the royalist excise administration of 1643–6 who reappeared in 1660. The same naturally was also true of the Hearth Tax, which was only instituted in 1663. In the Ordnance Office some royalists did return. In the Navy the only cases of continuity were with holders of certain posts in the dockyards. Pepys's republican predecessor as Clerk of the Acts was eased out and compensated with another position in one of the yards. Various members of the Pett family of shipbuilders and royal Shipwrights at Chatham and Deptford provide the most notable cases of continuity.

Some of the unsuccessful claimants, or their successors and dependants, were fobbed off in various ways. One lady was ordered to be paid £200 a year because her son had *not* become the Clerk of the Pastry; someone petitioning to be made Yeoman of the Wine cellar was put on a waiting list from which future servants were to be chosen; a son of the late Lord Chief Justice petitioned for three different offices and was granted a fourth (in the revived ecclesiastical courts).[12] Not surprisingly, conflicts arose between rival claimants. In 1662 there were disputes in progress over a Signet Clerkship of the Privy Council, and a Tellership of the Receipt.[13]

As was true before the Civil War, we can distinguish between those offices where appointment was in the king's direct gift, and those where entry might require royal approval, or at least not incur royal disapproval, but where the gift of entry belonged

---

[12] *CSPD, 1660–1*, p. 555; ibid., *1661–2*, pp. 100, 290–1.
[13] Ibid., *1661–2*, p. 369 (and p. 367).

to the head of the department or court in question, or occasionally to some other minister of state or senior figure. As late as 1678 it was apparently not clear whether the office of Groom Porter was in the gift of the King or of the Lord Chamberlain.[14]

The rate at which offices were filled illustrates the scale of the administrative reconstruction in 1660 and after (Table 3.1). It also suggests the extent to which heads of departments, brokers, and others receiving fees and gratuities from appointees are likely to have been able to profit from this. The grants which are tabulated here do, it should be noted, include some pensions and local posts (keeperships of this or that, etc.) besides offices under the crown as we have defined them here.

The renewed increase between 1672 and 1678 may simply reflect generational changes—more people dying who had come back or come in at the Restoration, but it seems more likely to have been due to the greater generosity, we might say prodigality, with the King's resources on the part of the Lord Treasurers Clifford and Danby during these years, compared with the Treasury Commissioners who preceded and followed them.

II. PATRONAGE

By 1662–3 something like normality had returned. To say that, in the days before public advertisement, formal interviews, and competitive examinations, most people entered office under the Crown through some exercise of patronage is broadly true but not very illuminating. We need to be more specific. A patron could be the master, even the employer of the client whose claims he advanced. At the other extreme, the applicant might be taking advantage of the most tenuous and remote connection, sometimes through a third party acting as intermediary in seeking the patron's help. In between these limits was a range of possible relationships: familial, local, regional, professional, ecclesiastical, party political. There is one particular problem of evidence in this area. A very large proportion of the approaches

---

[14] Ibid., *1677–8*, p. 570. See also ibid., 20–1.

TABLE 3.1. *Numbers of Patents*[15]

Date	Number
12 Charles II (1660–1, eight months only)	478
13 (1661–2)	158
14 (1662–3)	62
15 (1663–4)	51
16 (1664–5)	46
17 (1665–6)	44
18 (1666–7)	33
19 (1667–8)	54
20 (1668–9)	46
21 (1669–70)	41
22 (1670–1)	42
23 (1671–2)	70
24 (1672–3)	73
25 (1673–4)	87
26 (1674–5)	97
27 (1675–6)	128
28 (1676–7	103
29 (1677–8)	87
30 (1678–9)	58
31 (1679–80)	83
32 (1680–1)	40
33 (1681–2)	37
34 (1682–3)	40
35 (1683–4)	34
36 (1684–5)	35
1 James II (1685–6)	113
2 (1686–7)	59
3 (1687–8)	58
4 (1688, ten months only)	30
1 William III and Mary II (1688–90)	168
2 (1690–1)	73
3 (1691–2)	50
4 (1692–3)	40
1693 (by calendar year only)	39
1694	38
1695	34
1696	40

[15] Bodl. Eng. Hist. MS b.79, fos. 5ʳ–123ᵛ, entitled 'Offices Granted by Letters Patents since the Restoration of King Charles II as by the Docquet Books in the Signet Office', but extending to 1696 (after 1693 by calendar, not regnal years). I am extremely grateful to Dr Andrew Barclay for having drawn my attention to this valuable source, part of the archive of William Lowndes, Treasury Secretary, 1696–1724.

made by seekers of minor appointments, surviving in the State Papers, are to Joseph Williamson, Under-Secretary, 1660–74, and then Secretary of State, 1674–79. In part this reflects the fact that he was a compulsive record-keeper, whose papers were to remain in the public domain, whereas others similarly placed either kept more of their papers themselves, like Sir Edward Nicholas (much of whose archive was later to come back into the public domain in what are now the British Library's holdings), or perhaps did not bother to keep them at all, in the case of such aristocrats as Arlington, Conway, and Sunderland.[16]

There was also an institutional shift during the course of the reign. Lord Treasurer Southampton was honest and conscientious, but not—so far as the evidence goes to show—particularly active as a patron. In August 1666 a one-time Fellow of New College, Oxford who said that he had previously been an Excise Farmer, petitioned to be made a Customs Farmer, and this request came to Williamson. But from 1667 on anyone in their senses would have known that applications for revenue posts would require an approach, either direct or indirect, to the Treasury Commissioners, under whose aegis customs farming was to be brought to an end in 1671. When there were Lord Treasurers again (Clifford, 1672–3 and Danby, 1673–9) the trend towards Treasury control may have slowed down but it was certainly not reversed.

Non-revenue offices were a different matter. Even a peer, whose father had been an ambassador under James and Charles I, felt that he had to offer his services to the King through Arlington, but *via* Williamson, while a Channel Islander evidently knew that Arlington could be tetchy and asked Williamson to petition for someone's continuance in office when the Secretary of State was in a good mood.[17] Sometimes

---

[16] Henry Coventry's letter-books of his outgoing overseas correspondence (to envoys, governors, etc.) are in BL Add. MSS 25, 117–25; his surviving domestic correspondence (now at Longleat) is available on microfilm in the BL and the IHR. D. T. Witcombe, 'The Parliamentary Careers of Sir William Coventry and Mr Henry Coventry 1661–1681', Univ. of Oxford B.Litt. thesis (1954), is understandably less concerned with this aspect.

[17] *CSPD, 1666–7*, p. 39; ibid., *1667–8*, p. 453, 483. Admittedly Lord Aston was a peer of Scotland and so did not have a seat in the (English) House of

conflicts between individuals or between different departments had to be settled at a higher level. For example, there was a dispute between two courtiers (one of them admittedly the Treasurer of the Household) and the Lord Chief Justice about the disposal of the Seal Office in King's Bench—a profitable semi-sinecure.[18] A rather different kind of case is recorded by Pepys in his diary entry for 13 October 1668. He had heard that James Sotherne, a Clerk in the Lord Admiral's office, was trying to succeed the recently deceased Store-Keeper of Deptford dockyard, whereas the Navy Office had this place in mind for their own senior Clerk, Thomas Turner, so that one of Pepys's under-clerks, Thomas Hayter, could then succeed Turner. After Matthew Wren, York's Secretary as Lord Admiral, had left them, 'upon great discourse . . . we did resolve to shove hard for our Clerks, & that places of preferment may go according to seniority and Merit'. Turner did get the Deptford post; Sotherne and Hayter both later rose to the top as naval administrators.[19] When the customs came out of farm and were put under the management of salaried Commissioners, the Treasury Commissioners ruled that all London customs posts, save the very lowliest grade of Tidesmen, were to be passed and granted by them, with the Treasury Secretary receiving fees from the appointees proportionate to the value of the offices in question.[20] The Excise Farmers did once propose an additional Commissioner direct to the King, but this was simply referred back to the Treasury; the individual concerned served briefly as an Excise Farmer a year or so later.[21]

Some proposals failed to get any further. Dr Fell, the Dean of

Lords; moreover, both his father (d. 1639) and his son (who succeeded him in 1678) were avowed Roman Catholics (*Complete Peerage*, i. 285–6).

[18] *CTB*, ii. 146.

[19] Robert Latham and William Matthews (eds.), *The Diary of Samuel Pepys* (11 vols., London, 1970), ix. 327, 330; Sainty, *Office-holders in Modern Britain*, iv, *Admiralty Officials, 1660–1870* (London, 1975), 130, 151–2; ibid., vii, *Navy Board Officials, 1660–1832*, comp. J. M. Collinge (London, 1978), 109, 140, 145.

[20] *CTB*, iii. 942.

[21] Ibid., 1006, 3 Jan. 1671/2; PRO, E 351/1313, for Sir John Davis as one of six accountants for the excise revenues in 1673.

Christ Church who was about to become Bishop of Oxford, recommended the antiquary Anthony Wood for the next vacancy as Under-Keeper of the Records in the Tower,[22] though this might have been designed to get him out of the way, Wood not being universally popular and certainly not with Fell. It was not beneath the King's own dignity to recommend the Duke of Ormonde's ex-coachman to the Hackney Coach Commissioners for the next vacancy there, we must assume more fruitfully.[23] Sir William Godolphin, Ambassador in Spain and absentee Auditor of crown land revenues in Wales, sought to be succeeded in the latter position by his relative Sidney (the future peer and Lord Treasurer) and not by his deputy, Mr Tudor; in the event Sir William remained Auditor and Tudor remained reversioner to his place.[24] In spite of being nominated by the Lord Chancellor, Sir William Waller, the son of the parliamentarian general, did not succeed when the Minister Resident at Hamburg died there in 1678; the post went instead to Sir Peter Wyche, who had considerable previous diplomatic experience and presumably more effective sponsors.[25]

Sometimes a general directive was issued, rather than a specific recommendation being made. Thus in May 1675 the Lord Treasurer and the Chancellor of the Exchequer simply told the Excise Commissioners to appoint fit persons to be sub-commissioners, as desired by the excise farmers.[26] Alternatively, the right to nominate to a particular office was itself dispensed as an act of political or personal favour, as when Sir Courtenay Pole was granted the nomination of the next Customs Surveyor at Poole when the current holder's pending dismissal had taken effect; perhaps this was to compensate for the rejection of his nominee for the Collectorship at Lyme Regis, though the chronological sequence is not quite clear.[27] The man who was said to be the King's favoured candidate, Thomas Tupton, did

---

[22] *CSPD, 1675–6*, p. 121.   [23] Ibid., 206.
[24] Ibid., *1676–7*, p. 534.
[25] Ibid., *1678*, pp. 383, 409; Gary M. Bell, *A Handlist of British Diplomatic Representatives, 1509–1688* (RHS, 1990).
[26] *CTB*, iv. 737.
[27] Ibid., v. 1230; *Hist. Parl.*, iii. 255 (an excellent entry by J. P. Ferris).

not succeed to the Six Clerkship which fell vacant in 1682; instead it was to be held successively by the financiers and crown creditors, Richard Kent and Charles Duncombe.[28]

In some departments and branches of government there were often possibilities of alternative employment. For instance, an unsuccessful candidate for the Store-Keepership at Woolwich obtained the Clerkship of Survey at Deptford instead.[29] When Philip Warwick the younger (son of the better-known official and royalist historian) died in 1683, the senior Treasury Commissioner, Lord Rochester, asked Secretary Jenkins to recommend a successor. Since the post in the London customs held by Warwick junior had been a sinecure, executed by deputy (he had actually been serving as a diplomat in Scandinavia), this was a way of offering a favour to a loyal ally rather than look-ing for someone with professional qualifications.[30] Indeed it appears that the Customs Commissioners kept a list of persons recommended but not yet provided for, since two years before this they had been told to send their list of names to the Treasury.[31] One of the more unusual applications was when an ex-slave, liberated from Morocco, petitioned the king for a London Customs Waitership, with what success is unfortu-nately not clear.[32] Whether or not in relation to the post left vacant by Warwick's death, the Treasury Commissioners did query the fitness of the Poet Laureate, John Dryden, for a customs office (12 November 1683).[33] At the bottom levels of the Customs service appointments were ranked in a hierarchy: no one was to become a Land Surveyor who had not already been a Land Waiter, and no one a Tide Surveyor without having been a Tidesman.[34] The aspirations of quite humble individuals are reflected in a petition from a servant of the Clerk of the Pells in the Lower Exchequer, for a Quayman's post in the port of

[28] *CSPD, 1682*, p. 335; T. D. Hardy, *A Catalogue of Lord Chancellors, Keepers of the Great Seal, Masters of the Rolls, and Principal Officers of the High Court of Chancery* (London, 1843), sources as below, Ch. 4, for Kent and Duncombe; PRO, PROB 11/370, q. 81 (will of M. Blucke, the previous holder).

[29] *CSPD,1682*, p. 377.

[30] Ibid., *1683*, ii. 420.

[31] *CTB*, vii. 15, 24 Jan. 1680/1.

[32] Ibid., 506–7.

[33] Ibid., 949.

[34] Ibid., 1019.

London, he 'being about to settle himself in the world'.[35] Near the end of the reign, in the summer of 1684, a petitioner for a Deputy Land Surveyorship based his claims on his services for the royalist cause before the Restoration, nearly a quarter-century earlier, probably with little chance of success.[36]

There are instances where someone of supposed influence was asked to help, but was unable to oblige. In February 1676 Colonel Roger Whitley, then Deputy Postmaster, was approached by the local postmaster at Harwich, on behalf of a relative who was seeking employment. Whitley explained at some length why he was unable to assist, although he would have liked to do so:

the world is soe altered of late, to the disadvantage of young Gentlemen in point of Education, that there is little encouragement to be had[;] in times past (before the wicked rebellion) a Nobleman, or great Officer of State, or Court would have halfe a score or a dozen Gentlemen, to attend him but now all is shrunk, into a Valet de Chambre, a Page and five or six Footmen, and this is part of our cursed Reformation, and I wish this were all;[37]

Sometimes a philosophical view of other's people's better fortune was the best that could be offered, as when one minor functionary wrote to another in November 1683 on the continued advancement of Sir Stephen Fox and the promotion of Mr Fenn, an ex-Paymaster, to be a naval Victualling Commissioner: 'I would not have you so uneasy at the good fortunes of Mr. F. as some of your friends in the court are, the truth is they have great friends and good parts but their luck is bad, . . .'[38] There was in fact a well established way of getting an appointment blocked, so that it could be kept open for someone else, or for someone's nominee. This was known as granting a *caveat*. Thus a Page of the Backstairs in the royal Bedchamber obtained a *caveat* on any grant of the Customership in the port of Cardiff;

[35] *CTB*, vii. 15, 24 Jan. 1680/1, 1163.   [36] Ibid., 1209.
[37] Post Office Archives (Mount Pleasant), Ref.1/9, TS copy of letter-book, 1675/6–77, pp. 19–20. See Ch. 4, sect. xiii for a fuller discussion of these records.
[38] BL Add. MS 28,875, fo. 285, William Shaw to John Ellis, 6 Nov. 1683.

the ex-parliamentarian leader, Denzil Lord Holles got one put on the Keepership of Records in the Tower; a reversion to a Tellership in the Receipt was blocked because the King himself had promised it to the Earl of Manchester (son of the previous Lord Chamberlain) for his son; Arlington, when he was Lord Chamberlain, had a collective *caveat* put on all Chamber offices that were in his gift while he was absent from Court; likewise no grant of the Knight Harbinger's place was to pass unless the whole Board of Green Cloth had notice of it; Secretary Williamson secured a *caveat* on the Sergeantry at Arms to the House of Commons in 1675; and Secretary Coventry one on the Keepership of Royal Libraries; Mistress Gwyn's *caveat* on the Registrarship of Chancery (a notorious sinecure) was, however, cancelled—poor Nelly! One Charles Pigeon of Gray's Inn secured a *caveat* on the appointment of an Excise Appeals Commissioner, to which he had had a reversion, but all *caveats* on these posts, which had been declared to be specifically in the King's sole gift, were cancelled a few weeks later. Sometimes this blocking mechanism was simply, as with Arlington, a precaution taken by a head of department, so that he should not be bypassed. Such was the case with the Lord Chief Justice and the Clerkship of the Treasury in Common Pleas, and with the Master of the Great Wardrobe and the Clerkship there. But it could also be something obviously nearer to a financial racket, as when the amply favoured Edward Progers, Groom of the Bedchamber, was granted a stop on any reversion to the Chief Searchership of Customs in the port of London, to replace two existing holders who were in the process of being dismissed, perhaps for disloyalty since this was in the summer of 1679, a time of political crisis. More bizarrely the Master of the Mint's *caveat* on his own suspension from office had to be overridden by the Attorney-General, so that he could be eased out (July 1680).[39]

Changing patrons was always a tricky business, like changing

[39] *CSPD*, *1668–9*, p. 437; ibid., *1673–5*, pp. 111–12, 473, 533; ibid., *Addenda 1660–85*, pp. 444–5; ibid., *1675–6*, pp. 5, 288, 407, 563; ibid., *1677–8*, pp. 231, 285, 489; ibid., *1678*, pp. 52, 383; *CTB*, vi. 116, 617.

jobs today. The choice between sticking with one and switching to another was especially delicate for men on the make. A classic case here might be that of Samuel Pepys. He started out as a client, or servant, of Edward Montagu, then briefly became a subordinate of George Downing at the Exchequer of Receipt, then switched back to Montagu (shortly to become Earl of Sandwich). Later, being by 1668–70 sufficiently well established and highly regarded, he became a direct dependant of James Duke of York, losing office with the campaign to exclude York from the succession in 1679; whether on his return to office in 1683–4 he should be seen as temporarily a client of George Legge, Lord Dartmouth is doubtful. By then his career depended on the direct favour of the King himself and his brother. Hence James's overthrow at the end of 1688 was almost immediately followed by the end of Pepys's career in the royal service. There was also, going back to the 1670s, the (quite unjustified) suspicion of Popery from which he never entirely recovered.

Another, less-well-known instance is also instructive. In 1677–8 John Ellis was on the staff of Sir Leoline Jenkins, then Charles II's ambassador in the extraordinarily long-drawn-out peace negotiations at Nimeguen between Louis XIV, William III of Orange, and the other warring parties—England by then being neutral. The Duke of Ormonde's son and heir, the Earl of Ossory, was serving in the Dutch army, in a quasi-private capacity on account of English neutrality. Ellis wanted to transfer from Jenkins's to Ossory's service, on whose initiative is not quite clear. He received a friendly but firm note from Laurence Hyde (the future Earl of Rochester), warning him that Jenkins, a good man who might well become a great one—as Hyde put it—found his services indispensable, and that he should therefore only leave the Ambassador's employment for the Earl's with Jenkins's express approval.[40] Later evidence shows that Ellis took this advice, for he received the friendliest of letters from Jenkins when he had become Ossory's secretary, and again later when, after the Earl's tragic death at the age of only fifty-

40 BL Add. MS 28,896, fo. 121^{r-v}.

five, he had crossed over to Ireland and joined the secretariat in Dublin, under the patronage of Ossory's father, the Lord Lieutenant, and/or of his brother, the Earl of Arran as Lord Deputy. How high Ellis might have risen if he had stayed in Jenkins's service we cannot tell; but since the latter himself died in 1685, he would have had to find someone else in any case, unless (like Pepys by the time of Sandwich's death) he had by then been senior enough to have depended for promotion on being selected by the King. At the earlier stage Hyde's admonition was surely sound. As a well-known academic patron of the last generation once remarked to the present author: 'I don't mind X making use of me as he rises to fame and fortune, but I do object to feeling that I am being kicked away below him as he mounts to the next rung of the ladder.'

There was a reverse side to patronage. Clients and subordinates could seek to ingratiate themselves with their masters and seniors by offering entertainment and effecting introductions for others; this is partly what is meant today by networking. Examples can be found in many of the diaries and other autobiographical fragments of the time: those of Evelyn, Ashmole, Pepys, Anglesey, Whitley, to name among the most obvious. But it could misfire. In April 1668 James Hickes, the senior clerk in the Post Office, arranged an elaborate dinner party for Under-Secretary Williamson, so that he could meet the deputy Deputy Postmaster, Andrew Ellis and others, at the same time expressing his own hostility towards the Deputy, Arlington's brother, Sir John Bennet. Either the dinner never took place or it went off badly, for a month later we find the luckless Hickes writing a grovelling letter of apology to Williamson, with whom he had evidently fallen badly out of favour.[41] Bennet does seem to have been a difficult person to work with, or maybe just a bully towards his inferiors. The Postmaster at Dover expressed himself as utterly disgusted at having to act under him and Andrew Ellis, while a few years later Pepys too fell out with Sir John,[42] who would perhaps not have got as far as he did but for

[41] *CSPD*, *1667–8*, pp. 340, 344, 393.
[42] Ibid., 429; ibid., *1672*, pp. 23–4.

his much more talented younger brother. One archetypal disappointed place-seeker, who wrote disgruntled letters but perhaps did not do enough networking, was Heneage Finch, Lord Winchilsea. Having served as Ambassador at Constantinople in the 1660s, he held prestigious but unremunerative posts such as Lord Lieutenancies but nothing else thereafter, and wrote plaintively to successive Secretaries of State bemoaning his impoverished lot.[43]

To understand how offices were filled, it will thus be clear that the right to appoint was a key factor. But there was of course also the question of qualifications. For all revenue posts numeracy was essential, and in some of them creditworthiness too. For diplomatic and some secretarial posts linguistic skills were needed; for some legal offices a knowledge of Latin and 'law French', together with the ability to master the arcane legal 'hands' which were in use again from 1660. In 1670 the Exchequer Auditors had to be told to enter various kinds of particulars in English 'because many clerks understand not the Latin'.[44] Such general qualities as being industrious and conscientious, loyal, and honest may seem too obvious for further comment to be required, but in so haphazard a system even these could not always be taken for granted. We shall find instances where they were conspicuously lacking; but before turning to such topics as corruption and disloyalty, there are other features of the administrative system which demand our attention. These include the terms on which offices were held, whether or not they could be performed by deputy, whether there were or could be reversionary grants preventing entry to them except in strict sequence; not least how well the holders of particular offices were remunerated, and whether they were sought more for honorific or political than financial reasons, or as stepping-stones to something better.

There were two other modes of entry to office, which seldom operated in isolation from patronage but which were none the

[43] Ibid., *1675–6*, pp. 466–7; ibid., *1680–1*, pp. 181, 361; ibid., *July–Sept. 1683*, pp. 298–9; ibid., *1684–5*, p. 208. See also *DNB*; *Complete Peerage*, xii, pt. 2, pp. 777–9; PRO, PROB 11/396, q. 131.
[44] *CTB*, iii. 439.

less distinct from it. Moreover, by the standards of the time, these were by no means necessarily regarded as corrupt or improper.

III. PATRIMONY

Very few posts under the Crown were literally heritable. At the highest but largely honorific level, the office of Earl Marshal had become fixed in the Howard family, being held either by the Duke of Norfolk or the next most senior Howard peer if there either was no Duke or he was ineligible. Likewise the office of Lord Great Chamberlain was the property of the Berties, Earls of Lindsey. At a more modest level, in 1660 the Chief Ushership of the Exchequer was resumed by Mrs Mary Walker, widow of the anti-Independent pamphleteer Clement Walker, and—after litigation with another family member—was transmitted to her son John, who was to hold it for another forty years.[45] But what we may describe as patrimony was wider than strict heritability. The case of the Fanshawes of Ware as King's Remembrancers in the Upper Exchequer, and the Osbornes of Chicksands as Lord Treasurer's Remembrancers are well known and need not be repeated in detail here.[46] The Fanshawe succession was resumed in 1660 but collapsed in 1674, owing to the lack of adult male heirs.[47] The Osborne tenure was also resumed and thanks to longevity lasted for another thirty-five years.[48] Sir Robert Croke of Chequers took up his reversion to become Clerk of the Pipe, in succession to his father, the notorious Sir Henry, but the Croke succession came to an end in 1681.[49]

[45] Sainty, *Officers of the Exchequer* (List and Index Society, spec. ser. 18 (1983)), 147–8; Aylmer, *King's Servants*, index entry, 'Walker, Clement'; id., *State's Servants*, 292–3; Somerset Record Office, DD/GB 148 (Gore papers), Trinity Term, 1667.

[46] H. R. Trevor-Roper, *The Gentry, 1540–1640* (*Econ. Hist. Rev.*, suppl., 1 (1953)), 30; Aylmer, *King's Servants*, index entries; id., 'The Officers of the Exchequer, 1625–1642', in F. J. Fisher (ed.), *Essays in the Economic and Social History of Tudor and Stuart England in Honour of R. H. Tawney* (Cambridge, 1961), 172–3.

[47] Sainty, *Officers of the Exchequer*, 47–8.   [48] Ibid., 56.

[49] Ibid., 66; Aylmer, *King's Servants*, index entry, 'Croke, Sir Henry'.

Transmission of offices within families was not limited to successions from fathers to sons. Patrimony in this sense could extend to brothers, grandsons, sons-in-law, and nephews. Widows can be found petitioning to follow their husbands, for example as Anchor-smith at Portsmouth (heavy work if it was to be done in person), and for local Postmasterships; a son-in-law sought a customs post at Barnstaple; a widow and her son to be jointly Flag-makers. The craft of falconry seems particularly to have run in families, as evidenced by the Falconers under the Master of the Hawks, probably because of the particular skills transmitted.[50] At a rather higher level, Daniel O'Neile (alias O'Neill and Oneale), one-time secret agent, Groom of the Bedchamber and royal favourite, bequeathed to his wife, the Countess of Chesterfield, his interest in the management of the Post Office, asking Secretary Bennet (soon to be Lord Arlington) to advise her about this, also his share in the gunpowder manufacturing patent, with Colonel Legge (father of the future Lord Dartmouth) being requested to help her there.[51] When Justinian Pagitt made his will in January 1671 he had already settled his office of Custos Brevium in King's Bench on his brother Lewin, although this did not take effect until his death ten years later.[52] Offices which had been held under Charles II were sometimes not transmitted until later reigns. In 1696 Benjamin Coling left the Cryership of the court of King's Bench to his wife for her life, then to his two younger sons, his Ushership of the House of Lords and Keepership of the Council Chamber to his eldest son, together with his farm and Receivership of fines in King's Bench, though the latter was charged with payments of £200 for each of his two daughters. None of this took effect until his death in 1700.[53]

---

[50] *CSPD, 1668–9*, pp. 544, 549; ibid., *Addenda, 1660–70*, p. 691; ibid., *1670*, pp. 219, 449; *CTB*, iv. 570; *CSPD, 1682*, p. 583; ibid., *1683–4*, p. 201.
[51] PRO, PROB 11/315, q. 124.
[52] Ibid., 317, q. 145.
[53] Ibid., 458, q. 176 (proved 16 Dec. 1700).

IV. PURCHASE

Purchase as a factor in entry to office raises more complicated questions. It may be agreed at once that venality never existed in England on the scale, and with the fiscal significance for the Crown, that it did in pre-Revolutionary France.[54] The sale of revenue and judicial posts had been illegal since the reign of Edward VI, though the definition of these remained—to say the least—blurred at the edges. More to the point is the distinction which needs to be drawn between a brokerage fee, or gratuity, having to be paid to a head of department or to someone else in a strategically placed position, as a condition of entry, and a capital sum for which an office was bought from its existing occupant or sometimes from the holder of a reversion to it. Thus it was payments of the former kind which William Coventry agreed to forego when a salary of £500 year was settled on him as Admiralty Secretary in August 1664.[55] Something similar was arranged for William Blathwayt as Secretary at War under James II, when his salary was raised from £750 to £1,095 p.a. and the fees which he could receive from army officers were limited to one day's pay when a commission was first taken up and the same every time someone was granted leave.[56] It is a rather remarkable fact that seagoing naval commissions were never venal in the strict sense; even at the warrant officer level or below, only Purserships were sometimes bought and sold. By contrast, in the English—later the British—army, in spite of periodic royal attempts to suppress the practice, commissions in many regiments had to be paid for until 1871. As Dr David Davies has rightly reminded us, we must not think of the later seventeenth-century naval officer corps as having been exclusively meritocratic, free from patronage and favouritism.[57]

[54] See most recently and notably William Doyle, *Venality: The Sale of Offices in Eighteenth-century France* (Oxford, 1996).
[55] *CSPD, 1663–4*, p. 674. See also V. Vale, 'Clarendon, Coventry, and the Sale of Naval Offices, 1660–8', *Camb. Hist. J.*, 12 (1956), 107–25.
[56] *CSPD, 1686–7*, p. 371, no. 1474.
[57] J. D. Davies, *Gentlemen and Tarpaulins: The Officers and Men of the Restoration Navy* (Oxford, 1991), for purserships, pp. 21–2, 153–4; Michael

None the less, it is tempting to say that for England seapower was simply too important to be left to the vagaries of the market. Be that as it may, the contrast with the army is very striking.

In the civil government we find periodic attempts to restrict venality further, even to stamp it out. The Commons had a committee considering this in 1663; a bill to strengthen the 1552 Act was read twice and committed in 1667; in 1679 an order in Council was reported to have banned the purchase of all civil as well as military offices; and in April of that year the Earl of Essex, as senior Treasury Commissioner, introduced a bill in the Lords which might have extended the Tudor statute. But little came of all this, and debate tended instead to focus on which offices did and did not come within the scope of the prohibitory Tudor statute. Thus the sheriff of Dorset was accused of selling local offices in 1665, but it is not clear on which side of the line these would have fallen. In 1664 Sir Charles Lyttleton wrote to his friend Lord Hatton: 'I am in some treaty of buying a place in the Custom House, but that must not be spoke of, though I feare there is a worse reason to conceale it, because I han't money enough for the purchase.' When he was Lord Lieutenant of Ireland in 1674, Essex had said that Lord Ranelagh should not be allowed to sell the Irish Chancellorship of Exchequer to Sir James Hayes because it was a judicial office.[58] On the other hand customs posts as such were not all classified as revenue offices. In 1670 the Comptrollership at Bridgwater was said to be worth £50–£60 a year and to be on the market for £300–£400; the sale price of

Lewis, *England's Sea Officers: The Story of the Naval Profession* (London, 1939), 242–3. For the Army there is a whole literature: see John Childs, *The Army of Charles II* (Manchester, 1976), 44–6; Anthony Bruce, *The Purchase System in the British Army, 1660–1871* (London, 1980); R. E. Scouller, 'Purchase of Commissions and Promotions', *J. Soc. Army Hist. Res.*, 62 (1984), 217–26. I have not followed up all the primary source references on this subject.

[58] *CSPD, 1663–4*, p. 132; HMC, *Ninth Report*, app., House of Lords MSS, p.112; *CSPD, 1679–80*, p. 177; HMC, *House of Lords MSS, 1678–88*, pp. 119–20; *CSPD, 1664–5*, p. 431; *Hatton Correspondence*, i (Camden NS, 22 (1878)), 36; *CSPD, 1673–5*, p. 242.

the Customership of Great Yarmouth was estimated at £600. Waiterships in the port of London seem to have passed for money. Williamson's agent in Yarmouth, Richard Bower, told him in 1675 that the King's Searcher there, who held his place by patent, had recently died; he was said to have sold his office to someone who had just gone to London to get himself confirmed in it, but Bower believed that the dead man's patent was not good (i.e. that it was invalid), and went on to observe that the purchase price was £300–£400.[59] Perhaps more surprisingly the political economist Charles Davenant was said to have bought a Commissionership of Excise from Henry Frederick Thynne in 1678, whereas I have not found evidence of traffic in lesser excise posts, though this may be due to uneven survival of the sources.[60] Elsewhere—in the law courts, the household, and parts of the central executive—venality flourished; it would not be true to say that this went unchecked, because the transaction and the individual making the purchase normally had to have at least the tacit approval either of the King or of the head of department.

Clarendon seems to have had no doubt at all of his right to dispose of administrative offices in the Court of Chancery. Years later he told his eldest son that he would have felt fully justified in selling the Clerkship of the Patents for £2,000; but, because the King had already promised this post to Sir Robert Howard (being unaware that it was in the Chancellor's gift, not in his), he had only accepted a present of a diamond worth under £100 from Howard. But when, four years later, Sir Robert had sold the Clerkship to Sir Thomas Vyner's son for between £2,600 and £3,000, he had thought it right and proper to accept about 300 gold pieces—in effect as a brokerage fee.[61]

---

[59] *CSPD, 1670*, pp. 49, 494; PRO, SP 29/288/14A, 368/128 (*CSPD, 1673–5*, p. 608).

[60] *CSPD, 1678*, p. 371.

[61] See P. H. Hardacre, 'Clarendon, Sir Robert Howard, and Chancery Office-holding at the Restoration', *Huntington Libr. Q.*, 38 (1975), 207–14, giving the full text of Bodl. MS Clar. 154, fos. 53–6, Clarendon to Cornbury, Montpellier, 9 Nov. 1669. I am grateful to Prof. Hardacre for having given me a copy of his article.

Sometimes we only know about such cases because something went wrong. Thus someone paid £300 for a place as Groom of the Privy Chamber supernumerary, only to find that the board wages and livery payments for it had been stopped; a later position on his behalf sought arrears of £376 14s. 10d. A Gentleman Usher's place in the Chamber had been bought for £500 but then had to be used as security for a loan of only £50, which looks like a rather poor bargain. Even a reversion to the Chief Clerkship of King's Bench (an exceptionally lucrative position) fetched £6,320, presumably involving an element of gamble on the life expectancy of the existing holder and of any prior reversioners.[62] William Prettyman said that he had paid £1,000 for the Receivership of First Fruits and Tenths (why was this not a revenue office?), but the Treasury ruled that it was not a genuine purchase, simply representing part of what his brother, Sir John, had left office (under a cloud) owing to the King.[63] The Duke of Buckingham was said to have paid the Duke of Albemarle either £20,000 or £24,000 for the Mastership of the Horse, on the understanding that he would receive £2,400 a year for twenty years on the Irish establishment in consideration of the same. No wonder that Ireland's financial resources were chronically overstretched; and perhaps no wonder too that Buckingham was to die a bankrupted pauper.[64] Not that this transaction did the Monck family much good either, for the second Duke of Albemarle (who succeeded in 1670) was an utter spendthrift who died of drink in the West Indies. The value of a Secretaryship of State seems to have levelled off at £6,000; before his promotion to this rank, Williamson had been offered £1,600 for his Clerkship of the Privy Council and £600 for his Keepership of the State Paper

---

[62] *CSPD*, 1668–9, pp. 216–17, 391; ibid., 1672–3, p. 516.

[63] *CTB*, iii. 370, 397, Feb.–Mar. 1670.

[64] *CSPD*, 1672, pp. 618–19; ibid., 1672–3, p. 510; Frank T. Melton, *Sir Robert Clayton and the Origins of Deposit Banking, 1658–1685* (Cambridge, 1982); North Yorks Record Office, Duncombe Park papers (the financier Charles Duncombe acquired the Duke's Yorkshire estates from the ultimate mortgagees, but never lived there himself); forthcoming *New DNB*, article on Charles Duncombe; Bruce Yardley, 'The Second Duke of Buckingham', Univ. of Oxford D.Phil. thesis (1989).

Office—a position which he in fact kept as Secretary of State, indeed to the end of his life.[65] The going rate for a particular office could naturally vary for different reasons. The Wiccamical autobiographer John Potenger beat down the asking price for the Comptrollership of the Pipe from £1,800 to £1,700, but he believed that he should only have had to pay £1,200 for it except for the greed of the Chancellor of the Exchequer's secretary. Since he was to hold the post for fifty-six years, this might none the less be considered to have been a good investment.[66] If Sir Thomas Robinson had not died of injuries from jumping out of an upstairs window to escape the 1683 fire in the Temple, his place as Chief Prothonotary of Common Pleas would have been worth £5,000.[67] Clerkships of the Council seem to have varied in price according to the ages and expectations of those involved: Sir Richard Browne sold to Williamson for £1,000 plus a lease on some crown property; whereas Sir George Lane sold to Sir Robert Southwell for £2,000, and Southwell, with his letters patent to hand, in turn sold to Francis Gwyn for £2,500.[68] When a fee of as much as £300–£400 was offered to Williamson by someone who wanted a Chancery Mastership, the borderline between brokerage and venality in judicial offices would seem to have been fairly flexible.[69] The same was true with the definition of a revenue office when Brooke Bridges bought the Auditorship of the Imprests from Robert Wylde (or Wild) in the spring of 1672.[70] How much such transactions affected the value of offices and the wealth of their holders is a difficult matter to which we shall have to return. Occasionally such traffic simply resulted in a net loss to the Crown, as in the case of Buckingham and the head-ship of the royal stables; or in a different instance when the King

[65] *CSPD*, 1672–3, pp. 321–2; 1679–80, p. 82.
[66] *Private Memoirs of John Potenger . . .*, ed. C. W. Bingham (1841), 39–40; Sainty, *Officers of the Exchequer*, 77.
[67] J. H. Baker, 'Sir Thomas Robinson (1618–83), Chief Prothonotary of the Common Pleas', *Bodl. Libr. Rec.*, 10 (1978), 27–40.
[68] BL Add. MA 38,861, fo. 9.   [69] *CSPD*, 1672–3, p. 236.
[70] *CTB*, iii. 1062, 1072 (giving Treasury approval provided that they reached agreement on the fees which had been due to the late Auditor Wood, d. 1670).

was said to have paid £5,100 for one of his sons, the Duke of Grafton, to have command of a company in the foot guards.[71] As we shall see when looking at the wider question of remuneration for crown servants, costs and liabilities could be involved as well as profits.

V. RETIREMENT

Part of the difficulty about succession to offices arose from the continuing lack of any regular provision for retirement. Exceptions can indeed be found. The elderly ex-royalist judge, Sir John Malet, was granted a pension of £250 a term (equivalent to £1,000 year) when he was superannuated from King's Bench in his eighties.[72] Sir John Doleman was allowed to retain the profits of his Council Clerkship when he retired in January 1685, though two weeks later he had to petition for four and a quarter years' arrears.[73] Lower down the scale, the Doorkeeper to the Excise Appeals Commissioners sought leave to surrender his post, in exchange for a lump sum from his prospective successor, after seventeen years' service. Earlier than that, an aged and infirm Watchman in the port of London had petitioned for an allowance from his successor.[74] Sometimes we have to infer from the very silence of the sources that voluntary surrender would involve a cash payment from the incoming postholder; but this was by no means an invariable rule. It is perhaps not surprising to find that it was in the new revenue services—the Excise and the non-sinecure side of the Customs— that anything like regular retirement pensions were first to emerge. An isolated case is found in the London customs at the end of Charles's reign, and then an actual superannuation fund, based on a compulsory 1.25 per cent annual levy, in the excise

[71] Scouller, 'Purchase of Commissions and Promotions'; C. Dalton, *Army Lists*, i. 289, 315, shows that Grafton became *Colonel* of the King's Foot Guards in 1681, which makes this very large sum more plausible.

[72] CSPD, 1673–4, p. 188; CTB, i. 533; DNB; Sainty, *Judges*.

[73] CSPD, 1684–5, pp. 282, 284, 295.

[74] CTB, vii. 1397; ibid., iv. 50.

under his successor. The customs did not get a regular superannuation fund for another generation, not until near the end of Queen Anne's reign (1712). The only detailed study of these developments is concerned almost exclusively with the customs scheme, perhaps owing to the relative paucity of excise records from a sufficiently early date.[75]

VI. TENURE

Clearly the value of offices, and hence a large part of their attractions for prospective purchasers and other aspirants, would depend to some extent on the security of tenure enjoyed by their holders. Earlier in the century the preponderance of posts were held for life, with a significant number of major offices being held during the King's pleasure or during the good behaviour of the incumbent.[76] Under the Long Parliament and then the Commonwealth there was a marked but by no means complete move away from life to pleasure tenure; under the Cromwellian Protectorate there was a slight swing back the other way, to life tenure.[77] At the Restoration, the initial assumption seems to have been that everything would be as it had been before 1642, and that grants with life tenure would thus again be the norm. However, we soon find evidence pointing the other way. As early as 1662 a Bill was in draft to nullify all grants of offices carrying survivorships or reversions in the areas of justice, finance, the customs and military garrisons; those procuring such grants were to be punished by being rendered permanently incapable of holding any office at all.[78] In November 1663 it was ruled that the King could dismiss officers who had been sworn in but did not hold by patent, for

---

[75] Ibid., vii. 603, 1043–4, 1068; ibid., viii. 1173; Marios Raphael, *Pensions and Public Servants. A Study of the Origins of the British System* (Paris and The Hague, 1964), based on a Ph.D. thesis written at the London School of Economics under the supervision of Prof. Richard Titmuss; for the Excise see pp. 124–6.

[76] Aylmer, *King's Servants*, ch. 3, sect. iii, and via the index.

[77] Aylmer, *The State's Servants*, ch. 3, sect. ii.

[78] *CSPD, 1661–2*, p. 613.

committing misdemeanours, regardless of their formal tenure.[79] But there was no general move away from life tenure until 1667–8, and Sir John Sainty is surely correct to associate this campaign with the Treasury Commissioners (of 1667–72). His tables of appointments and reversions show a dramatic shift in the Exchequer (though here there was to be a subsequent return to life tenure by the next century), in the Ordnance Office, at the Mint, in the King's Works, among the Clerks of the Privy Council and the Sergeants-at-Arms. Except in the Exchequer, these changes proved permanent and irreversible.[80]

Any government wishing to exercise closer control over its servants might have been expected to see the benefits of abandoning life tenure. This would have been as true of a parliamentary republic as of an absolute monarchy; with increased efficiency goes at least the possibility of greater power. Sainty also points out that the tenure of the twelve common-law judges was changed from good behaviour to pleasure at the very same time, and here the motive was quite clearly to have tighter executive control over the judiciary, marking a step towards what Andrew Marvell and others called 'arbitrary government'. The reversal of this and a return to good behaviour (amounting to almost total security of tenure) for the judges was to be one consequence of the gradual shift towards constitutional or parliamentary monarchy after the Revolution of 1688, although it was not achieved until William III was forced onto the political defensive in 1701. As for Charles's reign, by the 1670s there could only have been a handful of offices held by patent from the Crown during good behaviour, while the number held for life was steadily diminishing owing to deaths and resignations. Sainty even discerned a slight swing back to grants for life in the Exchequer under Lord Treasurer Danby, which was to be reversed again under the second Treasury Commission (of 1679–85).

[79] Ibid., *1663–4*, p. 358.
[80] Sainty, 'The Tenure of Offices in the Exchequer', *Eng. Hist. Rev.*, 80 (1965), 449–75; 'A Reform in the Tenure of Offices during the Reign of Charles II', *Bull. IHR*, 41 (1968), 150–71, esp. app., pp. 165–71. The Lowndes MSS strongly support his conclusions: see references in n. above and below.

VII. REVERSIONS

Reversionary grants of offices were a long-established and wide-spread feature of the old administrative system, but like other aspects easier to describe than to evaluate. The prevalence of reversions was closely related to the modes of entry and appointment and to the forms of tenure, but not so much so that the whole system can simply be subsumed under these headings. During the parliamentary and republican regimes of 1642 to 1660 there had been an almost total cessation of such grants.[81] Not surprisingly they reappeared more or less automatically with the welter of claims and counter-claims which we have observed in 1660 and immediately thereafter. A reversion was basically a cheap way of doing someone a favour; and depending on the accidents of mortality such a grant might never take effect. For instance, in 1662 the Secretary of State and the Keeper of the Privy Purse secured a reversion to the exceptionally lucrative Chief Clerkship of King's Bench, but the former died in 1685 and the latter was killed in action much sooner (in 1665), while the then holder of the office lived until 1692.[82] From the applicant's point of view, a reversion could be a kind of 'consolation prize', for himself or a member of his family, to make up for not getting an office—or perhaps a pension. There could also be disputes or uncertainty as to whose gift they were in. The power to grant a reversion to the Registrarship of the Prerogative Court of Canterbury was agreed to lie with the Archbishop, although this was essentially an office under the Crown.[83] The flow of such grants to legal, revenue, customs, and household offices continued for a time unchecked, although as early as 1662 a draft Bill would have prohibited them in all financial and judicial posts, at the same time that tenure was to be changed to good behaviour.[84] Perhaps predictably, no further move appears until the Treasury

[81] Aylmer, *State's Servants*, 77, etc.
[82] *CSPD, 1661–2*, p. 573; PRO, PROB 11/413, q. 9, Sir Robert Henley; *Hist. Parl.*, ii. 525.
[83] *CSPD, 1665–6*, pp. 175–6.
[84] PRO, SP 29/66/72 (partly illegible, at least on microfilm).

Commissioners took over, when they claimed a veto on (apparently) all reversionary grants, not only those in the revenue sector.[85] And, although it survives in the state papers and not in the treasury records, a list of reversions granted from May 1667 to September 1669 seems likely to have been compiled at their behest; at least eleven out of the eighteen named were to revenue or legal offices.[86] While any precise calculation is impossible, the Commissioners seem to have had less success with reversions than with tenure, although common sense suggests that offices held only during pleasure would be less attractive to those seeking reversions, whether for themselves, their close relatives, or as brokers on behalf of others. In 1678 the Treasury Secretary or one of his clerks minuted somewhat ungrammatically 'The King don't grant manors in reversion'—not that he still had many of which to dispose.[87] On the other hand, a general ban on reversionary grants does seem to have been in operation by 1682; whether this was for political reasons (to keep out those who might later prove disloyal), on grounds of greater administrative efficiency, or simply because the succession to some offices had become clogged with such grants and what were called survivorships is not clear.[88] However, grants made between that date and the King's death demonstrate that the ban was, to put it no stronger, less than completely effective, even if the flow had been checked by comparison with the early years of the reign.[89]

VIII. DEPUTIES

Among the conditions often laid down in the grant of an office, either by royal patent or by departmental warrant, was whether or not the holder could perform his duties by deputy; and, if so,

---

[85] *CSPD, 1667–8*, p. 1.
[86] PRO, SP 29/265/184, a list of offices granted for lives successively, also known as survivorships; all six have some connection with crown finance.
[87] *CTB*, v. 1356.
[88] *CSPD, 1682*, p. 557; *CTB*, vii. 667.
[89] *CSPD, 1683–4*, pp. 185, 360; ibid., *1684–5*, pp. 229, 275, 305.

on what basis the deputy was in turn to be appointed. In 1665 the Master of the Rolls certified that the Prothonotary of Chancery normally acted by deputy, and that the same was true of the Register (or Registrar) in that court.[90] This was by no means the same as the Lieutenant of the Tower having to seek special permission to be absent, and getting leave to appoint a deputy while he was away.[91] Lord Treasurer Southampton forbade any officer of the Lower Exchequer from acting by deputy except with special permission, while in the Upper Exchequer deputies to the Auditors were to be sworn and their names reported.[92] By contrast, Secretary Williamson seems to have appointed Sir Roger L'Estrange, who was already Surveyor of the Press, to be his deputy for licensing publications entirely on his own initiative; likewise the Duke of Monmouth made Lord Fauconberg his deputy as Chief Justice in Eyre south of Trent by deed poll when he was sent off to suppress the rising in south-west Scotland.[93] On the other hand, restrictions were set on customs officers who held by royal patent from having deputies. Waiters were said to have no authority to create their own deputies; in the outports, patent officers' deputies were to be officially approved and not to act on an occasional or irregular basis. Yet it seems to have been taken for granted that the Chief Searchership at Gravesend (a branch of the port of London) would act by deputy.[94] An unusual arrangement is found in the will of Sir William Bowles, Groom of the Tents, Toils, Hales, and Pavilions, deputy to his own son, William Bowles junior, who held the Mastership of the Tents, etc. on life tenure; but at New Year's Day 1679 Bowles senior reckoned that no less than £29,514 5s. 4d. was owing by the Crown to him and other officers of this sub-department of the Chamber. He disposed of the residue of these arrears, if they were ever

[90] Ibid., *1665–6*, p. 175; H. Horwitz, *Chancery Equity Records and Proceedings*, 11.
[91] *CSPD, 1667*, pp. 256, 280.
[92] *CTB*, i. 687; ibid., ii. 27, 129, 224 (The Treasury Commissioners, July 1667–June 1668).
[93] *CSPD, 1673–5*, p. 571; ibid., *1679–80*, p. 247.
[94] *CTB*, vi. 24–9; ibid., vii. 226–7, 415, 1521.

collected, to his two sons and five daughters in equal shares, making his other son (not his heir) executor of the will.[95] This can only have been an attempt to keep the office of Master in the family, though there would seem to have been only a slim hope of recovering such huge debts.

IX. ABSENCE AND ABSENTEEISM

Acting by deputy could arise from pluralism, in the case of an individual holding another office. But this was not quite the same thing as absenteeism. If the Lord Lieutenant was out of Ireland, he had to obtain royal approval for the appointment of a Lord Deputy, or else the King himself would appoint Lords Justices, as he often did during an interval between lieutenancies. Thus Ormonde had his two sons, Ossory and Arran, to act for him in turn as Lord Deputy when he was absent during his successive viceroyalties, but not because he was also Lord Steward of the Household. The Vice-Treasurer of Ireland was normally but not invariably also Treasurer-at-Wars. This was almost comparable to the Chancellor of the Exchequer also being the Under-Treasurer in England. More unusually, in 1673 the Master of the Rolls in Ireland was also to act temporarily as Vice-Treasurer there.[96] Absenteeism without express royal permission or the appointment of an approved deputy could be a cause for dismissal or, with a patent office held for life, at least of suspension. This can be seen in the Navy, including the royal dockyards, the Mint, and in Ireland. Even a seventy-year-old ship's cook was held to need the Lord Admiral's dispensation from attendance in order not to be classed as an absentee.[97] Absence due to illness was treated with varying degrees of sympathy. The Treasury Secretary was definitely unhelpful towards one of the Exchequer Auditors; by contrast the royal favourite and Bedchamberman Thomas Chiffinch got six weeks

---

[95] PRO, PROB 11/365, q. 40.
[96] *CSPD, 1673*, p. 586.
[97] Ibid., *1667-8*, pp. 329-30; ibid., *1668-9*, pp. 85, 110; ibid., *1672-3*, pp. 203, 362-3, 376; ibid., *1678*, pp. 237-8, 241; *CTB*, ii. 626.

leave plus authority to find his own substitute. It seems to have been tacitly recognized that the Lieutenancy of the Tower was so testing, if not stressful, a post that its holder needed periodic spells of leave.[98]

X. HOLIDAYS AND HOURS OF WORK

All this was the more understandable in that there was no provision for regular holidays, although officials in the courts kept the normal four law terms, while great officers of state often took a break when the King himself was out of town, unless of course they were required to attend on him at Newmarket, Windsor or wherever else. Some officers in the household and in the central executive attended in rotation, quarterly or monthly. There is even evidence of a kind of bargaining process with the dockyard workers at Deptford and Chatham in 1670 and 1671 demanding holidays to compensate for chronic arrears of pay.[99] The officers of the Lower Exchequer were warned not to take excessive and additional holidays, but what constituted the norm is not clear.[100] This may have been related partly to the hours of work. Those who called the tune for other officials and for members of the public who required their services, such as the Treasury Commissioners and the Auditors, specified the time at which they would be available to transact business, though in the former case these were constantly being changed. The Receipt of Exchequer was to be open for business from 8 a.m. to noon in summer and from 9 a.m. to noon in winter, but it seems unlikely that the officers there worked only a three-hour day for half the year. They were not allowed to take more than three weeks off without special permission; two years after this the Treasury Commissioners told them that their hours of attendance were not sufficient.[101]

[98] *CTB*, iv. 104; ibid., v. 1188; *CSPD, 1683–4*, p. 394; ibid., *1684–5*, p. 132.
[99] *CSPD, 1670*, p. 50; ibid., *1671*, p. 126.
[100] *CTB*, iii. 568–9.
[101] *CSPD, 1667–8*, pp. 459, 470; *CTB*, i. 686; ibid., ii. 3–4, 6, 104, 235, 247, 317, 463–4; ibid., iii. 954; ibid., iv. 326–7, and so on.

It is all but impossible to reconstruct the actual day-to-day routine of any one individual. For all its richness as a historical source even Pepys's Diary is tantalizingly difficult to use for this humdrum but by no means trivial purpose. Meetings of the Navy Board were held at fixed times, but as Clerk of the Acts he did not have to keep regular office hours.

XI. THE LOCATION OF OFFICES

Here too there was more continuity with the earlier part of the century than might have been the case if the Republic had endured. Parts of the Household were wherever the King was; the same was true with those on duty in the central executive, though here there was often a division between those in attendance and others who stayed in the capital. Charles spent prolonged periods away from Whitehall and St James's, regularly at Newmarket and Windsor, occasionally elsewhere, at Hampton Court and latterly in Winchester. Those departments and legal offices which had been based in and around the City had had mostly to find new premises as a result of the Great Fire; top priority was given to rehousing the Excise and the Customs Offices. The latter had to be on the main (north bank) waterfront. The Excise had to move twice, ending up with new, permanent premises in a court off Broad Street. The Navy Office escaped in 1666 but had to be rebuilt as the result of another fire in 1673. The common-law courts and Chancery sat in Westminster hall, but their offices were in the Temple and Chancery Lane respectively. The Ordnance Office and the Mint were located in the Tower, a source of much petty squabbling over the use of buildings and open spaces. The Exchequer and the Treasury, and the central executive (when not peripatetic) were in Whitehall. The public or royal records were divided between the Tower, the Rolls Chapel off Chancery Lane, and their respective departments.[102] Although it would have taken

---

[102] Besides numerous casual references in a wide range of sources see *The A to Z of Restoration London [The City of London]*, introductory notes by

less time than with present-day traffic conditions, Pepys had a considerable walk (when he did not go by coach or by boat) between the Navy Office and the Admiralty, and to attend on the King, the Duke, or the House of Commons, well over three miles away. (This would have been less of course 'as the crow flies', because of the curve in the river between Westminster and the Tower.) Other contemporary diarists record a great deal of coming and going, as well as 'wining and dining', but Pepys alone conveys for the reader the extent of 'face-to-face' contact; he knew, or knew of, an astonishing number of people, covering moreover the entire range of the social hierarchy from royalty, royal mistresses, and great ministers of state through the middle ranks to tapsters, porters, and orange girls. No doubt the fact that his duties, as well as pleasures, took him right across the city from east to west, gave him unusual opportunities to observe things and people; but then, as now, some human beings are more observant than others.[103]

XII. REMUNERATION

To explain how office-holders supported themselves, and what material rewards they received does not lend itself to generalizations. There is no doubt that, compared with the situation before the Civil War, more middle-ranking positions in the revenue departments and in the armed forces carried relatively generous salaries. There is also no doubt that the attempts to restrict, even to abolish the taking of fees and gratuities, made in the 1640s and 1650s, were simply abandoned at the Restoration. It would be convenient to be able to say that officers who did not receive payments from those who needed to

Ralph Hyde, index comp. by J. Fisher and R. Cline (London Topographical Society, 145 (1992)); and many vols. of *The Survey of London* (pub. for the LCC, then GLC, now Corporation of the City of London, 1900–).

[103] As well as the *Diary*, see vol. x, *Companion*, and the biographies by Arthur Bryant and Richard Ollard; although the former is more detailed, the latter is particularly successful at conveying the sense of Pepys as both observer and participant.

make use of their services had larger stipendiary fees or salaries from the Crown to make up for it; but this was only partly so. Great officers of state and those in specially favoured positions, such as the Gentlemen and Grooms of the Bedchamber, had generous stipends or pensions. In addition they might well receive presents as brokers or middlemen; some no doubt trafficked systematically or casually in lesser offices and other forms of royal favour, but they did not receive regular fees or gratuities. As Lord Treasurer (and effectively chief minister), Danby's salary was £8,000 a year (more than the landed income of many peers); by contrast his Secretary (and brother-in-law), Charles Bertie, and the clerks in the office would seem to have been wholly dependent on fees and gifts until later in the century.[104] Some salaries at the middle and lower levels may have been intended to justify the holder's not being entitled to take fees or gratuities. Why else should the Assay-master of Tin have merited £200 a year out of the Exchequer?[105] Sometimes additional stipendiary payments were authorized for extra work; each of the Ordnance Commissioners (acting in lieu of a Master of that office) was to receive an extra £500 for wartime burdens.[106] The Auditor of the Receipt and his clerks were awarded an additional £500 for the extra work involved by grants of parliamentary taxation.[107] Others were paid in poundage, a percentage on gross turnover. The Excise Commissioners were to have two pence in the pound (or 0.83 per cent), whereas Stephen Fox (that 'wonderful child of providence', as he described himself) got fourpence in the pound (or 1.67 per cent) on the newly raised land forces in 1667.[108] The Treasury Commissioners wanted the Treasurer of the Navy to have £2,000 a year in place of all fees; for a holder of this office who was both honest and efficient, it would have been cheap at the price.[109] At a lower level, the Treasury acting through the

[104] See Stephen B. Baxter, *The Development of the Treasury, 1660–1702* (London, 1957); Sainty, *Office-holders in Modern Britain*, i, *Treasury Officials, 1660–1870* (London, 1972); Henry Roseveare, *The Treasury: The Evolution of a British Institution* (London, 1969).
[105] *CSPD, 1666–7*, p. 213.   [106] Ibid., 339.
[107] Ibid., *1667*, p. 98.   [108] Ibid., *1666–7*, p. 601; ibid., *1667*, p. 223.
[109] *CTB*, iii. 375 (25 Feb. 1670).

Customs Commissioners, could vary stipends both upwards and downwards. Thus the four Searchers in the port of London were to have £60, instead of £40 p.a. each, but the Collector at Plymouth had his salary cut to £140 a year. In 1671 an exact scale was worked out so that the total cost of the Band of Gentlemen Pensioners could be kept to £6,000 a year: for the Captain £1,000, the Lieutenant £500, the Standard-bearer £310, the forty gentlemen £100 each, the Clerk of the Cheque £120, and the Harbinger £70.[110] When the £500 a year salary for the Lord Admiral's Secretary was confirmed at Matthew Wren's succession to William Coventry in 1667, the treasury minute records 'ordered by the King, for able men to enter his service'.[111] In order not to exaggerate the contrast between navy and army, we should remember the evidence for something similar being attempted with military commissions in the 1680s.

There was a formal distinction between stipends or salaries which were carried on a particular departmental payroll and those which were paid direct from the Exchequer. This in turn bears on the question of arrears, to what extent officers got paid as and when they should. For otherwise, as the north-country saying goes, 'fine words butter no parsnips'. Payment out of departmental funds would depend on whether the particular treasurer or paymaster received what he was due and was in turn punctual and honest in paying it out. Thus when dockyard workers were driven to the verge of industrial action, and sometimes even over it, because of their wages not being paid, this was usually because the Treasurer of the Navy and his various subordinate paymasters had more urgent priorities.[112] Yet those who were paid direct from the Exchequer could be in a more vulnerable position, as for example when in August 1663 the King was persuaded to direct the Lord Treasurer to stop the

[110] Ibid., 1184, 1231; *CSPD, 1671*, p. 131.
[111] *CTB*, ii. 188.
[112] For evidence of strikes and withdrawal of labour by dockyard workers see *CSPD, 1663–4*, pp. 242–4, 276 (Chatham); ibid., *1664–5*, p. 189 (Deptford); ibid., *Addenda 1660–85*, pp. 135, 139 (Woolwich); ibid., *1665–6*, pp. 30, 181–2 (Woolwich); ibid., 53, 317–24 (Portsmouth); ibid., 469, 471 (Harwich); ibid., *1667*, p. 453 (Woolwich); ibid., *1671*, p. 578 (Chatham).

payment of all pensions, although exceptions were soon being made both for named individuals and for special categories of people.[113] When the Treasury Commissioners got to work in 1667–8, they had lists made, showing who was how much in arrears, and many office-holders and pensioners were ordered to receive one year's payment. Even Lauderdale, the King's de facto viceroy in Scotland, who said that his £1,000 a year pension as Gentleman of the Bedchamber was four and a half years behind, had to put up with a single year's payment.[114] In November 1666, at the height of the Dutch War and towards the end of Southampton's Treasurership, the King's twenty-two violinists said that their pay was four and three quarters years in arrears and they apparently got an order for payment in full, whereas the Messengers of the Chamber, who claimed to be three and a half years behind, although they were perhaps more necessary to the functioning of government, received only one year's pay.[115] Other financial ups and downs in the course of the reign affected the regularity of officers' payment, though it is worth noting that the famous (or infamous) Stop of the Exchequer, which took effect in the winter of 1671–2, did not in itself lead directly to the cessation of stipendiary and salary payments. Much the most comprehensive table of arrears which I have found was compiled at the very beginning of the next reign and was based on the situation at Christmas 1684 (Table 3.2). It would naturally be unwise to say that the state of things on the eve of the King's death was typical of what it had been throughout his reign. When the first Treasury Commissioners had reviewed arrears in 1668 (setting aside bad debts from the Interregnum) no one could have been more than eight years in arrears even if they had been appointed at the Restoration and had received no pay at all. It could be argued that 1684 was untypical in two quite different, almost opposite ways: there might have been a general unspoken assumption in informed circles that the King did not have long to live and a corre-

---

[113] Ibid., i. 542, *et seq.*
[114] Ibid., ii. 230, 544–50, 554–9.
[115] CSPD, 1666–7, pp. 245, 248–9, 291, 446.

TABLE 3.2 *Arrears in ratio of money owing to annual payments due, Christmas 1684*[116]

Office	Arrears
Revels	13.90
Tents and Toils	12.50
Apothecaries, etc.	10.50
Surgeons	10.20
Surveyors of Woods, etc.	10.05
Ordnance Office	8.65
Keepers of Forests, etc.	8.42
Musicians	7.54
Physicians	7.40
Jewel House	6.90
Ceremonies	6.16
Pages of Honour	5.95
Keepers of Papers, etc.	5.94
Governors and Captains of Garrisons, Forts, and Castles	5.78
Falconers	5.66
Grooms of Bedchamber to King	5.42
Queen's Dressers	5.41
Office of Works	5.34
Secretaries of State	4.34
Heralds, etc.	4.30
Groom Littermen	4.12
Grooms of the Bedchamber	4.02
Gents of the Bedchamber	4.00
Counsel Learned	3.92
Queen's Maids of honour	3.62
Wardrobe and Robes	3.53
Stables	3.24
Keepers of Houses and Gardens	3.24
Divers Officers	2.90
Band of Pensioners	2.69
Clerks of Council and House of Commons	2.67
Huntsmen	2.29
Judges in Eyre	1.62
Upper Exchequer	1.55
Readers in Universities	1.37
Masters of Requests	1.31
Chancery Masters	0.50
Judges of Common Pleas	0.06
Judges of King's Bench	0.01
Judges of Chester	—
Exchequer of Receipt	—

[116] Bodl. Eng. Hist. MS b.99, fos. 3–18ᵛ, which can be taken in conjunction with MS b.100, fos. 2–23, the Arrears of Charles II's servants, with what was

sponding wariness about what his brother's succession would bring; in short, the whole system might have been like a clock running down. As against this, Charles had decisively defeated his political enemies and his overall financial position—provided that the country remained at peace—had never been stronger. So the tables of arrears from William Lowndes's papers in the Bodleian Library, while not necessarily representative of the whole reign, may not actually be so misleading. The Judges and the officers of the Exchequer were the most up to date in terms of pay received. Various offshoots of the Chamber and some categories of its staff were the worst off, in having the longest arrears owing to them. Conspicuously absent from the list are the officers of the Navy (shore as well as seagoing), Customs, Excise, and Hearth Tax, also the Tax Office and the Treasury itself. The slightly defeatist sub-heading by the author of the paper 'Officers of Divers Natures' includes the Constable of the Tower, the Poet Laureate, the Groom Porter, certain officers of the Mint, William Blathwayt in his capacity as Auditor of revenues arising from the American colonies, and others who might well have come under the various branches of the Chamber. The sub-headings are conveniently tabulated at the end of the document. On a total of £72,598 11s. 11½d. due to be paid annually, the amount owing was £259,790 18s. 3d., or an average of rather over three and a half years (3.58), whereas the median arrears for departments (on my reckoning) was just over four years (4.12). The paper also gives the tenure on which the offices were held, and can be shown to validate most strongly Sir John Sainty's case about the changeover from life to pleasure.

To take the case of one very influential individual, the Earl of Bath was owed £450 on an annual fee of £80 as Keeper of St James's House (= Palace), but much more seriously no less than

---

owed in full to midsummer 1679 and one-third of what was owing from then to Christmas 1684; this is more difficult to use than either of the other two Lowndes MSS. The author himself had problems with the grand total owing, giving it as £216,154 18s. 2d. and then as £112,916 17s. 9d., next splitting the difference at £118,895 13s. 5d., and finally in despair crossing out all three totals (fo. 21).

£16,500 on stipendiary fees and pensions of £5,000 a year as Groom of the Stole and First Gentleman of the Bedchamber. Another document in the same collection offers an alternative set of calculations, giving debts owing from before 1679 in full and then at one-third for the last five years. On this reckoning Bath was owed £10,370 18s. 0d., excluding the St James's post. When we find so many office-holders with their stipendiary pay from the Exchequer so grossly in arrears, two different conclusions might be drawn. Perhaps many courtiers were not serving the King for material reward or pecuniary gain at all, but for reasons of honour, status, and social or political ambition. There again, insofar as many of them clearly did depend on the material fruits of office for their well-being, if not their basic livelihood, then arrears on this sort of scale point to the importance of alternative forms of remuneration, both legitimate and otherwise.

For those receiving fees and gratuities a distinction may be drawn according to whether these were paid by other office-holders or by people outside the administrative system. Examples of the first type would be paymasters or receivers getting their accounts passed, or those needing to obtain a patent for promotion. Arlington had to pay £80 5s. 8d. on two warrants for £3,000; the Master of the Mint complained when the Clerks of the Privy Seal tried to take fees on an indenture, although the Signet Clerks were not doing so; Arlington again had to pay £14 10s. 0d. at the Privy Seal Office when he was raised to an earldom in 1672, though we need not feel too sorry for him since the Secretary of State's fees from Irish military commissions alone were said to be worth £2,000 a year. The Treasury Secretary got fees on all London customs appointments: £1 10s. 0d. on posts worth over £30 a year, 15s. on those worth £10 to £30, and nothing on those worth under £10 a year. It may seem strange but it is perhaps not so surprising that the total fees payable on a patent to become a King's Waiter amounted to £32 1s. 12d. when the official annual stipend was only £50. Richard Mounteney's important office as Receiver-General and Cashier of the Customs cost him £66 7s. 6d. in the Pipe Office alone; Williamson's promotion to the Secretary of

Stateship £18 16s. 0d. in all. Sometimes this could get out of hand. Bevil Skelton, Envoy Extraordinary to the Emperor and the Imperial Diet, put in a claim for £336 10s. 0d. to cover extraordinary charges from Michaelmas to Christmas 1676, of which no less than £146 10s. 0d. represented fees and payments to get his money authorized by Privy Seal; remarkably this was approved by Williamson. Yet all these and innumerable other such instances may fairly be thought of as exchanges within the system.[117]

The fees levied on members of the public, and the gratuities often needed on top of these, were a very different matter. Thus the owners and/or captains of all merchant ships trading in foreign waters required passes, for which detailed schedules of the fees payable were issued repeatedly. Those acting as sureties for local tax receivers had to pay fees to be registered as such. Even sheriffs of counties, who were appointed annually and were not themselves in receipt of any remuneration from the Crown had to pay fees for this burdensome privilege. It could apparently cost as much as £82 3s. 4d. (consisting of thirty different items) to become a knight. Those buying timber from royal forests had to pay 5 per cent poundage and/or fourpence on every tree marked for felling. Every individual passing through the port of Dover was supposed not to have to pay more than 2s. 8d. in fees as from November 1670, perhaps not so unreasonable if we imagine a charge of £5 to go through passport and customs controls today. Anything to do with parliament was notoriously expensive. For a family or a locality to see a private Bill introduced and passed as a private Act, the cost might run into £100s, with the Speaker and the Clerk of the House doing particularly well; and so on. Examples could be multiplied almost indefinitely.[118]

[117] *CSPD, 1667–8*, p. 525 (5–7 Aug. 1668); ibid., *1670*, pp. 457–8; ibid., *1671–2*, pp. 311, 357; *CTB*, iii. 971; PRO, 30/24/41/48, 12 (Shaftesbury Papers); *CTB*, iv. 651 (13 Jan. 1674/5); *CSPD, 1673–5*, pp. 505–13 (at the Hanaper £16 10s. 0d.; at the Privy Seal £6; in the Signet Office £1, 27 Sept. 1674); ibid., *1676–7*, pp. 578–9.
[118] *CSPD 1677–8*, p. 116; PRO, SP 29/379/140, 148; *CTB*, v. 440; Bodl. Eng. Hist. MS b.204 (Warcup Papers), fo. 84[r–v]; *CTB* vii. 795; *CSPD, 1670,*

So it is hardly surprising to find charges of extortion being brought against officials. The number of such cases where the accusation was not, in effect, one of corruption under another name, that is of soliciting or demanding bribes, and where the charge can be seen to have been substantiated, is in fact quite small. A letter to Williamson on limiting exactions by lawyers and minor legal officials (9 February 1670) is suggestive but does not take us very far. The Lord Lieutenant of Ireland issued a proclamation against excessive fees and litigious suits, with what consequences is not clear. Ironically the very same man who was serving as Secretary to the then viceroy was himself to be in serious trouble for illegal exactions not long after. Sir Ellis (alias Elisha) Leighton, son of the well-known Scottish episcomastix, who had been so severely punished under Charles I, was eventually convicted of extorting payments disguised as fees from English merchants trading in France, when serving as Secretary to the Ambassador in Paris. He escaped abroad but was sent back, surrendered himself and was re-imprisoned. In another potential *cause célèbre*, the Auditor of the Receipt Sir Robert Howard—that man of letters miscast as an administrator—was summoned to answer accusations by Pepys's protégé and friend, William Hewer, of having taken excessive fees for payments which he had made to Hewer in his capacity as acting Treasurer for Tangier, when these were not covered by the regular establishment for the garrison there. There would seem to be no good reason for Hewer to have fabricated this, but predictably Howard got away with it.[119]

There was some renewed agitation, from both inside and outside the system, for more effective control over the levying of fees. An anonymous draft of 1668 proposed the restriction of all

pp. 583–4; Orlo C. Williams, *Historical Development of Private Bill Procedure and Standing Orders in the House of Commons* (1948); Sheila Lambert, *Bills and Acts: Legislative Procedure in Eighteenth-century England* (1971); Maurice F. Bond, *Guide to the Records of Parliament* (1971), 70–83.

[119] *CSPD, 1670*, pp. 59–60, 349; Robert Steele, *A Bibliography of Royal Proclamations . . . 1485–1714*, ii, pt. i (Oxford, 1910), 101, nos. 810–13; *CSPD, 1676–7*, pp. 347–8, 355, 365–6, 373–7, 379–80; PRO, SP 29/385/252, 386/40; *DNB*, 'Ellis Leighton' (less than adequate), *CTB*, vii. 773 (25 Apr. 1683).

fees relating to royal revenues to those which had been taken in the reign of James I. And in 1676 the Treasury ordered that Charles I's commission on fees should be inspected and revived. Yet not until 1693 do we find any general order being issued for the publication and posting up of all fees which had been taken then and in Queen Elizabeth's time.[120] Compared with the fuss generated over 'exacted fees' before the Civil War, this would therefore not seem to have been so great a grievance after 1660; perhaps the ending of price inflation had reduced the financial pressure on office-holders and the consequent temptation to increase fees.[121]

On the other hand it would be naïve to infer that all was well on the financial side of the office-holding system. The King's Master Cook petitioned successfully against having £421 3s. 8d. deducted from his pay for the cost of provisions; but the King's Embellisher (illustrator of formal documents) failed to get £236 which was owing to him, due to a dispute between the Treasurer of the Chamber and the Auditor of the Receipt. The ex-Clerk of the Cheque at Harwich dockyard feared that he would be arrested and imprisoned for debt if he showed his face in London. The Deputy Prothonotary of Chancery sought £108 13s. 4d. for his expenses and pains in engrossing, passing, and enrolling commissions over a four-year period (March 1664 to March 1668); since he would presumably have been receiving fees for this work, it looks a little like a case of what Francis Bacon (in his *New Atlantis*) had called being 'twice-paid'.[122]

Benefits in kind could be important subsidiary sources of income. In January 1669 the Navy Commissioners were allowed to take 'lop and top' of all trees felled for the navy, notionally to cover the costs of transportation, though it seems unlikely that they would otherwise have had to meet these out of their own pockets. No wonder that Christopher Pett, an under-officer at Woolwich, who had been involved in procuring

[120] PRO SP 29/243/102, I; *CTB*, v. 438; *An Exact Table of Fees of all the Courts at Westminster. . .* (I have used the 4th edn. of 1702; the 1694 edn. is Wing, *STC 1641–1700*, E 3705).
[121] Aylmer, *King's Servants*, ch. 4, esp. sect. ii.
[122] *CSPD, 1666–7*, pp. 25, 60, 74; ibid., *1667–8*, pp. 319–20, 542.

supplies of timber for shipbuilding, wrote disconsolately to the Commissioners, 'I am troubled that . . . I should beat the bush and another catch the bird'. In the royal dockyards the taking of 'chips' (wood cuttings and shavings, possibly also sawdust) was a major issue. Pepys drew, or tried to draw, a distinction between large and small chips and said that the Carpenters were only entitled to the latter, but he failed to provide any clear definitions by either size or weight. In June 1670 the Porter of Deptford yard was told to stop taking out any deal chips; in the same year the Duke of York as Lord Admiral, apparently issued an order forbidding the taking of all chips in any circumstances. What had been allowed as a legitimate perquisite thus became a crime—of theft or embezzlement. Back in 1664–5 Navy Commissioner Thomas Middleton had pointed out that pilfering and the taking of illegitimate perquisites could only be stamped out if wages were increased and were also paid on time. The travails of other Commissioners, both at Portsmouth and in other yards, to be found in subsequent correspondence, suggest that more than a fiat from James was needed to put such matters to rights.[123]

So the importance to many officials of legitimate extras needs no emphasis. These could take a wide variety of forms. The Clerk of the Cheque at Chatham proposed that Messengers should receive 4s., not 3s., for every trip to London on official business. The Privy Seal and Signet Clerks petitioned for an additional £5 apiece for the extra writing which they had to do for the Exchequer Auditors. Eight Clerks to the four Tellers of the Receipt were awarded £80 for extra work involved with parliamentary taxes. At the end of the same year (1670) the Auditor of Receipt was awarded £200 and the Clerk of the Pells £100 for extraordinary services. Riding Surveyors of the

---

[123] *CTB*, iii. 2; *CSPD, 1667–8*, p. 63 (6 Dec. 1667); *CTB*, iii. 86 (16 June 1669); *CSPD, 1670*, p. 280; ibid., *Addenda 1660–85*, p. 321. Middleton's trenchant letters are in *CSPD 1664* and the vols. following. From 1673 to 1684 such correspondence is in PRO, ADM 106/281–379; I have used the excellent, very full calendar covering June 1673 to Dec. 1675 (ADM 106/281–314). Whether I shall manage to complete a separate study of naval administration, using the rest of that series in the originals, remains to be seen.

Customs (in effect itinerant trouble-shooters) were allowed
20s. a day for expenses. The Registrarship of the High Court
of Delegates was alleged to have been worth £500 before 1641
(in the days of the High Commission); the present holder who
said it was now worth nothing at all, was to have £40 a year
(December 1672). On the other hand, the Lord Treasurer
rejected a claim for ten years' arrears when a Falconer's place
changed hands, but offered either two to three years' or £150
cash down instead. The Earl of Anglesey recorded in his
diary—apparently with pained surprise—that some people
disapproved of his both having a pension of £3,000 a year and
receiving the full profits of the Privy Seal. The Comptroller-
General of Customs was awarded an extra £100 on top of
£400 a year; he and his clerks were granted exemption from
jury service and military or civil office. The Collector of
Customs at Milford Haven was given a rise from £20 to £40 a
year on account of the port's size and the number of its
branches (called creeks or members). The Postmaster of
Salisbury sought 13s. 6d. for having had to make a special
journey of forty-six miles. At the upper end of the scale, John
Shales, already an Exchequer Auditor, was to have £400 a year
as Inspector of naval accounts; this was authorized by his
patron, Lord Treasurer Danby. The pensions which Stephen
Fox told the House of Commons (in May 1679) were being
paid out of the Secret Service money (and thus without having
to be audited) included several either to compensate for loss of
office or to supplement existing salaries and/or fees. These
examples could be multiplied.[124] They leave an overall impression of haphazardness; some people who were working hard in
a demanding job were well rewarded, others badly. Favoured
courtiers, cronies, political allies, and the like enjoyed benefits
far in excess of what they could be said to earn, while others
more deserving went unrewarded altogether. In short, favour
trumped desert. General campaigns for retrenchment, economy

---

[124] *CSPD, 1670*, p. 12; *CTB*, iii. 457–515, 708, 1315; *CSPD, 1672–3*, p.
270; ibid., *1673*, p. 360; BL Add. MS 40,860, fo. 46; *CTB*, iv. 162, 840;
CSPD, 1677–8, p. 250; *CTB*, v. 673, 683–4 (Shales, Jun.–July 1677); Anchitell
Grey, *Debates of the House of Commons* (10 vols. 1769), vii. 323–4.

drives in royal expenditure, as in 1662–3, 1667–8, and later in the reign, invariably exempted certain specially favoured individuals and categories of people. The principle, that it would normally be an economy to pay reasonable salaries and wages punctually, seems to have been tacitly accepted, but it could never be acted upon regularly and uniformly across the whole face of government.

XIII. CORRUPTION

How important were the gains from office on the wrong side of the line? This leads us into the complicated question of what was held to constitute corruption in later seventeenth-century terms, and to assess the scale and significance of what might today be called the 'sleaze factor'.

The most lucrative but also most risky perquisite enjoyed by treasurers, receivers, and paymasters was the right to use the cash balances which they held in hand for their own advantage. It was accepted that holders of such financial offices could use the king's money in this way between the time of its receipt, either from taxpayers or from the Crown itself, normally via the Exchequer, and the time when it had either to be disbursed or paid in and the account rendered for it. Not surprisingly some of them speculated unwisely, or made unsecured loans, or simply lived too extravagantly; a few actually made away with the money. It is impossible to say how many made legitimate fortunes in this way and how many were undone. There are striking individual examples of both types, and in some cases there is genuine, even insoluble doubt as to whether they acted improperly or not.

One of the earliest was that of Sir John Prettyman, Bart., Receiver of clerical tenths and first fruits in the Exchequer. An active royalist in the 1640s and 1650s, his debts were estimated at £15,000 by 1667; in 1669 the Crown was said to be owed £16,000 on his account. Prettyman lost his office and his seat in parliament and died in the King's Bench prison as an insolvent debtor, though the management of this branch of the revenue remained in the hands of other members of his family. As to whether he was deliberately dishonest or just incompetent and unlucky, the sources do not really permit of a firm answer. It is perhaps a little suggestive that his brother, Sir William, the Remembrancer of the same office, also got into difficulties. In 1677 his debt to the Crown of £8,465 17s. 8d. was amortized, on the basis that he would pay £400 every half year until 1687; but a year later things were said to have got worse and he in turn was suspended from office. These revenues arose in part from regular taxation of the clergy, in part from the windfall profits of vacant bishoprics. According to Chandaman, the Convention Parliament of 1660 was correct in estimating their average value at £18,000 a year, though his own figures for receipts and assignments show that for much of the reign the actual yield fell well short of this. If that total is accepted, then even Sir John Prettyman's debt would only have represented the equivalent of less than one year's arrears, and that of his brother less than six months' arrears.[125]

The case of Robert Hope, Esquire, Chief Clerk of the Spicery in the Household, was slightly different. He did not account direct to the Exchequer, but came under the control of the Board of Green Cloth, and it was they who suspended him when he was found to owe £6,355 in March 1665. The fact that pensions were granted to his daughters after his death in 1686 either indicates remarkable forgivingness or a tacit recognition that Hope had somehow been hardly treated.[126]

The story of Pepys's one-time friend, Thomas Townsend, is different again. He was co-Clerk of the Great Wardrobe from 1664/5 and sole Clerk from 1667; but he also acted in practice as deputy to the Earl of Sandwich, the Master of the office, and as its disbursing and accounting officer. Complaints soon began to pile up against him for extortion; he was suspended and then in effect also superseded. His accounts were still caus-

---

[125] Num. refs. in *CSPD* and *CTB*; *Hist. Parl.* iii. 284–5; C. D. Chandaman, *The English Public Revenue, 1660–1688* (Oxford, 1975), 115–17, 348–63.
[126] PRO, LS 13/170, fo. 172; LS 13/255, p. 32; and refs. in *CSPD*.

ing trouble well into the next decade, indeed possibly still at the time of his death around 1680. By 1668 the diarist seems to have come round to the Treasury Commissioners' view that Townsend was 'a knave and a fool', whose appointment reflected ill on his and Pepys's own patron.[127]

Perhaps the most shocking case was that of Sir William Doyley, knight and baronet. As one of the four Tellers in the receipt of Exchequer, he held a particularly sensitive position with discretionary control over in and out payments. His father, Sir William senior (*c.* 1614–1677), was proceeded against for £871 wrongly collected as a Hearth Tax receiver, but the son's offences were much more serious. He was found to owe the Crown £12,508, but this was disproportionately heinous in someone occupying a post of such special financial trust. Moreover, a double marriage settlement and a will which was never brought to probate apparently prevented the money which he owed from ever being collected.[128]

The undoing of Henry Slingsby had certain similarities with that of Doyley, although in most ways he was a more reputable figure. The younger son of a Yorkshire royalist family, he was co-Master and then Master of the Mint for most of the reign, and thus also in a position of particular financial responsibility. Investigations into his alleged irregularities were begun in 1677; he was suspended from office in 1680, and eventually forced out altogether in 1686. Of how much he actually cheated the Crown, as opposed merely to failing to present proper accounts, is not clear. By 1683 he was said to owe only £1,934, but at the end of Slingsby's life his friend John Evelyn remarked that he was in 'very deplorable circumstances' because of his debts both to the King and to private creditors. The diarist recorded trying to persuade the Treasury Commissioners to handle Slingsby as gently as they could; but by the next reign his debt to the crown was reckoned to be £12,697. Finally his widow had a total sum of no less than

[127] *Pepys Diary*, iv. 102; ix. 41, 52; x; PRO, LC 3/1, 61, 73; refs. in *CTB*, iii and v.
[128] Num. refs. in *CSPD* and *CTB*, iii–vi. A full account is given in Baxter, *Treasury*, 151–6.

£22,621 15*s*. 2*d*. written off in May 1690. And so he disappears from view.[129]

Then there was our old friend Colonel Roger Whitley. He was pursued relentlessly for having misdirected royal revenues into his own pockets, both as Deputy Postmaster (1672–7) and as a Commissioner for disbanding the forces (1678–9). But, as we shall see, his real offence was probably his exclusionist support for the Duke of Monmouth. On the opposite side of the political divide, the one-time Shaftesburyite-Whig client, turned court examining magistrate, Edmund Warcup, had been accused of fiddling the prize goods accounts and of forging his master's signature as early as 1666, but he was always on the winning side in politics and thrived on to fortune. At the highest level, Pepys's patron the Earl of Sandwich was disgraced for having allowed prize cargoes to be broken open and the contents distributed, before their value had been appraised for the King's share to be thereby safeguarded. This was in the famous case of the Dutch East India Company vessels captured in 1665; at the very least the Earl was guilty of culpable laxity towards his subordinates—as we have also seen in the case of Townsend.

By contrast the Earl of Orrery (Roger Boyle, known as Lord Broghill in Cromwellian times) was more successful in rebutting the charges brought against him when he was about to be impeached in 1669. One article charged him with having, in effect, exacted a political levy from ex-parliamentarians in Ireland, when advancing their claims in the post-Restoration land settlement there, and then having diverted the money so raised to his personal use. Another article charged him with having caused various branches of the Irish revenue to be undervalued, and thus leased at too low a rent, because he was secretly involved with some of the prospective farmers of these revenues. To the first count, he responded that far less had been

---

[129] Sir John Craig, *The Mint: A History of the London Mint from AD 287 to 1948* (Cambridge, 1953), ch. 10, pp. 176–8; C. E. Challis (ed.), *A New History of the Royal Mint* (Cambridge, 1992), 354–5; *Diary of John Evelyn*, iv. 567; *CTB*, viii. 49–50 (some of this was owed by Slingsby in other capacities), ix. 665–8, and many other refs, in *CTB* and *CSPD*.

raised than was alleged, and that in any case it had all been spent on the unavoidable costs, in fees and gratuities, of advancing actions in the courts and promoting legislation in parliament. The second he denied outright, arguing that he had actually helped to get the rental for these revenues raised to a higher figure than had at first been proposed and was about to be accepted. Whether or not Orrery was wholly innocent, this illustrates that with the costs involved in political lobbying and in the manœuvres associated with tax-farming, there was not so much a strictly defined line as an amorphous zone between what was and was not regarded as permissible.[130]

XIV. LOSS OF OFFICE

Just as new posts could be created, as for example in the Great Wardrobe, the Ordnance Office, the Customs, and the Excise, so others could be abolished. And here the matter of compensation, or alternative employment was obviously a vital issue, perhaps a matter of life and death, though some squealed before they were hurt. The two provincial Presidencies in Ireland, those of Munster and Connaught respectively, were abolished in 1673. Lord Berkeley of Stratton had already enjoyed two years as Lord Lieutenant before the ending of his Connaught Presidency; he pleaded and wheedled for a compensatory pension, though he seems also to have been out of pocket on his Lieutenancy pension at his death in 1678; as against this he held at least one sinecure office in the law courts at the end of his life.[131] Orrery, however, was apparently allowed to keep all his allowances when he lost the Munster Presidency and enjoyed

[130] See *A Collection of the State Letters of the Right Honourable Roger Boyle, The First Earl of Orrery, Lord President of Munster in Ireland* (fo. London, 1742), app. to the Revd T. Morrice's Life of Orrery, 51–4 and 55–8, for the art. against him and his answers. The fullest modern study is Kathleen M. Lynch, *Roger Boyle: First Earl of Orrery* (Knoxville, Tenn., 1965).

[131] *DNB*; *CSPD, 1673*, pp. 389–90, 430–1; ibid., *1675–6*, pp. 356–7; *CTB*, iv. 555; v. 807. His will shows him to have been more concerned about his share of the profits from a sinecure office in the Court of Common Pleas than about Ireland (PRO, PROB 11/358, q. 107).

additional financial favours; even so his widow was reckoned to be owed £8,000 after his death in 1679.[132]

The case of John Collins, FRS, the mathematician was much sadder. His office as Accountant of the Excise was abolished in 1668. The small compensatory pension which he was awarded seems not to have been paid; despite switching to the service of Henry Slingsby, then Secretary of the Trade Commission, and when this body was in turn wound up being given a place in the Farthing Office by Slingsby as Master of the Mint, Collins seems to have ended his days in poverty, though he or someone of the same name died holding an office in the royal Stables.[133]

As we know well today, not filling a post when it falls vacant, is by no means the same as making someone redundant. Such was the case with the Remembrancership of First Fruits, when its holder took over from his delinquent brother, the Receiver.[134] The same was true when the Mastership of the Ordnance in Ireland was temporarily merged with the Mastership in England; also when a Riding Surveyorship in the Customs was ordered to be left vacant.[135] By contrast, the Third Clerk of the King's Kitchen was awarded £700 cash down on the suspension of his post in August 1677.[136] On 8 July 1668 the thirty Gentleman Pensioners who were to be kept on were ordered to pay £3,000 to the twenty who were being 'reduced'; perhaps not surprisingly, the order authorizing such an intrinsically unreasonable form of compensation was rescinded only five days later.[137] This kind of arrangement would only have been tolerable if the total income from all sources (including fees, gratuities, and perquisites) was either constant, or rising,

---

[132] DNB; Lynch, *Roger Boyle*; CSPD, *1672*, pp. 430, 628; ibid., *1673*, p. 502; ibid., *1673–5*, pp. 146–7; ibid., *1675–6*, pp. 47, 337–8; ibid., *1679–80*, p. 431; CTB, v. 219; CSPD, *1683* i, p. 153; ibid., *1683–4*, p. 99.

[133] DNB; M. Hunter, *Establishing the New Science: The Experience of the Early Royal Society* (Woodbridge, 1989); S. P. Rigaud and S. J. Rigaud, *Correspondence of Scientific Men of the Seventeenth Century* (Oxford, 1841), ii, 174–9, 217–21, 548–9; CSPD, *1668–9*, p. 441; CTB, iii. 103; vi. 152; CSPD, *1677–8*, pp. 542–3; PRO, PROB 11/379, q. 17 (if the same man).

[134] See above; CTB, iii. 467.   [135] CSPD, *1673–5*, p. 27; CTB, iv. 563.

[136] CSPD, *1677–8*, p. 286.

[137] Ibid., *1667–8*, pp. 477, 484.

regardless of the number of people holding a particular office, and thus where those remaining in post were set to earn proportionately more. But that was not at all true with the Pensioners, as it might have been if—for the sake of argument—the Six Clerks in Chancery had been reduced to five or fewer, or their sworn Under-Clerks reduced from sixty to something less. One of the most ambitious compensation schemes has already been mentioned, that for the royalist officers of the Court of Wards and Liveries, when its abolition was confirmed by statute in 1660–1. How much they actually received is another matter.[138] A somewhat different case, not quite the same as compensation for loss of office, followed from the abolition of customs farming in 1671. The members of the abortive farm of 1670–1 were clearly held to have suffered consequential losses arising from the sudden decision to change over to direct management by Commissioners (who were in this case a different set of individuals). The nominal chairman of the Farm, though possibly a 'front man' for the City tycoons also involved, was Charles Paulet, then Lord St John, who was to succeed his father as Marquis of Winchester in 1675 and to be created Duke of Bolton after the Revolution of 1688. The Crown's complicated financial relations with him can be traced forward through the rest of that decade and into the next.[139]

Reduction and even redundancy are one thing; dismissal or removal from office quite another. Here, whatever the grounds might be for getting rid of someone, the tenure on which the post was held was invariably a significant factor but not always decisive. Although Peter Pett was suspended soon after the Medway disaster of June 1667, his patent as Master Shipwright at Chatham was still in the process of being revoked over a year later, in spite of the fact that it was only held during pleasure.[140] By contrast, Sir William Coventry's downfall, for having dared to challenge the Duke of Buckingham to a duel, was swift and irreversible, but should be seen as a political rather than an

[138] *Commons Journals*, viii. 219–20.
[139] See Ch. 1, sect. iv above; *CSPD, 1671*, pp. 407, 520, 591; ibid., *1671–2*, p. 270; *CTB*, iii. 1259.
[140] *CSPD, 1667–8*, p. 612.

administrative event—not least because the King had come to find Coventry extremely tiresome.[141] The same was true of Sir John Duncombe's dismissal from the Chancellorship of the Exchequer in the mid-1670s, because he could not work harmoniously with Lord Treasurer Danby and lost the King's favour in consequence.[142] Although the concepts of politicians and civil servants as distinct species were far from yet being fully formed or strictly defined, the relative ease and difficulty in removing individuals of the two types is apparent; some such cases have already been cited. Evidence of how difficult it was to get rid of non-political office-holders even when their presumptive guilt, usually of corruption, was overwhelming, can be shown from several other instances. These included that of the Customer of Carlisle and the Deputy Postmaster of Canterbury in 1669, the Receiver of the honour and castle of Windsor and one of the Clerks in Common Pleas in 1676, and the entire Southampton customs staff in 1674–5.[143] Others were purged more easily, such as the Receiver of the Excise in 1671/2, the Clerk to the Secretary of the Customs in 1677–8 (although the same man was later restored and eventually promoted), Watchmen, Waiters, and Tidesmen in the port of London, Warders of the Tower (for suspected Whig leanings in 1682–3), more surprisingly the two Surveyors-General of the Customs in 1679, but more understandably two Northamptonshire forest officers 'as men criminal in their trusts', and at the very end of the reign the Surveyor-General of Customs in Ireland and the whole staff at Carrickfergus—for collusion in frauds.[144] In general, those holding office by treasury warrant were more vulnerable than those holding by patent from the Crown. All this, however, must be seen in terms of what was considered permissible and impermissible behaviour, likewise in the context of factional and party political divisions.

[141] *DNB*; other standard sources; *CSPD, 1668–9*, p. 222.
[142] *DNB: Missing Persons.*
[143] *CSPD, 1668–9*, pp. 252, 490–1, 561; ibid., *1676–7*, pp. 127–8; *CTB*, ii. 241; iv. 297.
[144] *CTB*, iii. 1006; iv. 75, 105, 812–13; v. 920–1, 955, 1271; vi. 324–5; vii. 290–2, 1514; *CSPD, 1682*, p. 305; ibid., *1683* ii, p. 329.

XV. OATHS AND TESTS

The special requirements of professing Anglican beliefs and taking communion in church, imposed by the first Test Act 1673, had surprisingly little impact in the administration. Apart from the famous cases of the Duke of York and of Lord Treasurer Clifford, and the solitary, exemplary resignation of Dr Benjamin Worsley, there were allegations against various other individuals for failure to take the oaths and to receive communion as prescribed, but much less of a purge than we find later in the reign, during the Exclusion Crisis and the court-Tory reaction which followed (1679–84). In September 1682 a general order was issued to the Commissioners both of the Customs and of the Excise, to get rid of all disloyal or disaffected persons in their respective services.[145] The relative unimportance of the ordinary oaths prescribed to be taken on entry to particular offices can be seen in the standard manual of these which was republished after the Revolution. This volume was simply that of the 1630s unchanged save for a very few additions of oaths prescribed for the holders of newly created offices, such as those in the Excise. If anything, too much is made of these oaths in my first book dealing with 1625–1642.[146] Ideological tests were another matter. Although probably not written until the early eighteenth century, the reflections of John Potenger, who became Comptroller of the Pipe in 1677, are relevant to this:

I have thought it one of the greatest inflictions of my life to be cast in a time of great revolutions, for upon frequent changing of princes there are still required fresh assurances of the subject's loyalty; Kings believing by such methods to fix the sceptre firmer in their hands. But imposing of oaths often proves but a weak support to the crown;[147]

---

[145] *CTB*, vii. 602.
[146] Richard Garnet, *The Book of Oaths* . . . (1689, Wing, *STC 1641–1700*, G 264–5); Aylmer, *King's Servants*, ch. 3, sect. vii.
[147] *Private Memoirs of John Potenger*, author's preface, 22.

XVI. PRIVILEGES AND PERILS

Many different kinds of officials enjoyed exemption from jury and militia service and from local office-holding. Thus the staffs of the Mint, the Navy, and the Ordnance Offices were excused normal obligations as residents in the wards and parishes of the City. It may seem more surprising that a Master of Requests should have been excused from having to serve as termly reader in his Inn of Court.[148] Then as now, liability to taxation could be a tricky matter. It was ruled that the Excise Appeals Commissioners were not to be assessed by the Middlesex tax commissioners because they constituted collectively a court of judicature; they scarcely functioned as such but were a parliamentary-appointed body consisting largely of MPs, so this has the look of a racket. Civil lawyers at Doctors Commons were to enjoy the same fiscal immunities as judges and sergeants at Sergeants' Inn.[149] On the other hand, excise officers had to pay 2s. in the £ poll tax on their salaries; customs staff in London seem to have been exempted, but those in the outports also had to pay; a few years later the second Treasury Commission ruled that the officers of the customs house too must pay normal parliamentary taxes.[150] The payment of taxes by office-holders had actually been debated by the House of Commons in 1670 with speeches by such well-known figures of opposite political persuasions as Sir Thomas Clifford and Colonel John Birch.[151] Liability to assessments and poll taxes must be distinguished from the duties on legal documents and proceedings—the proto-Stamp Tax—levied specifically on lawyers and legal office-holders from 1671 to 1680, which have already been discussed in the previous chapter.[152]

---

[148] PRO, SP 29/249B/118–20; *CTB*, ii. 566; ibid., iii. 1194.
[149] *CTB*, iv. 324, 417, 808.
[150] *CTB*, v. 1122–5; vii. 605.
[151] Joan Thirsk and J. P. Cooper (eds.), *Seventeenth-century Economic Documents* (Oxford, 1972), 674, no. 50 (from *Debates of the House of Commons from the year 1667 to the year 1694, collected by the Hon. Anchitel Grey Esq* (10 vols., London, 1769), i., 323–7).
[152] See above, Ch. 2, sect. iv, for refs to Stamp Duties.

Liabilities could take some curious forms. In 1670 it emerged that the Six Clerks in Chancery were enjoying an extra £800 a year on a £10,000 mortgage executed by the Crown to their predecessors in 1627; when they showed marked reluctance to surrender this corporate perquisite, those hard-faced men the Treasury Commissioners told the Attorney-General to commence a prosecution against them.[153] Competition for benefits could sometimes involve status as well as money and degenerate into undignified wrangling. Such was the dispute between the Lord Chamberlain and the Lord Great Chamberlain as to which of them was responsible for the erection of scaffolding for the trial of a peer in 1676.[154]

As we should expect, revenue officers were exposed to the greatest risks. The days of pitched battles between smugglers and the customs and excise men for the most part lay ahead, in the eighteenth century. And it may indeed be thought that the level of serious violence involved in tax collection was surprisingly low. In 1671 an Excise Sub-Commissioner was assaulted in Newcastle-upon-Tyne and a Tide Surveyor likewise in the port of London. A Hearth Tax officer was said to have been dangerously wounded in 1675/6; proceedings were ordered to be set in motion, but ten days later he was reported to have made a complete recovery and those who had been arrested were ordered to be released; when two Excise collectors were attacked in a pub at Stratford-on-Avon, they killed one of their assailants in self-defence. They were indicted for murder at the Warwick assizes but the Lord Treasurer intervened and told the judges to forbear passing sentence on them. The redoubtable William Culliford was shot in the back at the London customs house by a disgruntled ex-officer who had lost his job in the west country and then wanted to be taken over to Ireland by Culliford in his capacity as a Revenue Commissioner; but the wounded administrative reformer recovered well enough to complete more than another thirty years' service under the Crown.[155] Potentially more serious, because it

[153] *CTB*, iii. 457, 463, 692, 697, 744.   [154] *CSPD, 1676–7*, p. 206.
[155] *CTB*, iii. 1144, 1151; v. 22, 138, 151; BL Add. MS 28,875, fo. 364; *CSPD, 1676–7*, p. 459; ibid. *1677–8*, p. 6.

involved a clash between the civil and the military arms of the state, in 1679 the Southampton customs officers alleged that they had been badly beaten up by some army officers stationed at Titchfield (on the coast by the Solent), when they had been investigating the smuggling of wine, some of which they had quite properly seized. The outcome of this is unfortunately obscure.[156]

Dr Michael Braddick has included resistance to tax collection in his valuable recent studies of seventeenth-century fiscality, and there is no point in going over the same ground. But the contrast with France may fairly be emphasized a little more strongly; there the level of extreme violence on the part of both resisters and enforcers was very much higher. A Hearth Tax collector did indeed die of the injuries sustained when stones were thrown at him in Bridport, Dorset (in 1668), though it is not clear that anyone intended to kill him. An inquiry was mounted by the local justices, the county coroner, and the officers of the borough; six men were arrested but then bailed. Thereafter the trail runs cold, until more than eight years later when the Farmers of the Hearth Tax were allowed £110 for their costs incurred in the prosecution of the man's alleged killers. In France a troop of dragoons would probably have arrived and have started to ravage the town.[157] It was not only tax gatherers who might meet a violent end. At Doncaster in 1680/1 the deputy Postmaster was unwise enough to take part in a game of cards—presumably for money—with a short-tempered Scottish peer, who ran him through with his sword, later petitioning the King that he might not be tried for manslaughter. Was alcohol also involved?[158] But for every

[156] *CSPD, 1679–80,* pp. 124–5.
[157] Michael J. Braddick, *Parliamentary Taxation in Seventeenth-century England: Local Administration and Response* (1994); ibid., *The Nerves of State: Taxation and the Financing of the English State, 1558–1714* (Manchester, 1996); *CSPD, 1667–8,* pp. 222, 224; *CTB,* v. 318–19; F. J. Pope, 'Dorset Assizes in the Seventeenth Century', *Dorset Nat. Hist. Arch. Soc. Proc.,* 34 (1913), 17–30.
[158] *CSPD, 1680–1,* p. 155; Sir John Reresby, *The Memoirs of Sir John Reresby,* ed. A. Browning (Glasgow, 1936); 2nd edn., ed. Mary K. Geiter and W. A. Speck (London, 1991), 213; *Complete Peerage,* v. 22, 'Eglinton, Earl of'.

office-holder who paid the supreme penalty or otherwise came
to grief, there were obviously very many who did well enough
and some who throve greatly. It is time to return to the value of
offices and wealth of their holders.

XVII. THE ECONOMIC SIGNIFICANCE OF OFFICE-HOLDING

This topic can be approached in two different ways, each of
which helps to advance our understanding. One involves the
attempt to assess aggregate totals, the other rests on case studies of families and individuals. And there is a real difficulty in
how best to relate these two approaches to each other. As we
shall discover again in the next chapter, when looking at individual career patterns and different types of crown servants,
there are regrettably few cases where reliable documentation
enables us to establish with any accuracy the profits of office in
relation to other sources of wealth or to levels of expenditure.

Sometimes there are fragments of evidence which point in
contrary directions. Professor Christopher Clay draws an interesting contrast between Lord Treasurer Danby who used the
profits of office to enlarge his landed estate and the Earl of
Sunderland who used his landed wealth as a means of attaining
high office and political power.[159] In writing the life of his
brother Francis, who was successively Attorney-General, Chief
Justice of Common Pleas, Lord Keeper of the Great Seal, and
finally Lord Chancellor, Roger North dwells on the modesty of
his estate, his absolute probity, and his reluctance to seek
anything additional from the King; according to Roger, each
successive promotion seems to have led to a positive diminution
of his income. As Chief Justice Francis North borrowed £4,100
(giving a bond for £8,000) from a distinguished civil lawyer
who was also an Excise Farmer, and he renewed the bond after
he had become Lord Keeper. Yet from items in the family papers

---

[159] C. G. A. Clay, in *Agrarian History of England and Wales*, v. *1640–1750*,
ed. Joan Thirsk (Cambridge, 1984), ii. 188–9.

we know that he himself lent large sums to various court nota-
bles, including the notoriously rapacious and extravagant
second Duchess of Lauderdale. Lord Guildford, as he had by
then become, seems to have been owed about £12,700 at his
death; figures for the last full year of his life show receipts
totalling £20,766 and payments £15,061, so his net disposable
income that year should have been some £5,704. None of this
actually contradicts the version given by his hero-worshipping
younger brother, but does qualify it somewhat.[160] Guildford
had been an executor for his own original patron, Sir Geoffrey
Palmer, who was Attorney-General from the Restoration to his
death in 1670. The surviving executors' accounts certainly
suggest a larger turnover for that office in Palmer's case, but do
not provide a reliable cross-check on Roger North's statement
that the office was worth £7,000 a year, and in any case there
might simply have been more business for the chief crown prosecutor in the 1660s than in the 1670s.[161] Much of the evidence
about the total annual value of particular offices is, if not anec-
dotal, too piecemeal for any firm conclusions to be based on it.
Senior members of the government themselves sometimes
wanted to know what an office was worth. When the
Mastership of Chancery in the Alienations Office fell vacant in
January 1685, the Treasury Secretary had to ask the other
Alienations Commissioners what legal qualifications were
needed by its holder and what was its annual value.[162]

Other criteria of wealth which might be applied to the office-
holders of these years, as they have been to those of the pre-
Civil War period, include house-building both in London and
the country, and providing for the erection of elaborate and
expensive funeral monuments. The most systematic attempt to
put the building of large and costly houses on a quantitative

[160] *The Lives of the Rt. Hon. Francis North, Baron Guildford, the Hon. Sir
Dudley North, and the Hon. and Rev. Dr. John North By the Rt. Hon. Roger
North together with the Autobiography of the Author*, ed. A. Jessopp (3 vols.,
1980), i. 215, 255, 371, 423, 435; Bodl. North MS b.8, fos. 89, 142, 144, 146,
167, 200, 261.
[161] Bodl. North MS b.73, fos. 35ᵛ–38ʳ, Roger North, *Lives*, i. 125.
[162] *CTB*, vii. 1516.

chronological basis unfortunately excludes urban building: for example, the famous case of Clarendon House, Piccadilly, which the Lord Chancellor believed had aroused enough envy and resentment to help bring about his political downfall. At the same time Clarendon was spending heavily on the rebuilding of Cornbury Park in Oxfordshire, and his finances were probably in quite a precarious state at the time of his loss of office and flight to France. More major country houses were built in the 1680s than had been in the 1660s or the 1670s; this peak was in turn surpassed in the 1700s and, most dramatically of all, by the widest margin in the 1720s; but the respective proportions being built by office-holders are not clear, since the author of this valuable study only has a separate category for 'civil servants' below the level of baronets. To give an example of the sort of difficulties involved, Sir William Lacon Childe had succeeded his father as a Chancery Master in 1673 and held this post until 1710, but his nephew and heir's building of Kinlet Hall, Shropshire in the early 1720s is counted (technically correctly so) as that of a landed gentleman not of an office-holder.

Some of the peers who were having large houses built in the 1660s had not yet reached the summits of their careers in the Crown's service and were evidently drawing on other financial resources: for example, Lord Arlington, the Earl of Sunderland, and the Marquis of Worcester. The Earl of Arlington's building of Euston Hall in Suffolk might seem to be a clearer case, but he was borrowing quite heavily from Sir Stephen Fox, and was possibly in debt to others also. Fox's own rebuilding of the house which he had bought in Chiswick could be said to have been financed from the profits of office; but, as we have seen, Fox was no ordinary office-holder so much as a major financial undertaker for the Crown, and by the 1680s his income was coming from a wide variety of sources (interest on money lent, estates, annuities, etc.). He also endowed his native parish of Farley in Wiltshire, very generously, with a new church, alms-houses, and a school, the north transept of the church containing family monuments with a burial vault underneath. To take another prominent administrator, Sir George Downing, like

Henry Jermyn Earl of St. Albans, was more of an investor in urban property development than a housebuilder as a form of conspicuous expenditure. Colonel John Birch's building work at Garnstone, near Weobley in Herefordshire, might appear to be a more straightforward case, except that Birch had contrived to retain a good part of the wealth which he had already accumulated before 1660. Sir William Jones, a highly successful lawyer, whose tenure first as Solicitor- —then as Attorney-General—ran from November 1673 to his death in May 1682, would have had no difficulty in paying for what Pevsner describes as a 'moderate-sized brick mansion' at Ramsbury, also in Wiltshire, besides a 'swagger-monument' for himself in the church there. It is, however, hard to see that John Ashburnham could already have made enough as Groom of the Bedchamber and holder of a local keepership to have rebuilt most of the church at Ashburnham in East Sussex by 1664–5. The likeliest explanation is that he had married two heiresses in succession, and according to one source had sold his house in Chiswick to the King (who wanted it for his son, the young Duke of Monmouth) for £7,000; even so, he was expelled from the House of Commons in 1667 for having accepted a £500 bribe, and acknowledged debts of over £2,000 when he made his will. On the other hand, his brother William, who was Cofferer of the Household from 1660 until his death in 1679, would have been much better able to complete the embellishment of the church with its family monuments, to rebuild the nearby Ashburnham Place, and to have another Ashburnham House built in Westminster, out of the more or less legitimate fruits of office. To take another individual more comparable to Fox and Downing in his quality as a Crown servant, it is extraordinarily difficult to estimate how far William Blathwayt built Dyrham Park, just north of Bath, in the 1690s out of the profits of his various offices, and how far through having married an heiress who died soon after. The main building work undertaken by Thomas Osborne, Earl of Danby and then Duke of Leeds, at his family home of Kiveton in West Yorkshire, during the years 1698 to 1704, came long after his Lord Treasurership and indeed mostly after his final loss of office under William III. On the other hand, although his father had been Strafford's Deputy as Lord President of the North (from 1633 to 1640), Sir Edward's income in the 1640s was reckoned on one estimate to have been only around £800 a year, on another £970; and besides Thomas Osborne's marriage into the aristocratic Bertie family, his own income as an office-holder from the late 1660s must have made a very considerable, if not a decisive, difference to his fortunes. While much fascinating information about expenditure on buildings can be assembled from a wide variety of sources, I have not found it possible to present it quantitatively in any meaningful way.[163]

Funeral monuments are another form of conspicuous expenditure for which there is a great deal of evidence. But there is nothing like a comprehensive listing of tombs, monuments, and inscriptions, especially where the sculptor's or mason's name is unknown; moreover, very large numbers of these structures have been destroyed, altered, or moved since they were first put up. Some individuals had tombs built, ready to receive them in death, while they were still alive; others made detailed specifi-

---

[163] Charles Saumarez Smith, 'Supply and Demand in English Country-House Building, 1660–1740', *Oxford Art J.*, 121 (1988), 3–16 (chronologically on target, but omits London, and does not classify office-holders above the rank of knight); Lawrence Stone and Jeanne C. Fawtier Stone, *An Open Elite? England 1540–1880* (Oxford, 1984), app. 1 and tables following p. 458 (this is a work based on a staggering amount of research, and statistically very sophisticated, but it is mainly based on the three counties of Hertfordshire, Northamptonshire, and Northumberland, and does not use the categories required here for the owners and builders of houses). I have also used some volumes of the *Survey of London* (published successively for the LCC, the GLC, the Corporation of London, and the *HMC*, 1900–); H. Avray Tipping, *English Homes*, Period IV, i, *Late Stuart, 1649–1714* (London and New York, 1920); Oliver Hill and John Cornforth, *English Country Houses: Caroline 1625–1685* (London, 1966); James Lees Milne, *English Country Houses: Baroque, 1685–1715* (London, 1970); N. Pevsner, *et al.*, *Buildings of England* (Harmondsworth, 1950s–1970s); Howard Colvin, *Architecture and the After-life* (New Haven, Conn., and London, 1991), and *A Biographical Dictionary of British Architects, 1600–1840*, 3rd edn. (New Haven, Conn., and London, 1995). It would require a team of scholars to construct a database from these and other works, such as *The Victoria County History* and older county histories, in order to be able to arrange house-builders by date, location, status, and probable sources of wealth. For the Ashburnhams see also PRO, PROB 11/338, q. 47, 362, q. 34; F. W. Steer (ed.), *The Ashburnham Archives: A Catalogue* (East Sussex County Council, Lewes, 1958); *Hist. Parl.*, i. 552–4.

cations in their wills, which might include setting financial ceilings on costs. Sometimes it seems safe to relate the splendour of a person's tomb or monument to their public career, or that of their spouse. It is unlikely that Henry Coventry, although he was the younger son of a Baron, who had himself been Lord Keeper, would have had so fine a monument (now in Croome church, Worcestershire), if he had not been Secretary of State. Nor would Elizabeth Pepys have had a handsome memorial in St Olave's, Hart Street, London, if her grief-stricken husband had not been Clerk of the Acts and already a man of some substance when she died in 1669. Tobias Rustat would not have been commemorated, let alone so splendidly, in the chapel of Jesus College, Cambridge, if he had not been a major benefactor; and that in turn was only possible because he had held office as Yeoman of the Robes throughout Charles's reign, had lived frugally, and had no direct heirs. Turning to another famous legal family, his income as (successively) Solicitor-General, Attorney-General, Lord Keeper, and Lord Chancellor would have more than sufficed to cover the cost of the grand and magnificent monument to Heneage Finch, first Earl of Nottingham, at Ravenstone, in Buckinghamshire. Whether his earnings as an Envoy and then an Ambassador would have provided enough for his brother Sir John Finch's joint monument for himself and his inseparable friend Dr Sir Thomas Baines, in Christ's College, Cambridge, is less clear. However, since each of them left £2,000 to the College, they must either have saved enough when abroad or have inherited money from their respective families. (Baines's official position was that of Physician to the Embassy when Finch was Ambassador in Constantinople; he was also Professor of Music at Gresham's College, obviously *in absentia*.) Again, examples could be multiplied but any systematic comparison of office-holders with others of similar status is sadly far out of reach.[164]

---

[164] John le Neve, *Monumenta Anglicana: Being Inscriptions on the Monuments of Several Eminent Persons* ... (3 vols., London, 1717–18), covering 1650–1715 and including texts from monuments and tablets which no longer exist; Katherine A. Esdaile, *English Monumental Sculpture since the Renaissance* (London, 1927); *English Church Monuments, 1510–1840*

As we have already seen, in many cases there is a problem of whether the individuals or their heirs and executors who spent money in these and other ways did so out of the profits of office, out of their income from land and other investments, or by borrowing. The last alternative suggests a different approach, that is by trying to assess the extent to which office-holders were either net lenders or net borrowers. Here the reader may be forgiven for thinking of the old adage that it is a bad workman who blames his tools, if I say that the evidence can only provide a basis for the most tentative conclusions. The index volumes to the recognizances for loans on Statute Staple, which were cited extensively in my first book, come to an end in the 1670s. It also appears that both these, and the recognizances entered on the Close Rolls in Chancery, tended increasingly to involve entering into obligations to do, or not do, this or that (such as obeying a forthcoming court decision or observing the terms of a family settlement), rather than genuine credit transactions. Even with loans we have to ask why people lent or borrowed. In the former case they might simply having been doing a kindness to a friend or relative. More often we need to relate lending to the alternative kinds of investment which were available; by the 1660s–1680s these included various shipping, trading, and colonizing ventures, the purchase of stock in the Royal African and the East India Companies, deposits with one or more of the goldsmith-banking houses, or sometimes—the riskiest of all— lending to the Crown, besides the acquisition, enlargement, or improvement of landed and urban property. The same is true with borrowers. They might need to raise loans because they

(London, 1946); Rupert Gunnis, *Dictionary of British Sculptors, 1660–1851* (London, 1953); Margaret Whinney, *Sculpture in Britain, 1530–1830* (Penguin History of Art, Harmondsworth, 1964); and most recently Adam White, 'A Biographical Dictionary of London Tomb Sculptors, c. 1560–c.1660', *Walpole Soc.*, 61 (1999), 156–60, 'index of persons commemorated'. Again, I have used Pevsner, *Buildings of England*, and Colvin, *Architecture and the After-life*. I am extremely grateful to Howard Colvin for kindly providing additional references to memorial chapels. Proposals for a nationwide database have been aired in the admirable publications of The Church Monuments Society (London, 1985–), whether with any positive outcome is unclear. [A pilot study is under way at the University of Sussex under the direction of Dr Nigel Llewellyn.] For Sir John Finch, see also PRO, PROB 11/369, q. 1.

were living beyond their means, for example as compulsive and unsuccessful gamblers or on account of drink and other extravagances. Alternatively, it might be because they too wanted to enlarge or round out their existing estates, undertake agricultural improvements, drain mines, or speculate in urban development. As economic historians have pointed out, borrowing could therefore be indicative of financial health as well as embarrassment. Why, for example, should Sir Mundiford Bramston, Master in Chancery, have needed to borrow £350 from Edward Backwell, the famous goldsmith-banker and principal victim of the Stop, in 1673? Such cases could be multiplied, where lack of contextual information leaves too many questions hanging in the air. For Ireland, a complete database of surviving recognizances on Statute Staple (from 1597 to 1687) is available on CD-ROM; nothing so sophisticated and systematic is known to me for the English material. On the basis of those materials which I have consulted, office-holders, other than members of the Bed and Privy Chambers, do feature slightly more often as lenders than as borrowers; but this scarcely enables us to generalize with any confidence about their aggregate wealth or the profitability of their offices.[165]

So we have to approach the question, as it were, from the outside by trying to put the administrative system into a wider economic and financial context. Contemporary evidence and the interpretations of modern historians both point to the total

---

[165] See Lawrence Stone, *Crisis of the Aristocracy, 1558–1641* (Oxford, 1965), 517–24; Aylmer, *King's Servants*, citations from PRO, LC 4/ser. for 1620s–40s; Sir John Habakkuk, *Marriage, Debt and the Estates System: English Landownership, 1650–1950* (Oxford, 1994) and earlier arts. by the same author; *The Irish Statute Staple Books*, CD-ROM, ed. Jane Ohlmeyer (material drawn from Dublin City Archives and from BL Add. MSS 19,843–4 and 15,635–7); PRO, LC 4/186, index to statute staple bonds, 1655–75 (in poor condition); LC 4/205, entry books of recognizances, 1677–1712; LC 4/84–5, recognizance rolls, 1673–6. I am extremely grateful to Sir John Habakkuk and Prof. Ohlmeyer for their help on all this, also to members of the colloquium on credit referred to at Ch. 2 n. 54. To avoid any possible misunderstanding: Stone and Aylmer, in the 1960s, drew on the corrections by H. R. Trevor-Roper (now Lord Dacre) and J. P. Cooper to earlier work by Stone. A book with a splendid title, Norman Jones, *God and the Moneylenders: Usury and Law in Early Modern England* (Oxford, 1989) is stronger on the sixteenth than on the seventeenth century.

number of persons in civil, as well as naval and military offices having been on the increase under the later Stuarts. For the Crown's servants as defined here we can point to the revenue services, the shore-based administration of the navy, and the growth of the colonial empire, which more than made up for any shrinkage compared with early Stuart times owing to the suppression of the prerogative courts and the slimming down of the royal household. We might go on from this to argue that, unless the average financial value of individual offices was decreasing (which is by no means impossible), the aggregate earnings of all office-holders must have been growing. How it was changing as a percentage of total national wealth is, of course, quite another matter. And it may be that, while twenty-five years is a long time in the life of any one individual (proportionately more so then than now), it is still too short a period for meaningful trends of this kind to be established with any confidence. But it would be defeatist to leave things there.

The most authoritative recent estimates of national income (NI) for England and Wales in the period 1492 to 1707 provide two alternative sets of figures based on different assumptions. One is that NI grew at the same rate as population; the other that it grew at the same rate as the real wages of building craftsmen in southern England geared to population, in both cases using the figures provided by the authors of the standard and best history of population, and for the second also well-known work of the 1950s on prices and wages. The sets of figures for NI based on these two different assumptions converge in 1715, but for the 1660s to 1680s are quite wide apart. Going back to the 1630s, the first assumption gives a figure in the mid-£40 millions; the second suggests only about £30 million, which perhaps coincidentally is much the same figure as I myself suggested for the 1630s back in 1961. The total public revenue as calculated by Professor O'Brien and Dr Hunt for their chosen earlier date (which is not exactly the same as mine) is between 1.5 and 1.9 per cent of NI on their first assumption and between 2.3 and 2.9 per cent on their second. In Charles II's reign, their figures for the peacetime year 1664 give them an NI of just under £49 million on the first but only £35.68 on the second assumption, with revenue as either 2.7 or 3.8 per cent of these totals. Coming forward in time to 1685, they have NI as either £45.11 or £38.81 million, with either 2.8 or 3.2 per cent for public revenue. They have very laudably tried to provide figures for one full year of peace and one of war in each successive decade. On either of their sets of assumptions, what Henry VIII was getting out of the country back in 1545—a staggering 8.4 or 8.9 per cent of NI—was not to be exceeded by a clear margin until 1707, although on the second assumption it had just been topped under William III in 1695. As an amateur in the fields both of demographic and quantitative economic history, I must none the less register some unease about using building work-ers' wages as the sole variable apart from total population figures. On the other hand, the first assumption, the direct correlation of NI with gross population totals, produces some curious-looking fluctuations. For instance, NI of over £60 millions in 1649 was only to be reached again with the total for Great Britain (that is, Scotland as well as England and Wales) in 1712, while the totals for 1671, 1674, and 1689 are all in the same range (mid-£40 millions) as those for the 1630s. None of this is logically impossible, but it does look a little implausible, presumptuous as it would be for me to question the O'Brien-Hunt figures. It is tempting but probably unacceptable to split the difference between their two sets of totals.[166]

Total public revenue figures are another matter. Here the problem is what proportion of these represent payments to office-holders, other than those in the armed forces, and what sort of amount should be added on for earnings from fees, gratu-ities, perquisites, bribes, the use of cash balances, and so forth. If we are interested in the overall fiscal burden of state upon soci-ety, then we can simply add the hypothetical total from all these sources, less those paid within the system (e.g. fees to officers by

[166] Patrick K. O'Brien and Philip A. Hunt, 'The Rise of a Fiscal State in England, 1485–1815', *Hist. Res.*, 66 (1993), 129–76, esp. app. 3, 'Conjectures for National Income', pp. 174–5, table 3. Their population figures are from E. A. Wrigley and R. S. Schofield, *The Population History of England, 1641–1871: A Reconstruction* (1981). See also Aylmer, *King's Servants*, ch. 4, sect. v, ch. 5, sect. iv.

officers), to total crown revenues. Assuming the same kind of range for fee and gratuity payments in the central governments as I have suggested for the 1630s (somewhere between an upper level of £400,000 p.a. and a lower of £250,000) these could then be added to the O'Brien-Hunt revenue totals, which for 1660–88 are substantially based on those of C. D. Chandaman. If, on the other hand, our concern is with the total value of office under the Crown for those in post at any particular date, the calculation becomes more complicated, since it involves working out what proportion of annual public revenue was devoted to salaries, wages, and perquisites from the Crown, as opposed to money spent on buildings, furnishings, entertainments, ships, charitable and educational giving, weapons of war both by land and sea, and the amount actually blasted off in the form of cannon balls, musket shot, powder, and match. On top of the fee and gratuity payments, we should certainly need to add a substantial if unknown amount for gifts and bribes to members of the central executive and the household, especially some officers of the Privy and Bedchambers. So there is a good deal of subtracting and adding to be done, if we were ambitious enough to want to convert O'Brien-Hunt (and Chandaman) figures into Aylmer ones, of the kind put forward for 1625–42.

We can also turn this question round again and think of it from the point of view of families and individuals. There the economic and financial attractions of office-holding need to be put into the context of the country's economy as a whole and the relative profitability of alternative careers and forms of investment. For example, if we take the period as a whole, Clay points out that the rate of return on agricultural land was lower than that from lending by bond or mortgage; thus financially it did not pay to borrow in order to buy land. He quite correctly goes on to point out that there were often reasons other than financial why people bought land: to round out their existing estates, to enhance their social status, or simply to retire and live in the country.[167] As has already been suggested above,

---

[167] Joan Thirsk (ed.), *Agrarian History of England and Wales*, v, 1640–1750, ii, ch. 14, b, 3.

compared with the situation earlier in the seventeenth century, there was a wider range of alternative openings for investment. Measured against the great mercantile and contracting fortunes and those of some credit financiers, such as the goldsmith-bankers, or indeed those of the greatest landowners, the incomes of all but a very small number of office-holders were if not meagre at least modest. At the same time, the enhanced salaries to be found since the Interregnum in the upper-middle ranks of the revenue departments, the admiralty and the navy, with a few scattered elsewhere, would have been attractive to ambitious men from the middle levels of society and to the younger sons of all but the richest landowners. As to expenditure, courtiers and great officers of state often lived extravagantly and spent conspicuously, but office-holders in general were not necessarily more likely to do so than other people of similar wealth. We shall return to this in the next chapter, with particular reference to the evidence from wills. But at this stage it seems best to reserve judgement on whether office-holding was more or less attractive, for either economic or other reasons, during this quarter century compared to other periods of the same length earlier and later, setting aside the exceptional circumstances of 1642–60.

There is one other source, providing a possible alternative approach to this question. Gregory King's famous but far from reliable 'Scheme of Income and Expenditure of the Several Families of England Calculated for the Year 1688' proposes 10,000 'persons in offices' (on my understanding of his table, *below* noble and gentry rank), accounting for £1.8 million annually out of a total NI of £43.5 million. In spite of the perennial fascination of King's figures and the means by which he arrived at them, it would be rash—perhaps even positively unhelpful—to use his estimates for 1688 in order to attempt comparisons with other, earlier or later dates.[168] In the most

---

[168] Joan Thirsk and J. P. Cooper (eds.), *Seventeenth-century Economic Documents* (Oxford, 1972), s. viii, pp. 780–1, no. 7. See also Geoffrey Holmes, *Augustan England: Professions, State and Society, 1680–1730* (London, 1982), esp. ch. 8; id., 'Gregory King and the Social Structure of Pre-industrial England', *TRHS*, 5th ser., 27 (1977), 41–68. The late Prof. Holmes was even

general terms, my tentative conclusion is that the overall burden of state on society was beginning to grow again in the 1680s but that the rate of increase only really accelerated after 1688, during the wars of William III's and Anne's reigns.

XVIII. CONCLUSION

Much of this chapter has necessarily been concerned with individual examples and case studies. It is time to draw the threads together, and to ask, what if anything was distinctive about the years 1660–85 in these respects? Maybe similar examples and illustrations could be drawn from any quarter century going back as far as documentation exists (into the thirteenth century?) down to the epoch of civil service reform (*c.* 1780–1870). And I would not want to deny an element of truth in this. None the less there are more specific features which must be weighed in the balance: the Restoration of 1660 itself and all that it entailed, with a king aged thirty on his return to his kingdom who then reigned for almost exactly the notional length of a generation; the particular interactions of politics, war, religion, and finance which shaped the public history of the reign; the growing importance of navy, trade, and empire; the role of the Treasury Commissioners, especially in changing the tenure on which offices were held; finally, the partial but by no means negligible advance towards greater professionalism. This surely is enough to sustain a claim that these years do have a character of their own in English administrative history.

more wary than I am of any attempt to quantify the aggregate wealth of office-holders or the economic and fiscal burden of state on society.

4. What Kind of Men?

For reasons which will already be clear, it is not feasible to ask the simple question—who were the servants of Charles II?—and to expect a sensible answer. No single random sample or selection drawn from all those who held office and who qualify as Crown servants between the end of May 1660 and the beginning of February 1685 will enable us even to ask, let alone to answer the kind of questions needed to construct a meaningful group portrait or corporate profile. The method which I have adopted instead is to compile a list of all the offices of sufficient significance, from the very top to the middle levels, so as to give an approximate balance across the different branches of the court and the administration; I have then tried to identify their holders at ten-yearly intervals, in June 1663, June 1673, and June 1683. It may fairly be asked: why choose these particular years? Looking for three equal divisions of the reign, it might appear that the dates 1661–71–81, 1662–72–82, or even 1664–74–84 would have served equally well. But 1663 seemed to be late enough for the exceptional circumstances of the Restoration to have worked themselves out, yet to be before the further cycle of changes associated with the Dutch War of 1664–7 and the unusually high mortality from the Plague in 1665–6. The summer of 1673 is at the pivotal point of the first Test Act and the ministerial changes which followed; by 1683 the Court or Tory reaction had had time to take effect at the administrative as well as at the highest political level. Not altogether surprisingly it proved impossible to settle on exactly the same number either of offices or of individuals at all three chosen dates. The number of offices varied according to which senior posts were 'in commission' rather than having a single holder. In some branches of government, such as the Excise, the

Customs, the Navy, and the foreign Plantations, additional offices were created, for functional reasons and not due to mere bureaucratic proliferation. The numbers of diplomats stationed abroad and of temporary vacancies fluctuated likewise, while the number of individuals qualifying for inclusion varied according to the extent of pluralism. For example, in 1683 the amazing William Blathwayt held three if not four posts, any one of which would have secured him a place on the list for that year. By 1663 there was an establishment for a Queen Consort, as well as for a Queen Mother; by the 1670s Henrietta Maria was dead but the complex winding up of her estates and finances continued to require the services of revenue officers and trustees well into that decade. The establishment of James Duke of York grew more elaborate, and came to have greater potential for the future with the increasing likelihood of his succession to the throne. The most powerful contingent factor in the whole political history of the reign was the inability of Queen Catherine to have children. The only completely new branch of the revenue was progressively enlarged. In 1663 the Hearth Tax was the responsibility of the annually appointed, part-time, and unpaid sheriffs—possibly on the model of Ship Money in the 1630s. In 1673 it was in the charge of Receivers and Collectors; by 1683 there were national Farmers and under them local Collectors. The number of revenue personnel did not increase continuously but fluctuated with different fiscal experiments. Thus the Law Duties were only in operation at the second of our three chosen dates; likewise there was a special tax on wine, requiring Treasurers and Commissioners from 1671 to 1680 but not earlier or later. Although there was a naval war in progress at the second date (June 1673), the Navy's shore administration was only enlarged by having two or three additional Commissioners stationed in the various dockyards; qualitatively this may none the less have had a disproportionate effect on how things were managed.[1]

[1] Again, Dr Collinge's invaluable list underestimates this by excluding those resident in the yards and not technically members of the Navy Board. For the latter, resort may be had to Sir George Jackson, Bt., *Naval Commissioners from Charles II, to 1 George III, 1660–1760*, with notes by Sir G. F. Duckett, Bt. (priv. pr., 1889).

Clerics have been excluded. This may be most open to question in the case of those who held salaried posts in the Chamber, as Dean of the Chapel Royal, Clerk of the Closet, or Lord Almoner; there were twelve such individuals in all, but only four or five were of any administrative consequence.[2] The politically most significant prelates were those who were active members of the Council without holding any major office of state, as no bishop did between Juxon (Lord Treasurer, 1636–41) and Robinson (Lord Privy Seal, 1711–14): namely Gilbert Sheldon (Privy Councillor, 1660–77), Nathaniel Crewe (1676–9), Henry Compton (1676–85), and William Sancroft (1678–88). In this respect they are strictly comparable to those lay peers—also excluded—who were Councillors but not office-holders as defined here, such as Lords Dorchester, Salisbury, Bridgewater, Northampton, Strafford, and Ailesbury.

It may also be thought that I should have taken three exact dates, not months. But such a quest for absolute chronological accuracy would be in vain. Some appointments took immediate effect, even before the patents for them had been issued; others were dragged out over weeks or even months. A very few cases of double counting may thus have crept in, but this seemed to me preferable to leaving blanks, that is recording no holders of some posts. For example, Samuel Pepys appears to have moved from the Navy Board to the Admiralty on 15 June 1673, but his successors as co-Clerks of the Acts—his brother John and Thomas Hayter—officially only took over on the 19th. At the highest level there was indeed more of a hiatus. James ceased to be Lord Admiral on 15 June and the new Admiralty Commissioners were not appointed until 9 July. I have, perhaps a little arbitrarily, included James as Lord Admiral for June 1673, whereas I have reckoned John Pepys and Hayter as Clerks of the Acts. No doubt similar holes could be picked in the cases of June 1663 and 1683.

Further to the question of method, I was criticized by the late

[2] J. C. Sainty, *Office-holders in Modern Britain*, xi and xii, *Officials of the Royal Household, 1660–1837*, pts. i–ii, comp. id. and R. O. Bucholz (London, 1997–8), i. 55–7.

A. L. Rowse, on amongst other grounds, for being as a historian like a builder or architect who left the scaffolding standing up against his completed structure.[3] While this may have been a fair point, it is sometimes sensible to describe one's method in order to explain the nature of the finished work. Thus this chapter has required the attempted identification of many relatively obscure individuals, occasionally involving an element of (I hope) informed guesswork. For instance, we know from departmental records that one William Morgan, described as an Esquire, was Clerk of the Stables during the 1660s and 1670s; there seems to be no trace of him by 1680 and after.[4] No fewer than four men of that name had their wills proved in the Prerogative Court of Canterbury between 1677 and 1681. One was a rich man living in Holborn but with connections in Chelsea, where he wished to be buried; he also had lands in Surrey, Gloucestershire, Hampshire, and Middlesex; although some of this property had already been settled on his eldest son, he was able to leave £1,000 to each of his four younger sons, besides other, smaller legacies. There is, however, no evidence of any link with the royal stables; and, in spite of his evident wealth, he is described as Gentleman, not Esquire. Next there was a Colonel, living in Westminster, with very little by way of material assets of which to dispose beyond £40 in gold and £30 in silver (equivalent at most to a few thousand pounds in today's money); he was clearly related to the next one, the third William Morgan, who was another affluent landowner, and an Esquire. This one was seated at Tredegar in Monmouthshire, also having property in Newport and in Glamorganshire, and in a position to provide £500 for a younger son and £3,000 for an unmarried daughter, with other substantial legacies and benefactions. The fourth was also an Esquire, living in Gloucestershire west of the Severn estuary but not in the Forest of Dean; of more limited means, he was sufficiently interested in horses to specify one as a gift in his will, besides other farm animals and agricultural

[3] Reviewing *The State's Servants* (1973) in *Books and Bookmen*, it has to be said in a manner so critical as to verge on the hostile.
[4] Sainty and Bucholz, *Officials of the Royal Household*, ii. 65; PRO, LC 3/61, fo. 2.

accoutrements. We are left with five possibilities: that the Clerk of the Stables was one of these four, or else that he left no will (at least none proved in the Prerogative Court); moreover there seems to be no administration granted for the estate of any William Morgan dying intestate at around that date.[5] My inclination is to settle for the Colonel who died in modest but perhaps not actually impoverished circumstances. Incidentally there are other cases (as was true after the two World Wars of the twentieth century) of inconsistency in whether or not retired service officers were described by their rank. It may be said that there is only a one in five chance of my being right about William Morgan; fortunately there are very few if any other cases with so many alternatives for identification. An easier one to resolve can be taken from the end of our period. This is whether the Francis Russell Esquire, who was an Esquire of the Body to both Charles and James II (1679–87) and Groom of the Bedchamber to James (1685–7), was the same man who became Governor of Barbados and the Leeward Islands under William and Mary (dying out there in 1696). If so, he was the eldest son of Edward Russell, who was himself the younger son of the fourth Earl of Bedford and brother of the first Duke, and his younger brother was Edward, the Admiral and future Earl of Orford (c. 1652–1727). The only alternative is an otherwise unknown Francis Russell, who must have died intestate, which is not impossible but seems most unlikely.[6] This also illustrates the need to go on beyond our terminal date of 1685, indeed beyond 1688–9, in order to work out the life-spans and careers of Charles II's servants.

Having set up my definitions, I have tried to stick to them and not to cheat. The total numbers of individuals (all but a small handful being men) have worked out as follows: in June 1663 444; in June 1673 517; in June 1683 470 (Table 4.1). To

---

[5] PRO, PROB 11/354, q. 51; 363, q. 108; 363, q. 109; 366, q. 75 (see PROB 6 and PROB 2 for grants of administration to the estates of intestates). The Tredegar one was a housebuilder too (Howard Colvin, *A Biographical Dictionary of British Architects, 1600–1840*, 3rd edn. (New Haven, Conn. and London, 1995), 522).

[6] *Complete Peerage*, 'Bedford', 'Orford'; *Hist. Parl.*, iii. 359–68.

TABLE 4.1. *Turnover and Continuity, 1663–1673–1683*

Date	Continuity	Total exclusive	Total
June 1663	260 (58.6%) also qualify in June 1673	184 (41.4%)	
	112 (25.1%) also qualify in June 1673 and in June 1683		444
June 1673	260 (50.3%) from June 1663	143 (27.7%)	
	257 (49.7%) new in June 1673		
	220 (42.6%) also qualify in June 1683		517
June 1683	112 (23.8%) from June 1663		
	108 (22.9%) from June 1673		
	250 (53.2%) new in June 1683		470

avoid any possible misunderstanding, let it be clear from the outset that these were not necessarily the most powerful people in the country, or the richest, or the cleverest and most gifted, or the most interesting. If we were compiling a list of the 400–500 most influential and wealthiest, then several more peers, numerous MPs and other landed gentry, top lawyers, merchants, and financiers would need to be brought in, while the majority of middle-ranking office-holders would have to be dropped. While there were some remarkably talented people in the king's service, there were always individuals of at least comparable ability outside it. And the particular months chosen lead to some additional exclusions, but to some quirky inclusions too. Thus the philosopher John Locke only held office for two years in Charles II's reign, but he was Secretary for presentations to ecclesiastical benefices when Shaftesbury was Lord Chancellor (from the end of 1672 to the autumn of 1673), and so qualifies. In the slightly better-known post of Secretary to the Council for Trade and Plantations (from October 1673 to December 1674) he would not have done so; and he was not to hold office again until he joined the Board of Trade as a Commissioner in 1696. Other notable Crown servants, some of whom have already featured in earlier chapters and some of whom will appear again

in later sections of this chapter, also fail to qualify on chronological grounds. To list them socially, from the top down, they
include the Earls of Carbery, Craven, Conway, and Carlisle, and
among commoners Sir William Petty, Sir William Lockhart, Sir
William Jones, Sir Gabriel Sylvius, Sir Paul Rycaut, Sir Edmund
Andros, Colonels Thomas Middleton and Bullen Reymes, and
John Webb the architect. This is the unavoidable consequence
of laying down criteria and then sticking to them. In theory
someone could serve for nine years and eleven months (July
1663–May 1673 or July 1674–May 1683) and still fail to qualify. In fact, I have not found any such case, though certainly
some with several years' service between the chosen dates are
excluded, Jones coming nearest with service as a Crown law
officer from autumn 1673 to spring 1682; obviously also
excluded are any who had been appointed at the Restoration
but had already died before June 1663, and those who were
only appointed after June 1683. Four ladies, two of them peer-
esses and none of them a royal mistress, qualify for inclusion in
June 1663.

Thus there was a greater turnover between 1673 and 1683
than there had been between 1663 and 1673; but how much we
should make of this is not clear. Perhaps a little more purging
had taken place, owing to the political crisis of 1678–81, or
maybe it was simply that more individuals had died in office or
retired voluntarily. The figures given for continuity relate to the
holding of an office which qualifies someone for inclusion, not
necessarily the same office. For example, Henry Bennet Lord
Arlington was Secretary of State in 1663 and 1673 but Lord
Chamberlain in 1683. Joseph Williamson was Under-Secretary
in 1663; in 1673 he was also a Clerk of the Privy Council, but
the Keepership of the State Paper Office was the only post
which he held throughout, although he had come and gone as
Secretary of State between two of our chosen dates (1674–9).
The fact of a man having been (for example) a Gentleman of the
Privy Chamber—a post which I have not reckoned as qualifying
someone for inclusion—before or after holding some other,
more significant office shows that the person was not a
complete newcomer to court circles, or had not been wholly

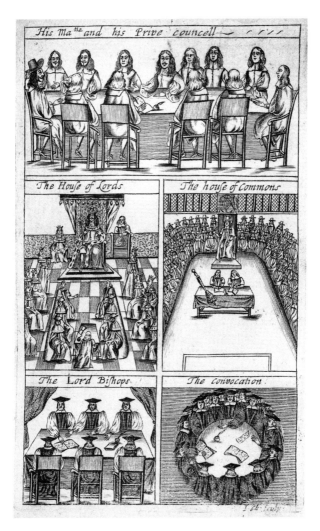

1. The Government of Charles II, 1660. Frontispiece to a pamphlet, *England's Glory*, 1661, listing office-holders. The Privy Councillors, chosen by the King, and responsible to him, undertook the day to day administration. King Charles (left) usually attended their meetings. The two Houses of Parliament are shown below. The King is present in the House of Lords; his heir, James, Duke of York, sits on his right. The Lord Chancellor with the Great Seal sits on his left. The judges sit below, with the peers on either side. In the House of Commons the Speaker is in his Chair; the Members fill both sides of the House and the two Clerks keep the minutes, with the Speaker's mace beside them. The upper house of bishops and the lower house of clergy of the Church of England are shown in the Convocation of the province of Canterbury. (Bodleian Library, Oxford.)

2. King Charles II's departure from Scheveling, Holland, and his arrival at Dover on 25 May 1660. (Ashmolean Museum, Oxford.)

3. The Restoration of the Monarchy and Charles II. The King is riding with General Monck and an escort. (Ashmolean Museum, Oxford.)

4. The procession entering the City of London on the eve of the Coronation of Charles II, which took place on St George's Day, 23 April 1661. Painting by Dirck Stoop. (Museum of London.)

5. A medal of Charles II and Catherine of Braganza, struck in 1662 to commemorate their marriage. (Ashmolean Museum, Oxford.)

6a. The Manner of his Majesties curing of the disease called the King's Evil, 1676. Scrofula, a form of tuberculosis, frequently affected children; the King 'touched' a very large number of his subjects. Records kept by the Clerks of the Closet show that they numbered some 28,983 during the last sixteen years of his reign (April 1669 to December 1684). (Ashmolean Museum, Oxford.)

6b. A touch-piece showing St Michael slaying a dragon, and on the reverse, a ship in full sail. These were produced to a similar design used for small coins, such as an angel. Those touched by the King were presented with a touch-piece; this one has been pierced for wearing. (Ashmolean Museum, Oxford.)

.7. A medal struck to commemorate the founding
of Christ's Hospital Nautical School in 1673, made
by Jan Roettier. A similar medal was also struck
to mark the founding of the mathematical school
intended to provide better technical training.
(Ashmolean Museum, Oxford.)

8. A View of Whitehall from St James's Park c.1677. The building on the far right,
Lord Lichfield's house, became No. 10 Downing Street; next to it is Treasurer Danby's
Cockpit Building; behind are the Palace of Whitehall buildings, and centrally, the Ban-
queting House. (Bodleian Library, Oxford.)

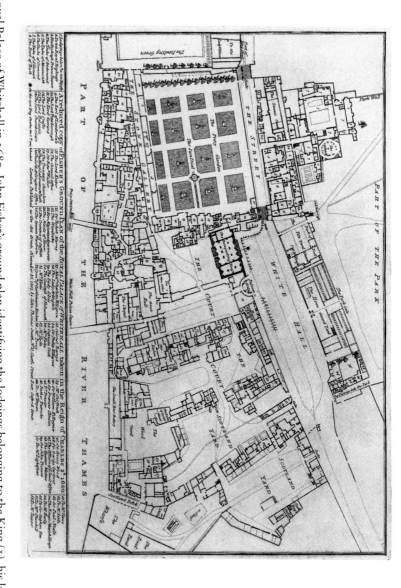

9. The Royal Palace of Whitehall in 1680. John Fisher's ground plan identifying the lodgings belonging to the King (1), his laboratory and bath (19), the Queen's apartments (23), the Treasury Chamber (18), numerous courtiers and office-holders, including the Duke of Ormonde (6), the Duke of Albemarle (7), the Earl of Arlington's office (20), and Sir Stephen Fox (56). (Bodleian Library, Oxford.)

10*a*. The Custom House in 1663, burnt in the Great Fire of London, 1666. Engraving by Bartholomew Howlett from *Chronicles of the Customs Department*.

10*b*. The Custom House from the River Thames, *c*.1775. This replaced the one burned in 1714, which had been built by Sir Christopher Wren after the destruction of the Old Custom House in the Great Fire of London in 1666. The Long Room on the first floor of the central part of the building served as the accounting offices of the Port of London, where customs duties were paid. (Museum of London.)

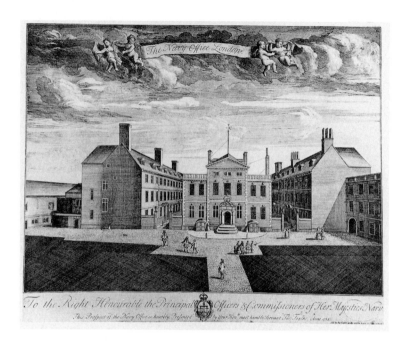

11. The Old Navy Office in Crutched Friars, Tower Hill. An engraving by
Thomas Taylor, 1714 (reproduced in *Defoe, A Tour through Great Britain,*
1724). As Clerk of the Acts, Samuel Pepys occupied a house in the Navy
Office between Crutched Friars and Seething Lane. (Museum of London.)

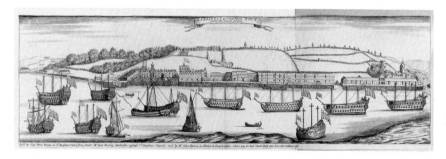

12. A View of Chatham Dockyard. It was one of the four main royal dockyards (the
others being Deptford, Portsmouth, and Woolwich), where the work of fitting out,
repairing, and supplying naval ships was carried out under the supervision of the Master Shipwrights and dockyards officials. (Ashmolean Museum, Oxford.)

13. The General Post Office, Lombard Street, in 1710. Formerly Sir Robert Vyner's house. A contemporary print by Sutton Nicholls. (Museum of London.)

14. Henry Bennet, first Earl of Arlington (c.1618–1685), by Sir Peter Lely. He was Secretary of State, 1662–74 and one of Charles II's inner circle of ministers in the early 1670s (the so-called 'cabal' from the initials of their titles, the others being Clifford, Buckingham, Ashley Cooper, and Lauderdale). (Private Collection. Photograph: Photographic Survey, Courtauld Institute of Art.)

15. James Butler, first Duke of Ormonde (1610–1688). Though not a great administrator, Ormonde served Charles II with loyalty and dedication as Lord Lieutenant of Ireland and head of the King's household below Stairs, these and other offices offered exceptional opportunities for the exercise of patronage. (National Portrait Gallery, London.)

16. Thomas Clifford, first
Baron Clifford of Chudleigh
(1630–1673). Clifford had
been appointed Comptroller
of the Household and later
Treasurer. He was closely
engaged in the conclusion
of the secret Treaty of Dover
in 1670. (National Portrait
Gallery, London.)

17. Sir William Blathwayt
(1649–1717). He achieved
success from quite modest
origins. He became a secretary to Sir William Temple,
Ambassador at the Hague;
in 1683 he purchased the
post of secretary-at-war.
He married the heiress of
Dyrham Park, Gloucester-
shire, and built the present
great house there.(Dyrham
Park, The Blathwayt Col-
lection (The National
Trust). Photograph: Photographic Survey, Courtauld
Institute of Art.)

18. Sir Stephen Fox (1627–1716).
Fox was a man of remarkable ability
and pleasant demeanour who rose
from humble origins to the position
of Paymaster in 1661, was a Treasury
Commissioner and managed the
nation's finances for over twenty
years. He became immensely wealthy,
according to John Evelyn 'honestly got
and unenvied, which is a near miracle'.
(National Portrait Gallery, London.)

19. Sir Robert Vyner (1631–1688), his wife, son, and step-daughter, by J. M.
Wright. Vyner was apprenticed to his step-uncle, a goldsmith-banker, and in
1661 became Goldsmith to Charles II. He assumed control of the banking
house, and was pre-eminent as a financier, but as the Crown's largest creditor he was ruined by the 'Stop' of the Exchequer payments of 1672. (National Portrait Gallery, London.)

20. George Monck, first Duke of Albemarle (1608–1670). A gruff professional soldier who commanded the army in Scotland; he played a leading part in negotiating the King's return in 1660. (National Portrait Gallery, London.)

21. Samuel Pepys (1633–1703), engraving after Sir Godfrey Kneller. His Diary, begun in 1660 when he was made Clerk of the Acts, gives vivid insights into domestic and everyday life, the workings of the Navy Office and government business. He was a most energetic and hard-working official, described by the Duke of Albemarle in 1665 as the 'right hand of the Navy'. (National Portrait Gallery, London.)

22. Catherine Wotton, Lady Stanhope and Countess of Chester-field (1609–1667), painted by Sir Anthony Van Dyck. She was made a peeress in her own right for financially assisting the King in exile. She married secondly a Dutch nobleman, John Kerckhoven, and thirdly a royal favourite and ex-secret agent, Daniel O'Neill; as Postmaster General he bequeathed to her his interest in the management of the Office, and she continued to receive the benefits as if she were Post-Mistress General. (Private Collection. Photograph: Photographic Survey, Courtauld Institute of Art.)

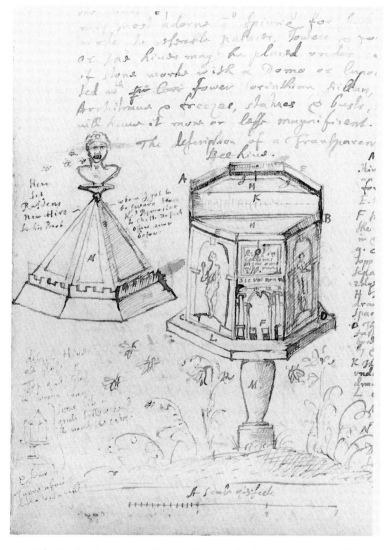

23. John Evelyn (1620–1706) made this sketch of a transparent beehive in the margin of his manuscript *Elysium Britannicum or The Royal Gardens*. The establishment of aviaries was one of the many topics which interested him, as 'an excellent virtuoso'. As a Commissioner for Trade and Plantations Evelyn received £500 p.a., but he was not an ambitious place-seeker. (The British Library.)

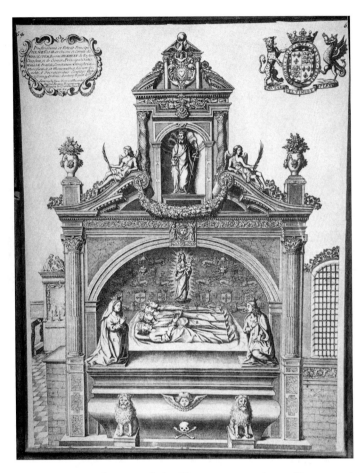

24. An engraved print of the Plantagenet tombs at Fontevraud Abbey, Anjou. In 1677 the Herald, Francis Sandford dedicated this plate illustrating his *Genealogical History of the Kings of England* to Henry Somerset, Marquis of Worcester (1629–1700), created first Duke of Beaufort in 1682, whose arms appear top right, and the dedication in Latin, top left. Somerset, who became President of the Council of Wales and the Marches, and a Privy Councillor in 1672, could claim descent in the male line from John of Gaunt, and so from the Royal house albeit via two illegitimate unions; but by 1677 the question of retrospective legitimization was currently a very sensitive political issue. (Photograph : Richard Dunn)

banished from them, as the case might be, but it has been beyond my powers to indicate such nuances in the totals of turnover and continuity.

The rate of change was far from uniform across the range of different offices, even in the same department. Within the Court of Chancery there were five Lord Chancellors or Lord Keepers between 1663 and 1683 but only one Master of the Rolls. Of the eleven subordinate judges there, the Masters of Chancery in ordinary, none held office throughout the reign, though two achieved a tenure of over twenty years. Thirty-three or thirty-four individuals appear to have held Masterships in ordinary, with an average tenure of 8.7 years, for what such a figure is worth. Turning to the senior administrative posts in that Court, through one of whose offices all suits had to be channelled, the Six Clerks, twenty-one men occupied these, with an average tenure of 7.1 years. Even allowing for the accidents of mortality, it may be significant that the Six Clerkships were distinctly more venal than the Masterships, more subject to speculative trafficking. As to the major revenue departments, no one held a senior post in the Customs throughout the reign, or even for the twenty years 1663–83, whereas for practical purposes Elias Ashmole the Comptroller and John Birch the Auditor did so in the Excise.[7] In the Upper Exchequer two out of seven Revenue Auditors spanned the whole period with an average tenure of ten and a half years, helped by the presence of one nonagenarian and one octogenarian; eight different individuals held one of the two Auditorships of the Imprests, with an average tenure of only 6.2 years. The Receiver-General of the Duchy of Lancaster held office throughout; despite the later eminence of his family, we know surprisingly little about Sir John Curzon of Kedleston, first baronet, beyond the fact that he was a successful side-changer. By contrast, no single person held the same office throughout in the Admiralty, Common Pleas (but two did so in King's Bench), the Mint, the Navy, the Ordnance, the Stables, or the Office of Works. Even Pepys, who filled key positions in the

[7] Appointed Oct. 1660 and Feb. 1661 respectively; there were no previous holders of these posts.

Navy Office and then in the Admiralty, suffered a forced interruption in 1679–84. Other major administrative figures whose
careers spanned the whole reign but in different capacities
included Stephen Fox and Robert Southwell; one of the Under-
Secretaries, John Coke, served right through. At the most intimate level of proximity to the King, four out of twelve Grooms
of the Bedchamber managed to achieve this; perhaps that is less
surprising if we remember that Charles II was restored at the
age of thirty and died at under fifty-five. The reasons for the
relatively premature death of an apparently healthy man, who
did not habitually eat or drink to excess, and until his last years
took regular exercise, remain mysterious. Perhaps the usually
unspoken explanation, of too much sex as he got older, is the
right one. Certainly, unless people were disloyal to him, Charles
liked to have the same individuals around him as the years went
by.

Unknown Warriors

Many years ago, when I was compiling a group profile of office-
holders under Charles I, it seemed reasonable to infer that virtually all those about whom I failed to discover anything beyond
their names and the offices which they held, came from social
backgrounds below the level of the gentry class. And maybe for
1625–42 that still holds good. But for 1660–85 it is striking that
many more of those whom I have had to discard as 'unknown'
seem to have originated in the gentry.[8] The near impossibility of
tracing them may be related to any or all of the following
factors: the incomplete coverage of the country by Heralds'
Visitations after the break in these from 1640 to 1660; the Civil
Wars and their aftermath having interrupted normal higher
education for many young men especially from cavalier families—hence the absence of entries for them in university or inns
of court admissions records; and perhaps more individuals
having died intestate. Other obstacles to identification are, as it
were, endemic and not peculiar to the years 1660–85: the

---

[8] At least twelve out of about forty in June 1663.

uneven survival of parish registers and the lack of detail in many which do; the fact of many English surnames having been location-specific; and of given (baptismal) names often having been family-specific.[9] The generally disruptive effects of the mid-century upheavals are hard to measure. Possibly there were more young men of illegitimate birth; but this had not stopped Mountjoy Blount, son of an earl and of another earl's sister, from himself attaining an earldom. The only other well-known case among Charles I's servants was Sir Thomas Stafford, whose latterly reduced circumstances were typical of many royalists who did not live to see the Restoration.[10] Looking forward in time, James Duke of Monmouth was the only one of Charles II's numerous sons to have been old enough to hold office—more than nominally—before the 1680s. When all these explanations have been weighed up, the majority of those who have had to be set aside as unknown were probably of sub-gentry status in 1660–85, but proportionately not as many as in 1625–42.

II. WILLS AND TESTAMENTS: A SHORT BUT NECESSARY DIGRESSION

The wills which individuals made before they died are often the most reliable source for their residence, status, family, and other connections at the end of their lives, and sometimes also give useful indications of their wealth. The last point has to be qualified in this way because a man's landed property, or much of it, had often already been settled, usually but not invariably on his eldest son, and is therefore not described in his will. Or to put the matter in a more negative way (your drink is half-empty; mine is half-full), the absence of a will is the commonest reason

---

[9] Strictly for illustrative purposes, there were at least two, if not three, more or less contemporaneous Gerald Aylmers in Cos. Kildare and Meath around this time; and a Jones family with connections in Somerset, Kent, and Virginia seems to have boasted at least three Cadwalladers.

[10] For the somewhat discreditable circumstances of his conception, according to the first Earl of Cork, see *Lismore Papers*, 1st ser., ed. A. B. Grosart (5 vols., 1886), ii. 103–4.

for losing track of someone, either altogether or in many respects. Moreover, wills can also help to establish where individuals came from; testators quite often remembered their place of birth or upbringing, by leaving money to the parish or by asking to be buried there. Records of the granting of administrations of estates, where no will had been found, are singularly uninformative.[11] And, as already suggested, it is all too easy to confuse two or more individuals of the same name who died at about the same date. Granted all these cautions, I have consulted the wills of some hundreds of individuals who held office in 1663, 1673, and 1683, besides a number of others from the years 1660–85. It is impossible to do more than offer general impressions as to what these sources suggest. Many of them clearly reflect the improved material circumstances of the testator since his early days, though even then we must be careful not to assume that this was entirely the consequence of his official service. Some wills, on the contrary, suggest impoverishment or at least very modest if not reduced wealth, perhaps arising from the loss of office at some earlier date, or from fees and wages not having been paid. Family ties naturally varied very widely, from those with a wife and a large number of sons, daughters, grandchildren, nephews, nieces, and other connections and dependents, for whom provision was to be made, to those with no close relatives at all, where a friend or neighbour was named as both heir and executor. Such variations would of course apply to all the wills made by those in comparable circumstances over the same period of time. The problem, as indicated, is to try to isolate what is specific to the testator having held office under the Crown. In at least one case a man of quite modest rank and wealth asked that the King himself might be gracious enough to accept a small present from his estate; others made gifts to a whole bevy of top people in church and state. If the testators had sons with their ways still to make in the world, this might have been a means of trying to ensure continued patronage; otherwise it would suggest that attractive, if all too rare human quality, disinterested gratitude.

Granted that these were technically ecclesiastical documents

---

[11] PRO, PROB 6. These do of course set a terminal date for the person's death.

which had to be processed in a church court, it is natural to ask what wills can tell us about people's beliefs. Since the publication of an important book nearly thirty years ago, it has become something of an orthodoxy to assume that the spiritual prologue which is found at the beginning of the overwhelming majority of early-modern wills reflected more what the professional scriptwriter (normally a cleric or a lawyer) considered to be appropriate, rather than expressing the testator's own theological convictions.[12] But the superb study on which this hypothesis was originally based related to the inhabitants of three Cambridgeshire villages, not to more or less educated professional people of the later seventeenth to early eighteenth centuries mostly living in or around London. It is true that many of those which I have read do have a fairly uniform (some would say a suspiciously standardized) opening, commending the testator's soul to Almighty God from whom it came, and/or expressing the hope, if not the conviction, of salvation through the merits (that is, the passion and sacrifice) of Jesus Christ. But some go well beyond this, to dwell on theological and ecclesiastical niceties, or to commend positively the doctrines and structure of the Anglican Church. In some cases clergy are named as beneficiaries; in others provision is made for nonconformist ministers. Such sentiments and bequests must surely reflect in the former case a strong attachment to the established Church, in the latter a continuing commitment to the defeated Puritan cause. Roman Catholics, who in many ways laboured under even worse legal disabilities than Protestant dissenters, of course should not have been holding office at all after the passage of the Test Act (operative from 18 June 1673).[13] None the less, in

---

[12] Margaret Spufford, *Contrasting Communities. English Villagers in the Sixteenth and Seventeenth Centuries* (Cambridge, 1974), ch. 13, pp. 320–44. See, however, Spufford, 'The Importance of Religion in the 16th and 17th Centuries', ch. 1, pp. 15–18, in *The World of Rural Dissenters, 1520–1725* (Cambridge, 1995), which is more positive on the use of prologues; also Christopher Marsh, 'In the name of God? Will-Making and Faith in Early-Modern England', in G. H. Martin and M. Spufford (eds.), *The Records of the Nation* (Woodbridge, 1990) 215–49.

[13] *Statutes of the Realm.* For those outside London, the Act took effect from August.

spite of the well-known resignations of the Duke of York from the Admiralty and of Clifford from the Lord Treasurership, some Catholics certainly did remain in office, but understandably their wills give little away. What are we to make of those testators who made no mention at all of religion, or only to specify their preferred place of burial? A will made very hastily in a sudden, fatal illness, sheer inadvertence, or forgetfulness may be adduced as explanations; but given the very strong conventions of the time, I would argue that such a void indicates at least relative indifference, and perhaps positive unbelief. The Exchequer Auditor Bartholomew Beale made his will over two years before he committed suicide by jumping from an upper window in Hatton Garden; it contains the barest acknowledgement of God's existence and of Beale's gratitude to Him.[14] William Clarke made his will on 23 April 1666, 'being to attend his grace the Duke of Albemarle in the present expedition against his majesties Enemyes the Dutch French and Dane and a greate part of the rest of the world . . .', and found no time to mention God; it is true that as Secretary-at-War he was a very busy man, but even so. . . .[15] By contrast, in 1684 Sir George Downing, who came from a strongly Puritan background which he had long since left behind him, more conventionally anticipated the resurrection of the body as well as hoping for eternal mercy and happiness.[16] Another ex-Cromwellian, the double agent and projector Sir Samuel Morland, Bart. only had time to thank God for his being of sound mind and perfect memory before proceeding to provide for the lady with whom he was then living (sometimes referred to in other sources as his third or even his fourth wife).[17] Edward Montagu, Earl of Sandwich, sought the blessing of God upon the Order of the Garter (to which he belonged) but made no other mention of religion.[18] By contrast, Matthew Pindar, a Six Clerk in Chancery and son of Sir Paul, the early Stuart tycoon, professed 'the true Christian

---

[14] PROB 11/344, q. 2 (Beale).   [15] PROB 11/321, q. 95 (Clarke).
[16] PROB 11/377, q. 139 (Downing).
[17] PROB 11/429, q. 240 (Morland, Dec. 1695).
[18] PROB 11/340, q. 113 (Sandwich).

faith according to the established Doctrine of the church of England . . .' (etc.).[19] These examples could be multiplied, and such distinct differences of content, not merely of emphasis, suggest something other than the scribe's view of what was meet and fitting; all the more so, in that some actually speak of having written their wills for themselves. In at least one case, what is normally the religious prologue about the testator's soul is tacked on at the very end, immediately before the witnesses' signatures: was this due to absent-mindedness, or to a nudge from the scribe or from someone else who was present?[20]

At the end of the century a book appeared telling people how to make their wills. Its clerical author laid down five rules: wills should be made while the testator was healthy and not on the point of death; in content they should be Christian, prudent, just, and charitable. He emphasized the need for a full and specific religious prologue, but wrote at greatest length about the necessity of giving to the poor, in particular not forgetting the widows and children of the clergy.[21] It is not easy to say how much should be read into these admonitions. While the vast majority of those who have left any evidence professed conventional religious beliefs, the ecclesiastical establishment was very much on the defensive by the 1690s–1700s.[22]

---

[19] PROB 11/374, q. 129 (Pindar).

[20] Sir Peter Apsley (1647–91 x 2), who was joined with his father, Sir Allen, as Master of the Hawks in 1671, and later as Treasurer to the Duke of York, becoming Cofferer of the Household on James's accession in 1685 (PROB 11/410, q. 138).

[21] William Assheton, DD, Rector of Beckenham, Kent and Chaplain to the Duke of Ormonde, *A Theological Discourse of Last Wills and Testaments* (1696, Wing, *STC 1641–1700*, A 4046), esp. pp. 3, 16–19, 97.

[22] John Redwood, *Reason, Ridicule and Religion: The Age of Enlightenment in England, 1660–1750* (1976); G. E. Aylmer, 'Unbelief in Seventeenth-century England', in Donald Pennington and Keith Thomas (eds.), *Puritans and Revolutionaries. Essays in Seventeenth-century History Presented to Christopher Hill* (Oxford, 1978), 22–46; Michael Hunter and David Wootton (eds.), *Atheism from the Reformation to the Enlightenment* (Oxford, 1992).

III. OFFICE-HOLDERS IN JUNE 1663

The themes of continuity and the resumption of places which had been lost in the 1640s and 1650s are reflected in the average or median ages of those holding office in June 1663. Of those whose date of birth is known or can safely be inferred, 240 had been born by 1620, i.e. were ten years or more older than the King, 53 were born between 1621 and 1630, and only 28 after 1630. So, while the young Cavaliers of the Interregnum were certainly present, they were as yet only a minority element. And age is likely to have contributed more to the turnover in personnel by the time that another ten and then another twenty years had passed than did either politics or religion.

If we consider their origins in terms of social status, the preponderance of the nobility and upper gentry is so overwhelming as to be almost a tautology. The fathers of at least 280 were of the rank of gentleman (or its equivalent) and above, while of these an even more remarkable 149 were the sons of knights or above. Only some 57 can be accounted as having definitely been the sons of sub-gentry families. But we should not exaggerate the significance of this, dramatic as the contrast is with the State's servants of 1649–1660. Many of the fathers of these Crown servants had themselves risen in rank, if not necessarily also in wealth, as a result of civil or military service under the Crown. It is not obvious at what stage in a son's (or daughter's) life their father's status is most relevant: birth, schooling or higher education, age of majority, marriage, or date of entry to office? Likewise we should probably not make too much of their place in their respective families. I have identified at least 153 who were eldest, eldest surviving, or only sons, as against 120 who were younger sons. Since I have only been able to consult selected parish registers, otherwise relying on printed pedigrees, mainly those in heraldic visitations, these figures are bound to be biased towards the armigerous gentry. I suspect but cannot prove that the preponderance of eldest sons would be even greater if we had reliable evidence for more sub-gentry families.

Their geographical origins (Table 4.2) may fairly be

TABLE 4.2. *Geographical Origins and Destinations, 1663*

County or other location of origin			Location of final residence	
Bedfordshire	7	(2)	7	(3)
Berkshire	5	(4)	7	(8)
Buckinghamshire	13	(4)	14	(9)
Cambridgeshire	2	(1)	4	(1)
Cheshire	5	(6)	4	(1)
Cornwall	7	(2)	3	(2)
Cumberland and Westmoreland	3	(1)	—	—
Derbyshire	5	(4)	5	(3)
Devon	18	(3)	7	(3)
Dorset	5	(4)	6	(3)
Co. Durham and Northumberland	4	(1)	2	—
Essex	12	(7)	8	(14)
Gloucestershire	10	(6)	5	(3)
Hampshire	6	(3)	8	(4)
Herefordshire	1	(1)	1	(1)
Hertfordshire	9	(8)	8	(9)
Huntingdonshire	5	(1)	3	(3)
Kent	25	(10)	32	(14)
Lancashire	6	(4)	1	(1)
Leicestershire and Rutland	3	(2)	1	—
Lincolnshire	3	(2)	1	(4)
Middlesex	22	(4)	44	(6)
Norfolk	8	(7)	3	8)
Northamptonshire	14	(4)	11	(4)
Nottinghamshire	4	(3)	3	(1)
Oxfordshire	10	(8)	11	(8)
Shropshire	9	(2)	3	(1)
Somerset and Bristol	24	(3)	6	—
Staffordshire	5	(4)	2	(1)
Suffolk	7	(9)	12	(6)
Surrey	12	(6)	21	(17)
Sussex	7	(7)	7	(6)
Warwickshire	8	(7)	6	(4)
Wiltshire	18	(2)	8	(1)
Worcestershire	8	(8)	4	(3)
Yorkshire	15	(3)	7	(4)
Wales and Monmouthshire	16	(2)	7	(1)
London (see below)	105	(33)	201	(83)
Ireland	26	(1)	28	(11)
Scotland	9	(12)	5	(7)
Channel Islands	3	(1)	2	(1)
North America and West Indies	1	—	4	—
Europe	9	(3)	12	(1)
Total Locations	494	(205)	534	(260)
Total known individuals	403	(172)	401	(170)

Figures in brackets from Aylmer, *King's Servants*, table 19 (pp. 267–3) give the location of final residence or main estate for 1625–42 office-holders contrasted with those of the servants of Charles I. Several features stand out clearly. Compared with 1625–42, Scotland is proportionately down; the age of the 'hungry Scots', if indeed it ever existed, was well and truly over. The total for Ireland is very much up; this may be partly due to my having paid more attention to office-holders there, but it surely also reflects the longer period for which the whole country had been under English rule and the intermingling of the ruling elites on the two sides of the Irish Sea. In the cases of London and Middlesex I have been particularly conscious of the growth of the capital city during the century. The boundaries of the City proper, even with its liberties, had long ceased to provide a meaningful definition of London as a great urban centre. By the later seventeenth century the city of Westminster too had spilt over its ancient bounds, to take in the parishes of St Giles (as well as St Martin's) in the Fields and St James's, Piccadilly. Where to put the limits of the suburbs, as opposed to commuter-occupied villages, is a knotty problem. Clerkenwell—then as now of somewhat mixed social composition—was effectively already part of 'Greater London', whereas Hampstead, Highgate, Hackney, and Stepney were not. Beyond Westminster, to the south-west, we may, I think, include Chelsea and Fulham but not Putney. The Surrey–Kent border, to the east of Southwark, is another debatable zone. Thus 'London' comprises the cities of London and Westminster, the borough of Southwark, and their immediate environs. Middlesex means the rest of that county, which still surrounded the twin cities on the north bank of the Thames.[23]

With the individual counties, nearness to London seems likely to have been the strongest single influence. Besides that, family linkages and patronage are plausible factors. For example, Devon's strong showing was largely due to the Monck-Morrice and Seymour connections. The case of Somerset is a little less obvious, but the Berkeleys and the Wyndhams go some

---

[23] Besides the magnificent but still incomplete *Survey of London*, and the equally invaluable Nikolaus Pevsner, *et al. Buildings of England*, I have relied chiefly on N. G. Brett-James, *The Growth of Stuart London* (1935), a pioneering work, too easily dismissed.

way towards explaining its prominence. Strong support for the royal cause in the Civil Wars may have had some influence, but not much or we should surely expect to find more people coming from Cornwall and Wales—and perhaps also from Shropshire and Worcestershire. But many of these individual totals are too small for much to be inferred either way. Looking across Table 4.2, to the locations of office-holders (where known) at the end of their lives, as might have been predicted we find a massive shift towards the capital and the neighbouring counties of Kent, Middlesex, and Surrey. Office-holders with two seats or principal residences, one of them in London (as defined here), were just as likely to have the other one relatively nearby as in a more distant part of the country. Oxfordshire and Suffolk are perhaps a little more surprising as counties to which office-holders were more likely to go than they were to have come from.

Experience of higher education brings few surprises, except for the large number of upper-class young men who had not been either to a university or to an inn of court. Unless there was a general trend away from higher education—for which there is some other, independent evidence—these rather low figures must reflect the general disruption of the 1640s and 1650s, especially affecting those of the officer class on the royalist side. We should not make too much of the relatively narrow

TABLE 4.3. *Higher Education, 1663*

Institution	Number
Cambridge	46
Oxford	57
Other universities	13
Gray's Inn	32
Lincoln's Inn	30
Inner Temple	30
Middle Temple	31
Other Inns	10

difference between cavalier Oxford and parliamentarian Cambridge, bearing in mind the purge at Cambridge in 1644–5 as opposed to that at Oxford in 1647–8, and the fact that the Engagement was enforced in both from 1649 to 1654. The figure for other universities can be almost equally divided between Dublin and Leiden. The total there might rise if I had been able to consult more admission, matriculation, or graduation records of European universities surviving from this period. As to the law schools, insofar as Gray's Inn had been more positively associated with the Puritan-parliamentarian cause than the other three Inns of Court, this was not yet reflected in such a way as to suggest any kind of disdain or revulsion; this might be expected to show up more for the cohorts of 1673 and 1683, if it were going to do so at all. More holders of legal offices might be found to have had at least a minimum of professional training, if more records had survived from the Inns of Chancery. Out of nine such institutions, there are admissions registers for only two, and fragmentary remains from a third, available at present.[24]

If we turn to politics in the partisan sense, we find the expected cavalier preponderance, though less overwhelmingly so than might have been anticipated. Of those whose allegiance during the Civil Wars and the Interregnum can be established with reasonable certainty, 217 had been consistent royalists and just over 100 may be classified as parliamentarians, Cromwellians, neutrals, and side-changers. In this last category there was obviously a difference between those who had

---

[24] Lawrence Stone, 'The Size and Composition of the Oxford Student Body, 1580–1910', ch. 1, in id. (ed.), *The University in Society*, i, *Oxford and Cambridge from the 14th to the Early 19th Century* (Princeton, NJ, 1974), esp. pp. 6, 19, and 92 (for Cambridge); Sir Robert Megarry, *Inns Ancient and Modern: A Topographical and Historical Introduction to the Inns of Court, Inns of Chancery, and Sergeants' Inns* (Selden Soc., 1972); *Pension Book of Clement's Inn*, ed. Sir Cecil Carr (Selden Soc., 78 (1960)), app., pp. 249–310; *The Admission Registers of Barnard's Inn, 1620–1869*, ed. Chris W. Brooks (Selden Soc., suppl. ser., 12 (1995)), 75–144; Clifford's Inn materials in the Inner Temple MS collections. I am grateful to Lord Bingham of Cornhill for the suggestion about Gray's Inn, to Prof. John Baker for facilitating my use of the unpublished Inner Temple admissions register, and to the Archivist of the Inner Temple, Dr Clare Ryder, for her help with these records.

switched—normally from parliament to king—in 1647–8 and those who had only come over in 1659 or even 1660; and we need to remember the additional category of those who had been firmly opposed to the Commonwealth of 1649–53 but had been reconciled to the Protectorate and some of whom had then moved back to royalism—open or concealed—in 1659–60. Having drawn these distinctions, I hope to be excused from going further into the great historiographical controversies of the last two generations (the 1940s–1990s) about the nature of the British Civil Wars or the English Revolution. It will instead be instructive to look more closely at the royalists among the 1663 office-holders. How far does this simply repeat what we have already noted about social background, measured by their fathers' rank or status? To put it in a slightly different way, to what extent are we in fact dealing with a semi-hereditary elite? This goes far beyond the extent of strict patrimonial succession to offices, which we saw in the previous chapter to have been of relatively modest importance. We need if possible to distinguish between the children of cavaliers in the widest sense, including MPs, army officers, and financial supporters of the royal cause, and those of royal office-holders as defined for 1625–42.

At or near the top it is not difficult to find examples. George Villiers, second Duke of Buckingham, was the son and heir of James and Charles I's great favourite. Charles II's Lord Chamberlain, the Earl of Manchester, was the son of his father's Lord Privy Seal, though to complicate matters he had been a parliamentarian General along the way. Sir William Compton, the Master of the Ordnance, whose early death Pepys lamented as the loss of one of the King's ablest and most trusty servants, was the grandson of the Lord President of Wales and the Marches (the first Earl of Northampton) and the son of Charles I's Master of the Robes (the second Earl). And Sir William's younger brother, Henry Compton, who became Bishop of London, was in turn to be an extremely active member of the Privy Council later in the reign (besides subsequently being one of the famous seven, who signed the letter inviting William of Orange to come over in 1688). Two of Charles II's most assid-uous servants, Henry and William Coventry, were younger sons of his father's Lord Keeper of the Great Seal. In 1663 Lord Chancellor Clarendon, himself a royal servant since 1642–3, had his two eldest sons already in post; both were later to hold the highest offices of state: Henry Hyde, second Earl of Clarendon, as Lord Lieutenant of Ireland and Laurence, first Earl of Rochester, as Lord Treasurer. The grandson of Charles I's Secretary of State, the heroic, doomed Lord Falkland, was to be the most honest if not quite the most perspicacious of Navy Treasurers in the 1680s. Two sons of Sir Edward Nicholas, who had been persuaded to retire from the Secretaryship of State in 1662, were already holding office and a third son soon followed them, though none ever achieved any great eminence or distinction.

Then there were what I have called the 'court' families. The Seymours had never had anyone at the very top since the ill-fated Duke of Somerset in the mid-sixteenth century, but had various members at other levels, including the then Duke of Somerset briefly as Groom of the Stole (he died in October 1660), Henry as Clerk of the Hanaper from 1660 to his death in 1686, and the future Sir Edward, who was to become Navy Treasurer and Speaker of the Commons. The Berkeley families of Gloucestershire and Somerset between them provided the Lord President of Munster, who was later to be Lord Lieutenant, and was also a Navy Commissioner, the Comptroller of the Household, the Keeper of the Privy Purse, the Treasurer of the Dunkirk garrison, and the Governor of Virginia. Some branches of the widely ramifying Howard family network were nearer to court and government than others. Barbara Howard, Countess of Suffolk, was first Lady of the Bedchamber to the Queen; she was also the sister of the other prominent George Villiers, Lord Grandison, who was Captain of the Yeomen of the Guard, 1663–89; Sir Robert, already mentioned, was the sixth son of the first Earl of Berkshire, a leading figure at the early Stuart court. A poor administrator, he none the less occupied a remarkable range of offices; his by then elderly father was a Gentleman of the Bedchamber until his death in 1669. There were other aristocratic Howards scattered about, though by this time some, like the Naworth branch, were quite remote cousins, represented by the successful side-changer Charles, first Earl of Carlisle, an ex-Cromwellian Deputy Major-General and a future Ambassador and Governor of Jamaica. With the Bertie family from Lincolnshire we encounter a rather different case, which may be a warning not to push this kind of explanation too far. The heads of this family, the successive Earls of Lindsey, had made good their claim to hereditary tenure in the office of Lord Great Chamberlain; Earls Montagu Bertie (d.1666) and his son Robert were privy councillors and the latter also a Gentleman of the Bedchamber. But the cadet members of the family, two of whom later (in the 1670s) came to hold the key posts of Treasury Secretary (Charles Bertie) and Secretary to the Customs Commissioners (Robert) did so because Thomas Osborne, who was by then Lord Treasurer and Earl of Danby, had married into the family back in the 1650s, though he scarcely owed his own subsequent political rise to this connection. Rather the cadet Berties were part of his, Danby's, political following.[25] Members of other courtly families owed their strategic advantages in varying measure to a single 'founding father'. Sir Humphrey May, Chancellor of the Duchy and then briefly Vice-Chamberlain of the Household (d.1630) had numerous sons, nephews, and cousins, some of whom appear in the service of Charles II, but he had not got to the very top, and this seems of limited force as an explanation. The Killigrews were an even more numerous and widely spread family, all originating from one stem line at Arwennack in Cornwall back in Tudor times but not owing much to this by the later seventeenth century. Enough has already been said about patrimonial succession in Exchequer offices. But the Pett family in the naval dockyards of Chatham, Deptford, and Woolwich, provide an even more remarkable instance. The continuous service of various Petts throughout the century survived even the disgrace and downfall of Navy Commissioner Peter Pett after the Medway disaster of 1667. Ship designing

[25] Note also Vere Bertie, King's Remembrancer of the Exchequer (1674–5) and then a Judge (1675–9); and Peregrine Bertie, Commissioner for Alienations, and Searcher, then Surveyor of Searchers in the Port of London (1675 on).

and construction cannot literally have been passed down in the genes, but an aptitude for applied mathematics and so for marine architecture may well have been. Legal dynasties, of whom the Finchs of Kent and the Atkyns of Gloucestershire are among the most prominent, raise similar questions: how much difference did a hereditary head start make?—not much surely unless the necessary aptitude and application were also present.

What of the contrary hypothesis, of an elite open to self-made men of talent? Some historians have argued that if the royalists had won the Civil War, a new elite would have risen to prominence through their contributions to such a victory,[26] much as was to happen—if only temporarily—with the republicans and Cromwellians of 1649–60. It could well be argued that, if the royalists lost the war, they did in the slightly longer run win the peace—in 1660 and after. Yet the mixed political and ideological background of Charles II's servants seems as evident at the level of administrators as at that of leading politicians. William Clarke, George Downing, Pepys himself were successful side-changers, while William Coventry and Stephen Fox were consistent royalists, the latter as self-made as anyone could be. The financiers and men of business of the 1670s and 1680s tended by definition to be younger and so further removed from the divisions and conflicts of the 1640s and 1650s; but, as against some of the aristocratic and courtly families already mentioned, we may there set such self-made men as William Blathwayt, Richard Kent, and Charles Duncombe. It is tempting to suggest that there might have been a kind of dichotomy between the staff of the royal household, the holders of semi-sinecure posts in the law courts, and the revenue administration on the one hand, as the quintessential preserve of a semi-hereditary upper class, and on the other hand the management of the armed forces, the central secretariat, the Treasury, and the actual running of the revenue services being open to talent as a necessary precondition of efficient government and

---

[26] See Ronald Hutton, *The Royalist War Effort, 1642–46* (London, 1982); and Martyn Bennett, *The Civil Wars Experienced: Britain and Ireland, 1638–61* (London, 2000).

the growing power of the English state. The historical reality looks a good deal more patchy, less neat and tidy than this, which is not to deny the element of truth in such a hypothesis.

Taking the definition of hereditary connection, to include grandfathers and uncles as well as fathers having been king's servants, this still only accounts for something between sixty and seventy of the 1663 office-holders. But the wider criterion, of having been a royalist or having come from a royalist family does, as has already been shown, produce a very much larger total (over 200 known cases). And this correlates quite strongly with the rank or social status of the office-holders' fathers.

The extent of the overlap which existed between office and parliamentary service may be more significant for political than for administrative history. For the allegedly excessive number of office-holders and royal pensioners in the House of Commons was to result in constant pressure for some kind of 'Place Bill', in order to reduce the strength of the Court or Crown vote. And eventually this led to the beginnings of the distinction between politicians and non-political civil servants.[27] Of the Crown's servants in June 1663, at least 138 sat in the Commons at one time or other; if we were to limit this to those who were MPs at that actual date, this would bring the total down considerably but still leave it large enough to underline the overlap between executive and legislature. Forty-four of our cohort sat in the House of Lords at some stage in their careers, of whom thirty were actually members of the upper house in 1663. Many of the Crown's servants as defined here also acted as lords lieutenant, deputy lieutenants, sheriffs, Justices of the Peace, high constables, grand jurors, county commissioners for tax assessment and collection, and so forth. This applied particularly to those who were landowners of noble and gentry status, and whose service in the royal household (principally the Chamber) was part-time, on some kind of rota basis. Royal service at the centre thus by no means constituted membership of a closed caste. The fact

---

[27] See Aylmer, 'Place Bills and the Separation of Powers: Some Seventeenth-century Origins of the "Non-Political" Civil Service', *TRHS*, 5th ser., 15 (1965), 45–69.

that at least 106 of those in post between 1660 and 1685 were Fellows of the Royal Society (in some cases after the latter date) may tell us more about the composition of that body than about the Crown's servants.[28]

Moving forward in time to the end of their careers—or of their lives—we have already noted the predictable geographical shift to London and the surrounding counties. Apart from the magnetic pull of London, Westminster, Southwark, and the surrounding districts of Middlesex, it seems fair to say that royal service tended to draw people away from Devon and Somerset to Kent and Surrey. The achievement of a rise in rank or status was so nearly universal that we must wonder whether it has any significance at all, or was almost a synonym for service under the Crown. Apart from those whose careers ended in disaster, either for pecuniary or political-cum-ideological reasons, the largest category of those who did not rise in status were the eldest sons of peers, baronets, and esquires, who inherited their fathers' titles or rank but did not rise any higher than that. Even so, the minimum total for those who did rise is 262; and I suspect that, if more information had been brought to light about the most obscure individuals, the figure would be a good deal higher than this—probably well over 300. We must bear in mind that, since knighthoods were not heritable, even the eldest son of a knight who was himself knighted had risen in rank; the eldest son of an esquire or equivalent attained that rank almost automatically on his father's death,[29] whereas younger sons would remain gentlemen unless upgraded. The younger sons of peers were known as 'the Honourable', ranking below knights but above all other esquires. Perhaps the most dramatic rise was achieved, very appropriately, by the man more responsible

[28] Michael Hunter, *The Royal Society and its Fellows, 1660–1770: The Morphology of an Early Scientific Institution*, British Society for the History of Science, 4 (Chalfont St Giles, 1982; corr. repr., 1985). Dr Hunter should not be held responsible if I have miscounted.

[29] In theory it took three successive generations before holders of positions equivalent to esquire and gentleman, such as doctorates and masterships of arts, could pass their status on, and enable these titles to become heritable in the senior male line.

than any other single person for the restoration of the monarchy: George Monck began life as the younger son of an impoverished knight and ended up as a duke and a knight of the
garter (the highest non-titular honour in the king's gift).
Edward Hyde rose from being the eldest son of an esquire to
an earl. By contrast, of Lord Keeper Coventry's two younger
sons, one—William—rose from being the Hon. to knight (of
which he was not stripped on his disgrace in 1669), while
Henry in spite of nearly eight years' service as Secretary of
State, remained Mr Secretary Coventry. Further down the
social hierarchy, a rise from being the son of a yeoman, a
merchant, or someone at the bottom of the clerical or legal
profession, could count for a good deal more than promotion
from gentleman to knight or even baronet being achieved by
someone who was already a member of the armigerous gentry
class.

Historians have disagreed about the continuing significance
of these, largely inherited social gradations, of which the
Heralds—as interested parties—were the most assiduous
upholders. It may be argued that the continued, indeed the
accelerating growth of the urban, commercial, and professional
sectors of English society had led to a blurring or loss of definition at the bottom of the gentry class, with Gent and Mister
being used interchangeably, especially among members of what
has been called the urban 'pseudo-gentry'.[30] None the less, rank
certainly still mattered a great deal to a very large number of

[30] See Alan Everitt, 'Social Mobility in Early-modern England', *Past &*
Present, 33 (1965); Stone, 'Social Mobility in England, 1500–1700', ibid., and
id., 'Social Mobility', ibid., 35 (1966); Aylmer, 'Caste, ordre (ou statut) et
classe dans les premiers temps de l'Angleterre moderne', in R. Mousnier (ed.),
Problèmes de stratification sociale (Paris, 1968), 137–57. More recently Prof.
Keith Wrightson has taken an informed and judicious view of this subject:
Wrightson, 'The Social Order of Early-modern England: Three Approaches', in
The World We Have Gained: Histories of Population and Social Structure.
Essays Presented to Peter Laslett on his Seventieth Birthday (Oxford, 1986),
177–202; id., 'Estates, Degrees and Sorts: Changing Perceptions of Society in
Tudor and Stuart England', in Penelope J. Corfield (ed.), *Language, History*
and Class (Oxford, 1991), 30–52; see also Corfield, 'Class by Name and
Number in Eighteenth-century Britain', ibid., 101–30.

people, in the years 1660–85 and after, even if the ways in which a rise in status could be achieved were becoming more varied and less subject to heraldic controls.

Finally we should of course like to be able to compare the wealth of individuals—in all forms: land, liquid capital, movables, etc.—at the end of their lives with what they had at the start of their careers in the Crown's service. Unfortunately this is all too seldom possible, except in the most rough and ready, impressionistic way. And that would still be true even if I had been able to read twice as many wills surviving from the 1660s to the 1730s as I have done. There are of course collections of family papers, many now in county record offices or other archival repositories, and others still in private hands, some of which I have been able to consult. But the survival of a continuous run of accounts or rent-rolls as well as of deeds and indentures, corresponding to the span of an individual's career is very unusual indeed. Even if I had been in a position to employ research assistants for this task, relatively little additional relevant evidence would have come to light. It would certainly not have been what might be called a cost-effective exercise. An alternative approach has been outlined at the end of the previous chapter.

Just as we looked back before 1660 in order to explain where these men had originated, so it is natural that we should follow the survivors among them forward, not only to 1673 and 1683 but also after 1685. About eighty of those holding office in June 1663 were promoted in the course of the reign. Of the 121 who are known to have outlived their royal master, thirteen had already lost office by June 1683. Silius Titus was very unusual, if not actually unique in having resigned his principal office, as Groom of the Bedchamber (in 1675), before going into political opposition. He was untypical in other ways too. His grandfather was an Italian immigrant, his father a London salter involved in the soap trade. Starting as an active parliamentarian, Titus had become a royalist by the later 1640s; in 1657 he was co-author, or editor, with the Leveller Edward Sexby of *Killing No Murder*, advocating Cromwell's assassination. He served as a Commissioner for Trade and then for the Plantations from 1668 to 1674; elected FRS in 1669, he was totally inactive in this capacity; in all he changed sides three if not four times between the 1640s and 1680s.[31]

Of the others who survived the King, something over fifty seem to have stayed level, more or less where they were, through the reign of James and the Revolution of 1688–9. Fourteen improved their positions under James but then suffered demotion or dismissal under his successors; of at least seven, the reverse is true, having lost their positions under James they were then either restored or promoted under William and Mary; about twelve stayed level under James but then went down if not out after 1688. A very few of the thirteen who had lost office before June 1683 recovered it after the Revolution; but, as we should expect, that event had most consequence for those who had either risen or fallen furthest under James. Some of these numbers are too small to tell us very much, and this is a topic which we shall need to look at again in relation to the cohorts of 1673 and 1683.

IV. OFFICE-HOLDERS IN JUNE 1673

Of those in post at mid-June 1673, 257 had entered the Crown's service since June 1663. As we should expect, they were as a group younger than those already in office by June 1663, though whether by an average figure of ten years there is not enough accurate information to say. Rather surprisingly, over eighty of them had been born before 1630. The commonest causes for relatively late entry to office were either that they had already been in the King's service but not in a post which qualified them for inclusion at the earlier date (for example, as Gentlemen of the Privy Chamber or as junior clerks in a court

[31] *DNB*; *Hist. Parl.*, iii. 570–4; Hunter, *The Royal Society and its Fellows, 1660–1700*, 62, 67, 208–9; Sainty, *Office-holders in Modern Britain*, iii, *Officials of the Boards of Trade, 1660–1870* (London, 1974), 19, 21, 23, 118; id. and Bucholz, *Officials of Royal Household*, i, 13, 176; *CSPD, 1661–73*, num. refs.; *CTB*, iii. 77; iv., 41, 173; PRO, LC 7/1; Bodl. MS Eng. Hist., b.79, fos. 6, 17, 19v. It is to be hoped that the *New DNB* will do fuller justice to Silius Titus's colourful career.

or department); or that they had been pursuing another career—legal, mercantile, military, naval, etc.—before entering civil office. There were, however, some remarkable cases of late entry, of men staging a 'come-back' after a decade in the wilderness. The palm here must be awarded to Sir Sackville Crowe, Bart., who had been born in 1600, was Treasurer of the Navy back in the late 1620s and Ambassador in Constantinople 1638–47. He had not been in total disfavour at the Restoration, becoming briefly a Trade Commissioner as well as being a Gent of the Privy Chamber. In 1671 he was eventually gratified with the semi-sinecure post of Secretary to the Council in the Marches of Wales, though whether he relocated to Ludlow is not clear. Crowe was chronically in debt. And having spent most of the years 1648–56 as a prisoner of state in the Tower, he ended his days in the Fleet Prison, the rewards of his Welsh office not having sufficed to keep his creditors at bay.[32] There were also some ex-Cromwellians or side-changers who took a long time to work their passage back into favour. William Ellis (1607–80), who had been Solicitor-General under the Protectorate, only became a Sergeant at Law in 1669, a King's Sergeant in 1671, and a Judge in 1672.[33] The case of Sir Hugh Wyndham (1603–84) is comparable. Unlike almost every other member of this large and active family, he was a parliamentarian and had acted judicially under the Protectorate. Although confirmed as a Sergeant in 1660, he only advanced to become a Baron of the Exchequer in 1670, and was promoted to be a Judge of Common Pleas three years later.[34]

Two men were to enjoy successful 'second careers' on the revenue side of government. Robert Huntington, son of a Norfolk yeoman, had served in the parliamentary army from 1642–3, rising to become the Major of Oliver Cromwell's own

---

[32] See the engaging notice by Robert Ashton in *DNB: Missing Persons* (Oxford, 1993).

[33] *DNB*; Sainty, *A List of English Law Officers, King's Counsel and Holders of Precedence* (Selden Soc., suppl. ser., 7 (1987)) and id., *The Judges of England, 1272–1990* (ibid., 10 (1993)).

[34] *DNB*; Keeler, *The Long Parliament*; *Hist. Parl.*, ii. 261–2; Sainty, *Law Officers*; id., *Judges*.

regiment from 1645 to 1648, when he resigned his commission, presenting a paper to the House of Lords shortly afterwards in which he gave as his reason that he had learnt that the conduct of his Colonel and the other senior officers of the Army was 'very repugnant and destructive to the honour and safety of the Parliament and Kingdom'. Considering that he had gone along with the Army in its resistance to the majority in the Commons the year before, culminating with the occupation of London in August 1647, we might be tempted to conclude that Huntington was rather a slow learner. Be that as it may, he took no recorded part in public life until he was restored by General Monck as Major of the same regiment in January 1660. Huntington's brother Richard was a leading political figure in Great Yarmouth; he conformed sufficiently to retain civic office after 1660, but worked consistently to ease the lot of dissenters and was to sit in the Exclusion Parliaments of 1679–81, dying in 1690, a few years after Robert; he was the despair of Sir Joseph Williamson's agent in the town, Richard Bower.[35] We can only infer that Robert pursued a successful business career, perhaps in London rather than Yarmouth after his regiment was paid off. He was appointed a Commissioner of the Excise in 1668, and in the 1670s was one of the four Receivers for the payment of the guards and garrisons, dying in 1684 with every appearance of very considerable wealth.[36]

William Webb is a more elusive figure. He was probably an officer of the London militia during the Civil War, and by 1647–9 was a large enough creditor of the Long Parliament to have acquired bishops' lands, either alone or in partnership with

---

[35] *Hist. Parl.*, ii. 620–1; Perry Gauci, *Politics and Society in Great Yarmouth, 1660–1772* (Oxford, 1996), *passim*; for add. refs. in Bower-Williamson correspondence see *CSPD, 1660s–1670s*.

[36] C. H. Firth and G. Davies, *Regimental History of Cromwell's Army* (2 vols., Oxford 1940), 200–9, 606; C. D. Chandaman, *The English Public Revenue, 1660–1688* (Oxford, 1975); Christopher Clay, *Public Finance and Private Wealth: The Career of Sir Stephen Fox, 1627–171*, 94–7, 121 (Oxford, 1978); Glenn O. Nichols, 'Intermediaries and the Development of English Government Borrowing: The Case of Sir John James and Major Robert Huntington, 1675–9', *Business History*, 29 (1987), 27–46; sev. refs. in *CSPD, 1670s–1680s*, and innum. ones in *CTB*, iii–v; PRO, PROB 11/376, q. 58.

others, to the value of £4,638. In 1648 he was made Examiner of the surveys of episcopal manors, and in 1649 he was promoted to the key post of Surveyor-General for the sale of deans' and chapters' lands, and a little later co-Surveyor for the sale of additional crown lands. Whether or not Webb had been trained as a land surveyor is unfortunately not clear. More significantly for the future, he seems to have become an art dealer, buying up pictures from the royal collection and reselling them—no doubt at a profit. In this way he became the object of unwelcome attention by the royal Commissioners appointed in the 1660s, who were appointed to recover more of Charles I's paintings and other possessions. However, in 1666 he was appointed Auditor to the farmers of the Hearth Tax; and in 1669 he submitted a scheme to the Treasury Commissioners for the more efficient collection of that levy, or at least for better accountability on the part of the sub-commissioners. And the Attorney-General was told to stay any proceedings pending against him in connection with the late King's goods, because of his valuable service in connection with the Hearth Tax. From 1669 until his death or retirement in the mid-1670s he was also one of the Tax Agents, often acting with Richard Sherwyn and Bartholomew Fillingham; they evidently made a formidable trio. Unfortunately Webb's only previous biographer was unaware of his second, post-Restoration career; and neither of us has succeeded in identifying him with any certainty as to place of origin or date of death.[37]

At the other end of the age scale, four of these post-1663 entrants to office were born in the 1640s or 1650s. The youngest was Christopher Monck, second Duke of Albemarle

---

[37] C. H. Firth and R. S. Rait, eds., *Acts and Ordinances of the Interregnum* (3 vols. 1911), via index of names; *CSPD, 1640s–1670s*; Bodl. MS Rawl. B. 239, nos. 10, 227, 314, 349, 354, 457; PRO, SP 46/109, fo. 44; SP 26/8; SP 28/286; E 351/453; *CJ*, vii. 226; *CTB*, ii–v; Sidney J. Madge, *Domesday of Crown Lands*, p. 53 n. 2 and pll. facing p. 128; Madge, *N&Q* 181 (1941), 114–16; C. H. Josten (ed.), *Elias Ashmole (1617–1692): His Autobiographical and Historical Notes, His Correspondence and Other Contemporary Sources Relating to His Life and Work* (5 vols., Oxford, 1966), iii. 1148, 1234 (and n. 6); E. S. de Beer (ed.), *Diary of John Evelyn* (6 vols., Oxford, 1955), ii. 154 and n. (Feb. 1649).

and the next youngest was Williamson's protégé Robert Yard, who was editor of the *London Gazette* from 1673 to 1702.[38] If there were enough evidence about dates of birth, the median for this cohort would probably be somewhere in the 1630s. Again we must remember that the individuals holding office in June 1673 might have entered royal service at a relevant level as early as July 1663 or as late as May 1673.

The place of these men in their respective families offers little to surprise us. Eldest, eldest surviving, and only sons predominate over younger sons by ninety-five to fifty-three. The general demographic background has to be borne in mind here. With the total population of England and Wales more or less stabilized, if not actually shrinking from the 1640s on, the number of younger sons would by definition have been smaller than it had been from the 1580s to the 1630s, though whether this trend was uniform at all social levels is another question.[39] In any case the number of individuals for whom date of birth is unknown makes it unprofitable to pursue this any further. Findings on the rank or status of their fathers are more interesting (see Table 4.4).

Bearing in mind the unavoidable bias of the evidence towards those from the upper ranks of society, this suggests a markedly aristocratic entry but with ample room for new men, again by no means a closed elite. As to their geographical origins, the absolute numbers are for the most part too small to be worth tabulating for every county. Nor can much be made of this by comparing places of origin with final locations at the end of their lives or careers. Cornwall goes down from five to three; but Devon only from eight to six; Gloucestershire from eight to three; Kent goes up, but only from nine to ten; Middlesex from eight to sixteen and Surrey from ten to fourteen; London (as

---

[38] Sainty, *Office-holders in Modern Britain*, ii, *Officials of the Secretaries of State, 1660–1782*, (London, 1973), 119, etc.; PRO, PROB 11/483, q. 152.

[39] E. A. Wrigley and R. S. Schofield, *The Population History of England and Wales, 1641–1871: A Reconstruction* (Cambridge, 1981); T. H. Hollingsworth, 'The Demography of the British Peerage', *Population Studies*, suppl. 18 (1965), 1–108; and an excellent county study, Philip Jenkins, *The Making of a Ruling Class: The Glamorganshire Gentry, 1640–1790* (Cambridge, 1983).

TABLE 4.4. *Social Origins, 1673*

Fathers	Number
Peers, including Irish and Scottish, and bishops	26
Baronets and knights	42
Esquires and gentlemen	80
Others (yeomen, merchants, etc.)	37
Total known with reasonable certainty	185

already defined) from forty-six to eight-nine; Wales falls from six to one; North America and the West Indies rise from none to five or six.

Higher educational experience shows a slightly greater majority for Oxford over Cambridge (thirty-seven to twenty-six, with other universities accounting for nine). The Inns of Court are just about level with each other: Gray's sixteen, Lincoln's eighteen, the Inner Temple twenty-two and the Middle sixteen, other Inns (and Doctors Commons) four. The most remarkable fact here is the large number of 1663–73 entrants who appear to have had no post-schooling experience, or none for which evidence has been brought to light. Foreign travel, with or without an attendant tutor (depending upon the wealth of the family), might include a spell at one or more continental universities, and I regret being unable to provide any figures for this.

As to the political background of those old enough to have been involved in the events of 1640–60, and for whom we have enough evidence, thirty-seven had been consistent royalists, while more than another forty came from cavalier families, with fathers or other close relatives who had been in the King's service or had fought on that side in the Civil Wars. Surprisingly, over forty had been parliamentarians, neutrals, or side-changers; insofar as these numbers are large enough to be meaningful, this shows if anything less of a royalist preponderance than for the cohort in post ten years earlier. The means by which they entered office continued to vary, with patronage in one form or another as the commonest factor, perhaps proportionately more so than direct royal favour, compared with those on the immediate post-Restoration scene in 1663. In 1673 several were actually the sons of men who had been holding office in 1663. And, as we should expect, proportionately more of them lived long enough for their careers to be affected by the change of monarch in 1685 and then by the dynastic revolution of 1688–9, in a few instances by the accession of Queen Anne and even by that of George I (Table 4.5).

Some eighty-seven sat in one or other House of Parliament, though not in all cases while holding office under Charles II. As with the 1663 cohort, this is a large enough proportion to remind us of the overlap between the different branches of government, and perhaps to explain the strictures of opposition critics on the so-called 'Pension Parliament' of 1661–79.

Turning to the rank or status which they achieved by the end of their lives or active careers, we find that at least 122 rose by one degree or more. Again, for many this seems little more than one aspect of holding office under the Crown. About ninety appear to have increased their wealth appreciably, and to have been able to pass it on to their immediate families, to more remote relatives, or else to endow charitable foundations. Again, further intensive research in record offices and private collections would probably bring this figure up somewhat. The significance of office-holding for the cohort as a whole was too varied for any generalization to be worth making; besides the

TABLE 4.5. *1673 Office-holders: Experience after 1685*

Experience	Number
Died or retired voluntarily before the death of Charles II	105
Removed during Charles II's reign	21
Held office during part, or all, of James's reign	62
Died, retired, or removed 1685–8	33
Still active (whether or not in office), 1689–1702	49
Still active (whether or not in office), 1702–	18

simple passing of ten years, account must be taken of the changed political (and religious) context since 1663, in particular the ministerial changes since 1667—the death of Southampton, the fall of Clarendon, the temporary eclipse of Ormonde, the dominance of the so-called Cabal, the oscillations in royal policy and in parliamentary reactions, and so forth. With the passing of the first Test Act and the King's apparent abandonment of his previous policies, a new political phase opens, with what effects for the personnel of court and government we must now investigate.

v. OFFICE-HOLDERS IN JUNE 1683

Again ten years had passed but the new office-holders could have entered the King's service, or have qualified for inclusion by having been promoted, at any date from July 1673. That said, their median date of birth was around 1640, with a surprisingly wide range, from the early years of the century to the 1660s (Table 4.6).

Insofar as the granting of reversions to offices had been contained (largely due to the efforts of the Treasury Commissioners of 1667–72) but not abolished, this would have tended to favour the sons or younger brothers of existing office-

TABLE 4.6. *Office-holders, June 1683: Turnover and Age*

Date	Number
Surviving from 1663	112
Surviving from 1673	108
New since June 1673, born by 1630	34
New since June 1673, born 1631–50	72
New since June 1673, born 1651–	31
New since June 1673, date of birth uncertain	113
Total	470

holders; we must also bear in mind that a son, son-in-law, brother, or nephew could be trained up by the holder of an office, with a view to his succession, without the formal grant of a reversion either by royal patent or by departmental warrant. And this certainly accounts for some of the younger entrants.

The place of these office-holders in their families shows a slightly less marked predominance of eldest and only, over younger, sons than in 1663 and 1673 (eighty-one to fifty-five); but this was hardly a big enough shift to indicate any new trend. The social status of their fathers continues to show much the same upper-class bias: sons of peers and bishops fifteen, baronets and knights fifty-seven, esquires, gentlemen, or equivalents seventy-six, non-gentry twenty-two. Bearing in mind that all the baronets and almost all the knights would have been Stuart creations (post-1612 and post-1603 respectively), their very strong showing points to the self-perpetuating element. As against this, several of those recorded here as Gentlemen or equivalents might well have been classified as non-gentry by the more strictly hereditary criteria operative a generation or more earlier. The proportions of those with some kind of higher education shows little change (Table 4.7).

Geographical origins likewise have few surprises, but the complete absence of entrants from Derbyshire, Lancashire, and

TABLE 4.7. *Higher Education, 1683*

Institution	Number
Cambridge	35
Oxford	42
Other universities	9
Gray's Inn	20
Lincoln's Inn	14
Inner Temple	28
Middle Temple	28
Other Inns	12

Nottinghamshire, and the dwindling away of those from Somerset and Scotland are worthy of note. Of the counties at a greater distance from the capital, only Devon, Lincolnshire, and Yorkshire really held up, with Cumbria and Herefordshire showing more positively than before; this and the strong presence of Norfolk probably reflect the influence of patronage and familial connections. Comparing origins with final destinations Kent stayed more or less level, Middlesex went up from eleven to thirty, and London from over forty to nearer sixty. Even allowing for Soho having become part of London by 1683, the strong showing of Middlesex suggests a preference for what we would call suburban living over residence in the inner city.

As we would expect, by this date there were few newcomers who had themselves taken any active part in the events of 1640–60. Twelve can be recorded as having been royalists—in arms or otherwise, and nine parliamentarians, neutrals or side-changers; again if family background is brought to bear, the cavalier preponderance becomes much more marked. Over fifty, and probably more like sixty, came from families with members already in royal service, or recently connected with it; again this is much larger than the number due to strictly defined patrimonial succession to office. Perhaps because of the political tensions of Charles's last years (notably 1677–83), it looks as if the recruitment of court and government personnel was narrowing, almost closing in on itself. This of course is not to overlook a number of outstandingly able new Crown servants from modest backgrounds and without prior connections in court or administration. Since, in the nature of things, proportionately more of them would have survived into the following reigns, their fortunes after 1685 and after 1688–9 are of particular interest (Table 4.8).

A large proportion of those who went out at the beginning of James's reign, before his religious agenda was apparent, were members of his brother's Bedchamber and Privy Chamber. This has been seen as part of a drive for economy and greater efficiency by the new monarch.[40] While I would not disagree with that

[40] Andrew P. Barclay, 'The Impact of King James II on the Departments of the Royal Household', Univ. of Cambridge Ph.D. thesis (1993).

TABLE 4.8. *1683: Experience after Death of Charles II*

Experience	Number
Withdrew or were removed during reign of James II, and did not return	32
Removed or withdrew but returned to office, 1689–1710s	22
Withdrew or were removed, 1688–90	45
Removed or withdrew but returned to office, 1690s–1700s	5
Appear to have remained in office until death or retirement	61

analysis, there does seem to have been a moral if not also an ideological dimension involved as well, plus the compelling need to reward those who had been in the Duke's service until his accession. The next commonest reason for dismissal or voluntary withdrawal under James arose from the policies pursued in Ireland by Tyrconnel from 1687, and proportionately more of those affected in this way were to be restored after the Williamite-Protestant reconquest of Ireland (in 1689–92). Relatively few individuals below the level of great officers and ministers of state left James's service on grounds of religious or constitutional principle. At the very top, Daniel Finch, Earl of Nottingham, George Savile, Marquis of Halifax, and Henry, later Earl Sidney are the best known of those who left office and then returned under William and Mary. We have already noted the less familiar case of Francis Russell, nephew of the first Duke of Bedford, who left the King's Chamber in 1687 and was to serve as Governor of Barbados and the Leeward Islands in 1694–6. Daniel Finch's younger brother, Heneage, later Earl of Aylesford, left his office as Solicitor-General, but did not return as a Privy Councillor until into the reign of Anne (1703) and reattained high office, as Chancellor of the Duchy, as late as 1714–16. At a somewhat lower level, but an important one bearing in mind Napoleon's dictum that an army marches on its stomach, Patrick Lambe was demoted from being the King's Master Cook to the position of Second Cook in April 1685, but was reappointed to the top post on 1 March 1689.[41]

[41] Sainty and Bucholz, *Officials of the Royal Household*, ii. 123.

John Robinson, chaplain and career diplomat, later to be Bishop of London and the last clerical minister of state as Lord Privy Seal, was out of royal service from 1687 to 1710.

As would be expected, more of those who were to re-enter royal service did so sooner rather than later, in fact between 1689 and the mid-1690s. If we turn to the Jacobites, the non-jurors and others who left office or were removed at or in the wake of the Revolution, definitely fewer recovered or recanted sufficiently to re-enter royal service. Another colonial Governor, Sir Nathaniel Johnson, left the Leeward Islands in 1689 and moved to become a settler or planter in Carolina, where he actually served as Governor years later (1702–8).[42] This is a reminder that the better-known cases of Francis Nicholson and Sir Edmund Andros, closely associated with James's policies in North America but who were reappointed to other governor-ships under William and Mary, were not unique.[43] Among the most controversial of those whose service was interrupted by the Revolution was the truly extraordinary Dr Sir Nicholas Butler, *bête noir* of Roger North. An MD of Cambridge from 1670, he had to obtain a pardon for bigamy in 1672–3; at some stage he entered the Duke of York's service and exchanged medicine for finance. He was made a Commissioner of the Customs in 1681, temporarily lost office under James, then converted to Catholicism and was restored to his Commissionership in 1686, withdrew or was removed again in December 1688, reconverted to the Church of England after 1689, and was again restored to his Commissionership in 1693. He died at Edmonton, Middlesex in 1700, with every appearance of affluence and success.[44] Four men may have lost office simply because the Hearth Tax was abolished by statute in 1689

[42] *Hist. Parl.*, ii. 655–6; *CSPC Am WI, 1680s–1700s*, via indexes.

[43] Although whether this validates the thesis of S. S. Webb in *The Governors-General: The English Army and the Definition of Empire, 1569–1681* (Chapel Hill, NC, 1979), about the progressive militarization of the colonial empire, is of course quite another matter.

[44] The account of him in Le Neve, *Pedigrees of the Knights* (Harl. Soc. 8 (1873)), 362, is at least partly fictitious. In addition to standard sources (*CSPD* and *CTB, 1670s–1690s*) see Roger North, *Lives of the Norths*, i. 279–80, ii. 192–5, 200, 232–3; PRO, PROB 11/457, q. 125.

and nothing else could be found for them, rather than because of their allegiance. The well-known political economist, Dr Charles Davenant (son of the poet laureate and, as some said, Shakespeare's grandson) was an Excise Commissioner under Charles and then under James; he did not re-enter crown service until 1703 and only attained a major revenue post (as Inspector-General) in 1705. A more straightforward, if in one respect unique, case is that of Richard Bulstrode, our only centenarian (1610–1711). He had actually been in royal service since the 1640s, but only held a post which qualifies him for inclusion here from 1674, as resident Envoy in Brussels. He was a committed Jacobite, though not on the evidence available a Catholic, and remained fit enough in body and mind to be active as an author into his nineties: a better advertisement than most for the royal court in exile.[45]

We must remember too that, if all those serving in 1673 and even in 1663, and who survived long enough, are taken into account, the number affected by the changes of 1685–9 would be appreciably larger. They included such eminent and remarkable figures as the first Duke of Beaufort, the second Earl of Clarendon, the Earl of Rochester, Sidney later Earl Godolphin, Sir Stephen Fox, Samuel Pepys, and the great philanthropist Tobias Rustat. We must not, however, overemphasize removals and interruptions. Among the groups or categories of those most adept at retaining office, or—should we say—those who were least affected by the political changes, were the members of the College of Arms, the holders of senior posts in the law courts (other than the common law judges themselves), and many middle-ranking and lesser revenue officers. Apart from

---

[45] *DNB*; *Bulstrode Papers*, collated A. Morrison, ed. A. W. Thibaudeau (1897); *Original Letters* (Bulstrode to Arlington, 1674), ed. E. Bysshe (1712); A. Lytton Sells (ed.), *Memoirs of King James II. His Campaigns while Duke of York, 1652–60* (London, 1962); C. H. Firth, 'Bulstrode's Memoirs', *Eng. Hist. Rev.* 10 (1895), 266–75; W. A. Shaw, *Knights of England* (2 vols., London, 1906), ii. 251; Godfrey Davies (ed.), *Bibliography of British History. Stuart Period, 1603–1714* (2nd edn., ed. Mary Frear Keeler, Oxford, 1970), nos. 92, 188, 413; Gary M. Bell, *A Handlist of British Diplomatic Representatives, 1509–1688* (RHS, 1990), no. SN30; some correspondence in Beinecke Rare Book and Manuscript Library, Yale University, New Haven, Conn.; and add. refs. in *CSPD, 1670s–1680s*.

the disappearance of the Hearth Tax and the Council in the Marches of Wales, the immediate consequences of the Revolution were not directly administrative so much as political. We might therefore expect to find some correlation according to whether or not office-holders were MPs or peers sitting in the House of Lords. Out of eighty-five MPs and peers from the 1683 cohort, twenty-six or -seven seem to have had their careers adversely affected by the events of 1685–9. Although the members of James II's parliament, unlike those surviving from the parliaments of 1660–81, were not summoned to the famous meetings held in Guildhall to discuss the future settlement of the kingdom (in December 1688), membership of the 1685 parliament did not as such disqualify individuals from future service under the Crown.

It is worth taking a cross-check on this by looking again at our select list of the twenty or twenty-one most noteworthy individuals who were excluded from all three cohorts through not having held relevant offices at any of the three successive dates, June 1663, 1673, and 1683. Twelve or thirteen were dead by James's accession in February 1685; one had already left office; one went out then and did not get back after 1688, and another did so in 1688–9; but four recovered their positions or positively advanced following the Revolution. The diplomat Sir Gabriel Sylvius seems to have retired voluntarily after 1688, but he was already a strongly committed Orangist long before then. The Earl of Craven indeed left the Privy Council in February 1689, but he was already well into his eighties. The military and construction engineer Sir Henry Shere went out permanently, and was regarded as a potential or crypto-Jacobite. So the June 1683 cohort does not seem to have been untypical in the way that its members were affected by these events.

Turning back briefly from politics to people's families and personal lives, their final places of residence or seats of their main estates have already been discussed. Their social rank or status was so generally improved as hardly to be significant. Obviously those who were executed, imprisoned, forced into exile, or otherwise proceeded against as Jacobites suffered a catastrophic loss of wealth and status, comparable to that of the regicides and other irreconcilable republicans after 1660. But a lasting increase in family wealth and rise in social standing was undoubtedly more typical, even if impossibly difficult to quantify. Such enhancement was achieved by at least 122 members of the 1683 cohort, as against seventeen who declined or disappeared, although some of these had previously risen in wealth and status. Jacobitism was easily the most powerful negative factor in their fortunes, even if it operated less strongly with administrators than at the highest political and ecclesiastical levels.

VI. THE NAVY COMMISSIONERS

The holders of these positions can be divided into those with and those without experience as seagoing naval officers. In the 1660s the former included Sir William Batten, Sir John Mennes, and Sir William Penn; and during the course of the reign Sir Thomas Allin, Sir Richard Beach, Sir Richard Haddock, Sir John Kempthorne, Sir John Narborough, Sir Jeremy Smith, Captain John Taylor, and Sir John Tippetts. The others were much more varied, and cannot be classified in any simple way. There was the courtier-virtuoso Lord Brouncker, the aspiring politician Sir William Coventry, the returned colonial Colonel Thomas Middleton, two shipbuilders or marine architects, Peter Pett and Sir Anthony Deane, the professional administrators, Pepys himself and later some of his one-time assistants, and one Puritan provincial merchant James Puckle.

Puckle is interesting, not for his service as a Commissioner which was virtually non-existent, but for who he was and what else he did. He was the son-in-law of William Burton of Yarmouth, who was an Admiralty and Navy Commissioner under the republic in 1653–4, was perpetually disqualified from holding office in 1660, and spent much of the next eleven or twelve years as a political refugee in the Netherlands.[46] In the

[46] For Burton see forthcoming art. in *New DNB* (forthcoming); meanwhile Aylmer, *State's Servants*, 277, 419 n. 11; PRO, PROB 11/342, q. 55 (will made 1671, proved 1673).

later 1660s Puckle was accused by the notorious Edmund Warcup of having sought to procure a pardon for his father-in-law by trying to bribe various influential people including Lord Arlington. The pardon would allegedly have been to exempt Burton from the King's proclamation of 1666, requiring all republican exiles to return to England forthwith or be treated as convicted traitors—a kind of attainder by royal fiat. In fact Burton later accepted (and presumably paid for) a more normal sort of pardon and did return to die at home in 1672. Shortly after this Puckle was appointed as an additional Navy Commissioner at a salary of £350 per annum (in June 1673). Perhaps he was unable to subscribe to the requirement of the Test Act; at any rate he never seems to have acted and was awarded a lump sum of £1,000 the following year—maybe as compensation for the interruption caused to his business career as a merchant and shipowner by this abortive appointment. Even more remarkable, in 1679–80 we find him in correspondence with Samuel Pepys, who was then himself in the Tower on trumped-up charges of treason and popery, helping him to compile the damning dossier on the nefarious 'Colonel' John Scott, professional rogue and adventurer, who was one of the principal witnesses procured by William Harbord and others to testify against the ex-Admiralty Secretary for supposedly having (along with Deane) betrayed naval secrets to the French. Puckle wrote these letters from Bruges and Brussels; the fact of his having left no will or any other evidence of his return to this country strongly suggests that he died overseas. Were his commercial activities in Flanders a cover for intelligence work on behalf of the Crown? That is only surmise, but his career is certainly not one which it would have been easy to predict.[47]

The extra Commissioners in charge of the royal dockyards had, on the whole, a harder time of it than the members of the Navy Board in London. Those whom we may fairly call the careerist bureaucrats—Pepys, Thomas Hayter, James Sotherne, William Hewer, Charles Sergison—served in the Navy Office or

---

[47] Bodl. MS Eng. Hist. b. 79, fo. 39v; *CTB*, iv. 1672–75, pp. 305, 367, 416, 725; Bodl. MS Rawl. D. 384, fos. 72–4; A 175, fos. 46r–57v. No will or administration found for Puckle.

the Admiralty and made only periodic visits to the fleet or the naval bases. Naturally there is more surviving correspondence to and from those in the yards. In this respect it is striking that in the 1670s and 1680s Beach was lamenting exactly the same weaknesses in the system—unpunctual payment of inadequate wages leading to chronic pilfering and other dishonesty—as Middleton had been in the 1660s. But Beach eventually caused such furious opposition at Chatham that the principal officers of the yard, led by Phineas Pett the third, then Master Shipwright there, counter-attacked with charges of impropriety against the Commissioner, although six years earlier he had asked the Board to consider a special pay rise for these very same individuals. Beach had to answer Pett's case before the Privy Council, over the heads of the Admiralty Commissioners as well as the Navy Board. But after a month of toing and froing the case was referred back to the Admiralty; on 24 July 1679 Beach was suspended by the Council for having 'violated the rules of the navy' (how is unfortunately not specified). However, on the King taking account of his long and meritorious service, the suspension was lifted and Beach restored exactly two months later. We are left tantalized as to whether his infringements of the rules had been merely formal or had involved impropriety (or worse).[48]

Some individuals, by contrast, could be around for a long time but leave little trace in the historical record, beyond strictly routine items. Sir John Tippetts (as he eventually became) had been an Assistant Shipwright at Portsmouth in the 1640s, and Master Shipwright there from 1650. He was reappointed on life tenure in August 1660, and in February 1668 was promoted to be an additional Commissioner. In 1672 he was promoted again to become Surveyor of the Navy, a post which he held until

<hr/>

[48] Beach's reports on the yard can be followed in *CSPD, 1672–73*, pp. 406–14, and ibid., *Addenda 1660–85*, pp. 364 *et seq.*; also in PRO, ADM 106/281–2, 290, 293–4; for the 1679 case see PRO, PC 2/68 (Council Register 1679–80), 25, 33, 46, 49, 87, 184, 210; for his promotion to be a member of the Navy Board and Commissioner in charge of victualling accounts in 1690 see Sainty, *Office-holders in Modern Britain*, vii, *Navy Board Officials, 1660–1832*, comp. Collinge (London, 1978), 23, 85.

1686. For the next few years he was Commissioner in charge of the 'old' (I assume meaning non-current) accounts; from October 1689 to his death in the summer of 1692 he was again Surveyor. There are regrettably few clues as to Tippetts's significance as a naval administrator. Some human weakness is perhaps suggested by his having asked the Navy Board for permission to take two weeks holiday in July 1661, but this is really more of a reminder to us that there was still no provision for regular annual leave, apart from celebration days when all offices were closed. He seems to have been feeling his way as a Commissioner when we find him asking Pepys in April 1669 where he should spend the coming summer. That autumn he found himself despatched to Hull with directions to review the possibilities of obtaining timber supplies from Sherwood Forest, an unlikely project given its distance from navigable waters. In August 1673 he and Haddock were sent to review the defences at Sheerness, to avoid any danger of the 1667 fiasco being repeated; that November he attended the King and the Admiralty Commissioners (James's successors as Lord Admiral), who then required the presence of the timber merchants (i.e. contractors). In 1674 he was first at Portsmouth, which he must have known almost too well, and then back at Chatham; later in the same year he explained to the Board that he had not felt able to sign a letter jointly with Beach; perhaps he was more meticulous. In 1675 we lose sight of him except as a member of the Board, but this may only be because the admirably full calendar of the relevant Admiralty Papers comes to an end then. In the early 1680s he himself became a contractor, for the construction of an additional large wet-dock in Chatham; this was regarded as a top secret undertaking, presumably through fear of the Dutch or the French copying the design. The ceiling cost was eventually set at £28,500 and Tippetts was to receive a reward of £1,500, over and above his salary, for seeing the project through to successful completion. Having survived 1660, it was perhaps predictable that Tippetts would come through the changes of 1685–9. Meanwhile, in July 1685 his nephew eloped with John Evelyn's daughter. The famous diarist was so outraged by

this that he disinherited her totally: an extreme step and a
reminder of the social mores of the time, but one which may
be thought to reflect poorly on Evelyn.[49]

Returning to the Navy Commissioners collectively, it is noteworthy that of those old enough to have been involved in public
life at any level between 1640 and 1660, only eight were
straightforward consistent royalists, while between twelve and
fourteen had been parliamentarians, Cromwellians, neutrals, or
side-changers (Table 4.9).

TABLE 4.9. *Navy Commissioners: Experience before the Restoration*

Royalists	Parliamentarians, Cromwellians, neutrals, side-changers
Slingsby	Batten
Mennes	Penn
Berkeley	Pepys
Brouncker	Middleton
Coventry	Tippetts
Seymour	Haddock
Allin	Harman
Beach	Puckle
	Smith
	Peter Pett
	Taylor
	Cox
	Ernle
	Phineas Pett

[49] *CSPD, 1660–85; CTB*, iii and vii; PRO, ADM 106/285–313; Bodl. MS
Eng. Hist. b. 79, fos. 9, 30, 37; *Pepys Diary* and *Companion*, via indexes;
Collinge, *Navy Board Officials*, 22, 24, 144; PRO, PROB 11/410, q. 135 refers
only to his own daughter and his grandchildren: *Diary of John Evelyn*, iv.
460–2.

VII. TECHNICIANS

Some men held office by virtue of their professional expertise. Of these, lawyers and financiers-cum-accountants are best considered separately, likewise linguists. The types of skill to be brought together here are marine architecture and shipbuilding, military engineering, land surveying and drainage, the design and construction of buildings, the design and production of coins, medals, and seals. This chiefly involves individuals employed by the Navy, the Ordnance, the Exchequer and the two Duchies, the Office of Works, and the Mint. Among the more interesting of such types were Peter Pett and other members of his family, Sir Anthony Deane, Sir Bernard de Gomme, the two Jonas Moores, Henry Shere, Sir Charles and William Harbord (and the more obscure Surveyors of Woods and Forests together with those for the lands of the two Duchies), John Webb and Sir Christopher Wren, Peter Blondeau, and the Roettier brothers. As always it is almost impossible to prove a negative. We cannot establish that all of these men and others like them would not have held office under the Crown without their particular expertise, though in some cases it seems nearly certain that they would not have done so. Therefore why should this not have been true of them all? To take the most famous, Wren came of a family with court and administrative connections; and he might have been called from academic life to some other position even if he had not become Surveyor of the Works and the Crown's principal architect for over a generation. William Harbord, whose surveying qualifications remain unknown, may have secured his place as Surveyor-General either as reversioner to his father Sir Charles or as a parliamentary politician in his own right. And some of those mentioned did not remain purely technical experts but became in effect general administrators; the most obvious exceptions to this are the foreign-born technicians at the Mint. Sir Anthony Deane, however, became so disillusioned (the King had done shockingly little to protect him from his accusers—William Harbord and others—in 1679) that he moved back into the private sector of business (although returning to royal service again after the Revolution).[50] Jonas Moore senior has been the subject of a definitive modern biography which demonstrates the interaction between his mathematical interests and achievements and his public career.[51] Henry Shere (typically for the time, his name is spelt in at least three different ways) certainly merits more attention than he has received. He was much the most successful of those involved in the building of the great mole (or breakwater) at Tangier, and then had to oversee its demolition in 1683–4; he played a decisive part in the defeat of Monmouth's army at Sedgemoor in 1685, and like Pepys he was too closely associated with James II to be re-employed after the Revolution, much to the State's loss.[52] The employment of foreigners, at least of men who were alien-born, is particularly evident in the Mint, first with Peter Blondeau and then with the several members of the Roettier family, especially John senior, who served there for about thirty years.

VIII. DIPLOMATIC REPRESENTATIVES

These included aristocrats and present or future ministers of state, usually sent on temporary special missions to peace conferences or to foreign courts. Denzil Holles, one-time Presbyterian leader in the House of Commons (1644–8), was unusual in holding the post of Ambassador Extraordinary in Paris for four years; otherwise, his only rewards, besides a peerage, were to be made a Privy Councillor, to serve as an Appeals Commissioner for prize ships and goods, and to hold various local offices; this was notwithstanding his record as a consistent royalist from before Pride's Purge and the regicide.[53] We may well agree with the historian of this subject that Sir William

---

[50] *DNB*; A. W. Johns, 'Sir Anthony Deane', *Mariner's Mirror*, 11 (1925), 164–93; Collinge, *Navy Board Officials*, 23–4, 96.

[51] Frances Willmoth, *Sir Jonas Moore: Practical Mathematics and Restoration Science* (Woodbridge and Rochester, New York, 1993).

[52] *DNB*; see also Aylmer, 'Slavery under Charles II: The Mediterranean and Tangier', *EHR*, 114 (1999), 378–88 and refs. given there.

[53] Patricia Crawford, *Denzil Holles, 1598–1680: A Study of his Political Career* (1979), chs. 10 and 11; *Hist. Parl.*, ii. 560–3.

Temple was the only Englishman of comparable distinction to the foremost European diplomats of the time; his career, however, belongs to the general history of foreign relations under Charles II, more than to administrative history as such and has been well delineated.[54] The only man who had comparable impact, although in the opposite direction to Temple for English foreign policy, was Sir George Downing. Nor should we overlook Sir William Lockhart, another ex-Cromwellian, who only entered royal service in 1673 and died too early for his achievement to be properly assessed. He had been the Protector's ambassador to the French court, latterly combining this with command of the republic's army in Flanders, and was well regarded on his return to France thirteen years later.[55] Ralph Montagu, ambassador in Paris both before and after Lockhart (1669–72 and 1676–8), was important less for his diplomacy than for his impact on the course of politics at home. Disappointed at being twice passed over for the Secretaryship of State, he was enraged by being punished for his affairs both with the King's ex-mistress (the Duchess of Cleveland) and with Charles's teenage daughter (the Countess of Sussex); then, having become an MP so as to be immune from normal prosecution, on 19 December 1678 Montagu blew the Lord Treasurer's cover over the subsidies which the Crown was receiving from France, thereby precipitating both Danby's impeachment and the end of the Cavalier Parliament. This may fairly be cited as an instance where someone's personal or private life did indeed have momentous public consequences. Refused a dukedom by William III, whose interests he had promoted in 1689 after having been a Monmouthite from 1679 to 1683, Montagu was then granted one by Queen Anne on the strength of his son's marriage to Marlborough's daughter. Effrontery and ruthless self-advancement are sometimes all too well rewarded.[56]

[54] Lachs, *Diplomatic Corps*, esp. pp. 50–1; K. H. D. Haley, *An English Diplomat in the Low Countries: Sir William Temple and John de Witt, 1665–1672* (Oxford, 1986).

[55] *DNB*; A. Robertson, 'Sir William Lockhart' (typescript), NLS (1914).

[56] The sources are copious. For a succinct account see *Hist. Parl.*, iii. 86–9;

Turning to those without high political ambitions, in the early years of the reign the Cavalier poet Sir Richard Fanshawe, a younger son of the long-time Upper-Exchequer family, served in both Portugal and Spain, dying there in 1666; his wife wrote his biography, an attractive but it must be said quite uncritical work which verges on hagiography. The longest-serving English envoy at the Spanish court has received less attention and perhaps deserves a little more. Sir William Godolphin, cousin of Sidney the future statesman, is easily confused with Sidney's elder brother, Sir William first baronet, who was an MP and held various local offices in Cornwall. Our man served as an Under-Secretary to Henry Bennet Lord Arlington from 1662 to 1665; he secured a reversion to an Exchequer Auditorship in 1664, succeeding to this post in 1668. Meanwhile he entered the House of Commons at a by-election in 1665. He accompanied the Earl of Sandwich, the Ambassador, as Embassy Secretary in Spain from 1666 to 1668, and returned to Madrid as Envoy in 1669, subsequently himself being promoted Ambassador. Goldolphin remained in that post until 1678, when he was denounced as a papist in the Commons and either resigned or was superseded. He tried unsuccessfully to transfer his Auditorship to Sidney Godolphin, but the rights of the deputy, a Mr Thomas Tudor, prevailed to prevent this happening. Godolphin continued to hold the position as an absentee until 1690, by which time Tudor was dead. At some stage Sir William did indeed become a Catholic; he stayed in Spain and died there in 1696. His oral will, giving his whole estate away to religious good causes, was contested by his nearest Protestant relatives. A much earlier written will still existed and this was eventually proved, in favour of his nephew and niece; the passage of a private Act of parliament was needed to uphold their rights while safeguarding a large charitable and educational bequest, also in the original will; attempts to get all the money released from Godolphin's bank account in Venice were still dragging on

and more lengthily E. C. Metzger, *Ralph, First Duke of Montagu, 1638–1709* (Lewiston, NY and Queenstown, Ont., 1987), chs. 4 and 5. For his house-building see Colvin, *Dictionary*, 509, 776.

until 1707 or later, though this can hardly have been the reason for the nephew's suicide in 1702.[57]

Looking at some of the others, more or less in order of age, the career of William Curtius as an English diplomat extended from 1632 to 1677 or 8. He was probably German by birth and became a naturalized Englishman, being rewarded with a baronetcy by Charles II in 1652. In the 1690s his eldest son assigned a debt of £14,255, allegedly owing to Curtius by the Crown, to his younger brother; how much of this was ever collected remains uncertain. The baronetcy became extinct in about 1700.[58] Richard Bulstrode has already been introduced to the reader and his career sufficiently described. William Swan (or Swanne) was probably the eldest son of a younger son from a gentry family with connections on both sides of the Thames estuary, in Essex and Kent. He was described as 'Captain' when he was knighted by Charles II in 1649 and served as a royalist envoy in the 1650s. After the Restoration he was made a Gentleman of the Privy Chamber and then held posts as Envoy at Hamburg and in the other Hanse towns of North Germany. He took a special copy of Elias Ashmole's book on *The Order of the Garter* to the Elector of Saxony at Dresden and wrote a rather pedantic account of his visit; he must have died very soon after writing to Ashmole about it, on 23 July 1678.[59] William

[57] *DNB*; *Hist. Parl.*, ii, 403–9; Sainty, *Secretaries of State*, 27, 80; id., *Officers of the Exchequer*, 130; F. G. Marsh, *The Godolphins* (Salisbury, 1930); PRO, PROB 11/435, q. 223; *CSPD, 1660s–1670s*; *CTB*, i–iv; NLS, MS 3420; *Diary of John Evelyn*, v. 505–6; HMC, *Eighth Report*, app. ii. 68, 90; *House of Lords*, ns, iii. 117–24; *Statutes of the Realm*, 9 William III, Private Acts c.19, orig. Act 31. The materials in the Cornwall Record Office all appear to relate to the other Sir William.

[58] *Complete Baronetage*, iii. 12 and app., 73; Lachs, *Diplomatic Corps*, 53, 56, 136, 142, 156; Bell, *Handlist*, E 96–8, G 92, 96, S 12–13; *Cal. Clar. St. Ps.*, i. 37, 148, ii. 133; PRO, SP 38/18; *CSPD, 1661–78*; *CTB*, v. 1388. No will appears to survive.

[59] Shaw, *Knights*, ii. 222; Bell, *Handlist*, G 109–10, H 26; Lachs, *Diplomatic Corps*, 56, 71, 84; PRO, LC 3/73, fos. 12v, 14v; Bodl. MS Eng. Hist. b. 79, fos. 27, 38; Josten, *Elias Ashmole*, 198–9, 204, 217, 1371, 1391, 1409, 1426, 1623, 1626; *CSPD* and *CTB*, refs. from 1660s and 1670s; *Cal. Clar. St. Ps.*, iii. 1655–7, pp. 65, 288, 292; *Nicholas Ps.*, i. 290 and n. 'a'; *Archaeologia*, 37 (1857), 147–53; *Visitation of Kent 1619* (Harl. Soc., 42 (1898)), 130–1; *Visitation of Essex 1634* (Harl. Soc., 13 (1878)), 494; PRO, PROB 11/358, q.

Perwich, whose despatches from Paris in the 1670s were edited in the 1900s, remains almost impenetrably obscure. He was most likely a member of a minor gentry family from Leicestershire and Northamptonshire. On the other hand he may have been the son of Robert Perwich of Hackney, whose wife ran a well-known school there; their daughter Susannah, who had a reputation both as a musical prodigy and as a pattern of religious devotion, is said to have had two brothers. Perwich seems to have lived permanently in Paris and simply to have acted as *chargé* when there was no resident Envoy or Ambassador.[60]

By contrast with some of these little-known individuals, Peter Wyche was the eldest son of an Ambassador who had ended his days as Comptroller of Charles I's household and a Privy Councillor.[61] In spite of academic and legal qualifications and his having been knighted just before the King's return to England in 1660, Sir Peter Wyche II did not fare very well. His mother had remarried, her second husband being the parliamentarian MP and army General, Sir John Merrick or Meyricke, who died in 1659. Lady Meyricke, previously Wyche, kept a detailed household account book, including memoranda of what Sir John owed her for housekeeping and had failed to pay, from 1650 to the time of her death in 1660; it was continued with some interruptions until 1678. For the last four years expenditure is classified under eight headings: House, Wife and Children; Myself; Servants; Stable; Taxes, Rent, etc.; Extraordinaries; and Total. For the last full year (May 1677 to April 1678) the total was nearly £1,300. The account book is now in the National Library of Scotland, and the authorship of the continuation is ascribed to Sir Peter's younger brother, Sir

133. Beware of confusion with Sir W. S., knight and Bart., of Lincs and Kent (1631–1680), as Cokayne points out (*Complete Baronetage*, iv. 26, n. 'c').

[60] Lachs, *Diplomatic Corps*, 32–3, 55, 61–2; Bell, *Handlist*, F 249, 265; *The Despatches of William Perwich English agent in Paris, 1669–77*, ed. M. Beryl Curran (Camden 3rd ser., 5 (1903)); *Visitation of Northants*, ed. W. C. Metcalfe (1887), 42; *Visitation of Leicestershire* (Harl. Soc., ii. 1870), 63; J. Batchiler, *The Virgin's Pattern* (1661, Wing, STC 1641–1700, B1077), 33.

[61] DNB, 'Sir Peter Wyche' (d. 1643); Aylmer, *King's Servants*, 92.

Cyril Wyche. This is certainly a case where the younger brother had the more successful career. Sir Peter served on the staff of temporary missions to Portugal, Russia, Poland, and Vienna on various occasions between 1666 and 1673, but only became an Envoy in his own right when he was sent to the Hanse Towns in 1678, where he served until 1682 and again under James II from 1685 to 1689. Cyril Wyche, who was also knighted in 1660, soon acquired one of the very lucrative Six Clerkships in Chancery, was Irish Secretary from 1676 to 1685 and again in the 1690s, became an Irish Privy Councillor, and was an MP in both England and Ireland. So he was in Dublin for the last two years covered by the account book, whereas Sir Peter was out of employment, except for the brief intervals noted, until 1678, and therefore might well have been living in the family home. The account book does not include income, so the evidence in favour of Sir Peter's authorship is incomplete; and it should be said that archivists are usually more accurate in such matters than historians, so I hesitate to contradict the Edinburgh catalogue.[62]

Bevil Skelton, second son of a Devon gentry family, obtained a coveted junior post as Page of Honour (on the ceremonial side of the royal Stables) in 1661 but sold it again the following year. He then pursued a military career without achieving any particular distinction before holding a succession of diplomatic posts from 1674 to 1688. He is said to have had neither aptitude nor qualifications for such a career, although he did eventually succeed in learning German (which, then as now, many English people found very difficult), and was rewarded by being made a Groom of the Bedchamber in 1684. His activities as Envoy in Paris led to his recall and imprisonment in the Tower from September to October 1688; then, with the sudden dramatic reversal of James II's policies resulting from William's invasion, he was released and made Lieutenant of the Tower himself in November or December. He went into exile after the Revolution

---

[62] *DNB*; Lachs, *Diplomatic Corps*, 54–5, 60, 62, 67, 87, 91, 136, 142, 155; Bell, *Handlist*, DK 63, E 101, H 31, 33, PL 17, POR 13, R 28, S 30; *CSPD, 1666–78*; *CTB*, iii. 1359; iv. 453; *Hist. Parl.*, iii. 770–2; *Handbook of British Chronology* (RHS 1986), 176; HMC, *Ormonde*, ns, iii. 343, iv–vii, *passim*; NLS, MS 1880.

and is said to have become a Catholic before his death.[63] Thomas Dereham was the son of a younger son and seems to have had no great expectations in his native Norfolk. In 1672 he became Carrier of the King's letters and despatches—a position of trust with obvious security implications—and in the 1680s was rewarded by being made Resident in Florence and Agent to the Grand Duke of Tuscany. His cousin, Sir Richard Dereham, the third baronet, was a hopeless spendthrift who had to sell the family estate, but Thomas had done well enough to buy it. He was unmarried and in his will left everything to his cousin's widow as trustee for her young son, the fourth baronet, which certainly showed strong family spirit. Apart from his having ingratiated himself with Sir Joseph Williamson in 1673, there is no evidence about Dereham's court or ministerial connections.[64]

At this middle level of diplomatic appointments, some of the foreign-born are easier to trace than the native Englishmen; Curtius was by no means unique. Bernard Gascoigne of Florence and Livorno had served in the royal army during the 1640s; he obtained a patent of denization in 1661, became a royal pensioner two years later, and went to Italy as embassy secretary in 1665 and was Envoy to the Emperor at Vienna in 1672–3. He died in London evidently out of employment and very exercised about his Italian property and dependents.[65] A much younger man, who was born and raised in the south of France, Gabriel de Sylvius, came to England as an Orangist refugee from the republican regime in the Netherlands during the war in 1666; his original contact and sponsor was Secretary

[63] Besides a very brief notice in *DNB*, see *CSPD, 1660s–80s*, Bodl. MSS. Eng. Hist. b. 79, fo. 69; Eng. Hist. b. 99, fo. 14r–v; Lachs, *Diplomatic Corps*, 55, 60, 62; Bell, *Handlist*, DK 66, E 102, F 274, 286, G 116, H 32, LC 171, 173.

[64] *CSPD, 1670s–1680s*; Bell, *Handlist*, IT 47, 50, 6, T 17; *Visitation of Norfolk 1664* (Harl. Soc., 85. 1933), i. 67–8; Shaw, *Knights*, ii. 170, 254–5; *Complete Baronetage*, iii. 206–7; PRO, PROB 11/436, q. 2.

[65] *DNB*; *CSPD, 1663–82*; *CTB*, ii–vii; Lachs, *Diplomatic Corps*, 37, 53, 54, 77, 142, 153; Bell, *Handlist*, E 100, IT 37, 41; HMC, *House of Lords MSS, 1678–1688* (11th Report, app. II), 69, no. 40; Bodl. MS Eng. Hist. c. 711, fo. 47; PRO, PROB 11/386, q. 22.

Arlington's Dutch wife. He proved extremely useful at first as an unofficial link between the Stuart and Orange courts, and then was soon employed as an English Envoy (from the late 1660s), although he did not achieve denization until 1679. His will shows that he still felt he had a claim to property in Provence (presumably within the House of Orange's enclave there); he offered a £500 reward to a French couple if they succeeded in recovering this estate for his wife, who was by then a Maid of Honour to the Queen.[66]

The historian of the later Stuart diplomatic corps does her very best for these men. To put it rather negatively, perhaps Charles II's foreign relations would have been even more muddled and inconsistent without the work of those discussed here and their other colleagues. Foreign policy was of course very much the personal preserve of the King and his most intimate advisers, notably Arlington and—later—Sunderland. No regular English diplomat signed the Secret Treaty of Dover, and the case of Ralph Montagu shows how much damage could be done by someone not absolutely loyal and trustworthy.

IX. SECRETARIES AND MEN OF BUSINESS

Those described under this heading included some of the most talented and remarkable of all Crown servants, several of whom we have already met in previous chapters or earlier in this one. As always, the classification cannot be completely hard and fast. For instance, the future Earl and Lord Treasurer, Sidney Godolphin, began in the royal Stables, advanced from there to the King's Bedchamber, then moved laterally into diplomacy but only temporarily so; next, again crossing functional and departmental boundaries, into revenue administration and financial management, although he was briefly Secretary of State in

---

[66] *CSPD, 1667–85*; *CTB*, v–vi; Bell, *Handlist*, DK 67, G 103, 113, LC 153, 157–8; Lachs, *Diplomatic Corps*, 52–3, 70; *Diary of John Evelyn*, iii. 471 and n. 3; iv. 123–4, 155, 447–8, etc.; PRO, PROB 11/436, q. 39; J. Hora Siccama, 'Sir Gabriel de Sylvius', *Revue d'histoire diplomatique*, 4th year, no. 1 (Paris, 1900), 598–630.

1684, before returning to the Treasury. How high Godolphin should rank as a statesman is not our concern here, but few individuals can have risen to the top on the civil side of government with so varied a range of experience behind them. Sir George Downing was Ambassador in the Netherlands (twice), Treasury Secretary and then a Customs Commissioner, but the only post which he held continuously from the time of the Protectorate until his death, was that of Teller in the Receipt, where he employed a succession of deputies. It will be helpful to look at some of the more characteristic figures in this category, more or less in chronological sequence.

William Clarke had already established his position as a military administrator before the Restoration as Secretary of the Army in Scotland. His close ties with General George Monck were both the making of him as a Crown servant from 1660 and (quite literally) the death of him in 1666. The most exciting and valuable part of Clarke's manuscript archive dates, of course, from 1647 to 1649 when he acted as scribe for the Army Council debates at Reading, Putney, and Whitehall. How onerous his duties were after the ex-Cromwellian army had been demobilized and paid off (in 1660–2) is not clear; the Clarke Papers (in the library of Worcester College, Oxford) do include some post-Restoration material but not much, nor of any great interest. There were only the two regiments of guards (Monck's and the King's) plus the royal lifeguard and the various garrison forces to be looked after until the enlargement of the standing army began, but most of this process took place after Clarke had died of wounds suffered on Monck's flagship in 1666. He has been much written about, and no more need be said here.[67] Joseph Williamson, another compulsive record keeper, while outwardly conforming to the necessary minimum extent, had

[67] *Sir William Clarke Manuscripts, 1640–1664* (with microfilm edn., Brighton, 1979): Aylmer, 'Introduction', 9–27; Lesley Le Claire, 'Civil War to Arcadian Dream: The Libraries of William and George Clarke', *Oxford Magazine*, 74 (1991), 6–9; *Clarke Papers*, i and ii (rep. in 1 vol., RHS, 1992), Austin Woolrych, 'Preface' (unpag.); Frances Henderson, 'New Material from the Clarke Manuscripts: Political and Official Correspondence and News Sent and Received by the Army Headquarters in Scotland, 1651–1660', Univ. of Oxford D.Phil. thesis, (1998); *New DNB* (forthcoming).

already established an underground royalist network as a
Fellow of Queen's College, Oxford, before the Restoration. His
transition from don to civil servant in 1660 seems so natural as
to have been almost automatic. The son of an obscure
Cumberland clergyman, he was almost as self-made in terms of
social origins as was Clarke. Williamson's intelligence activities
have been admirably described and assessed. It might fairly be
said that he achieved more as an Under-Secretary than as
Secretary of State, even if this was partly due to changed political circumstances over which he had no control and by which
he was eventually overwhelmed.[68] Nicholas Oudart was a naturalized foreigner who, because of his linguistic skills and continental contacts, was probably more valuable to the royalist
government in exile than he was in England after the
Restoration. He never got very far, ending his days in the semi-
sinecure post of Signet Clerk.[69] John Cooke, on the other hand,
who moved with great dexterity from Cromwellian to royal
service in 1659–60, became an Under-Secretary and later also
Latin Secretary; because of his exceptionally long service, he
may have been more important in the central executive for his
knowledge of precedent (in drafting documents and so on) than
for his actual grasp of contemporary events.[70]

[68] See refs. to Williamson in Chs. 2 and 3 above; F. M. G. Evans (Mrs.
C. S. Higham), *The Principal Secretary of State. A Survey of the Office from
1558 to 1680* (Manchester, 1923); *Hist. Parl.*, iii. 736–40; Alan Marshall,
Intelligence and Espionage in the Reign of Charles II, 1660–1685 (Cambridge,
1994), *passim*, esp. pp. 33–7 and 63–73. For his eventual marriage into a
branch of the Stuart royal family, see *Complete Peerage*, xx–xxi. 709–12,
'Thomond'; and on the building which he paid for in his old College see Royal
Commission on Historical Monuments, *An Inventory of the Historical
Monuments in the City of Oxford*, i (1939), 97; Victoria County History,
Oxfordshire, iii, *The University of Oxford* (Oxford, 1954), 134, 138; Colvin,
Dictionary, 631, 1089.
[69] PRO, LC 3/73, fo. 13; Bodl. MS Eng. Hist. b. 79, fos. 15, 27; *DNB*;
Sainty, *Secretaries of State*, 47, 94; Lachs, *Diplomatic Corps*, 130; Bell,
Handlist, LC 138; *CSPD 1663–84*; PRO, PROB 11/370, q. 88.
[70] John Venn and J. A. Venn (eds.), *Alumni Cantabrigienses* (10 vols.,
Cambridge, 1922–54), I. i. 385; H. M. Innes, *Fellows of Trinity College,
Cambridge* (Cambridge, 1941), 32; J. Twigg, *The University of Cambridge and
the English Revolution, 1625–1688* (Woodbridge, 1990), app. 4, p. 296; *Pepys
Diary*, i. 62 and n. 2; Sainty, *Secretaries of State*, 27, 47, 72; PRO, PROB

The career of Robert Southwell (1635–1702) also straddled different branches of government, though not at such a high level as that of Sidney Godolphin. His father had settled in Ireland and was Governor of Kinsale, except for a brief interval during the Cromwellian reconquest, from the early 1640s to his death in the 1670s. Robert was at school in both Ireland and England, attended Queen's College, Oxford, and Lincoln's Inn, and then travelled on the Continent; he married into the influential (and royalist) Kent family of the Derings. By the early 1660s he was back in Ireland; and, although a close friend of William Petty, of whom the restored Lord Lieutenant had a poor opinion, commended himself to Ormonde from an early date. In 1664 he bought a Clerkship of the (English) Privy Council, a post which he was to resell in 1679, apparently exhausted by the attendance required during the Popish Plot investigations; but he actually spent much of his time abroad, on missions to Portugal (twice) and to the Spanish Netherlands; he was made an Excise Commissioner (whose main responsibility was to oversee the Farmers) in 1671 and sold this post too in 1681. In 1680 he was again sent overseas, as Envoy to the Great Elector of Brandenburg-Prussia. He seems not to have held any central office from 1681 to 1689, but to have been quite happy setting himself up as a country gentleman at Kings Weston, in south Gloucestershire (now part of north Somerset or Greater Bristol). A supporter of James II at least until 1687, he contrived to keep out of the way successfully in 1688, until the outcome of events was clear. Having been an MP from 1673 to 1679 and again in 1685, he was not re-elected after the Revolution, but was made a Commissioner of Customs and attended William as Secretary of State (for Ireland) on the expedition of 1690. The sources appear to conflict as to whether or not he remained in this office until his death, but this is due to a confusion between the Secretaryship of State for Ireland and the (senior) Secretaryship to the Lord Lieutenant, Lord Deputy or Lords Justices in Ireland. Although increasingly inactive and

11/406, q. 186 (brief and uninformative; he left one son and three daughters); scattered refs. in standard sources but no body of material. I am grateful to Sir John Sainty for the suggestion about him as an authority on precedent.

no longer resident in Ireland, there seems to be no doubt that
Southwell was allowed to continue in the former post until the
eve of his death, when he resigned it in favour of his son,
Edward, who—just to make confusion worse—was at least for
a time both Secretary of State and Chief (or senior) Secretary.
Robert Southwell remained on the Customs Commission until
1694 but was at the same time also temporarily a Lord Justice
and an Accounts Commissioner in Ireland (1693). What most
of his previous biographers have underplayed is the closeness of
Southwell's relations with the two successive Dukes of
Ormonde. From having been a subordinate client and dependent of the first Duke back in the 1660s, by the 1680s he had
become a close personal friend, the Duke's chosen or 'authorized' biographer, and the person recommended most strongly
to the young Earl of Ossory, by then heir apparent to his grandfather, to act as his confidential adviser. The shame is that
Southwell's life of James first Duke of Ormonde is bland and
apologetic in content, almost unctuous in tone; none the less his
career is remarkable for the range of his services both to the
Crown and to the Ormonde Butlers. His son, Edward, was to
rebuild the house at Kings Weston, where Robert had enter-
tained King William, employing Vanbrugh as his architect
(though, as Colvin has shown, several builders and architects
had a hand in it as eventually completed).[71]

If Samuel Pepys inevitably stands out above all the other
Navy and Admiralty officials of his time, this is not to underrate

[71] T. Carte, *Life of Ormonde* (folio edn.), ii; Bodl. Carte MSS, via index vols;
MS Eng. Hist. b. 79, fos. 24v, 25v, 35, 66v; HMC, *Ormonde*, NS, esp. ii, iii
and iv; HMC, *Egmont*, ii; *CSPD, 1660s–80s, CTB*, ii–vi; *DNB; Hist. Parl.*, iii.
459–60; Dorothy Margaret Gardener, 'The Work of the English Privy Council,
1660–1679 (with Respect to Domestic Affairs)', Univ. of Oxford D.Phil. thesis
(1992); Colvin, *Dictionary*, 509, 1007; Lachs, *Diplomatic Corps*, 27, 42, 53–4,
73, 78, 142, 155–6, 165–72; Bell, *Handlist*, G112, LC 169, POR 10, 15, SN
219; *The Dukes of Ormonde, 1610–1745*, ed. T. C. Barnard and Jane Fenlon
(Woodbridge, 2000), refs. in chs. 1, 2, 4–6, 8. For his life of Ormonde see Lord
Mountmorres, *The History . . . of the Irish Parliament . . . 1637–1666* (2 vols.,
London, 1792), i. 180–313. I am grateful once again to Sir John Sainty for
confirming that the Secretaryship of State for Ireland and the Chief
Secretaryship of Ireland were distinct offices, certainly by the 1680s, possibly
earlier than that.

the capacities of his colleagues and subordinates. Nor should we always rely too much on his snap judgements of other people. If we compare some of his references to William Hewer in the 1660s with Pepys's later reliance on this one-time client and servant who, in effect, became his landlord and closest friend, we can see—to say the least—a mellowing process at work. Of the others, Thomas Hayter and James Sotherne went more or less their own ways, thereby escaping both the perils of the Popish Plot and the overthrow of James II in 1688, which Pepys himself and Hewer did not. Charles Sergison, to be important later as a keeper of naval records second only to Pepys, was still too junior to be brought on stage here. Richard Gibson qualifies for inclusion in 1683; he too had proved his ability in a junior capacity before then. These men, and others on the accounting and victualling sides of naval administration, were second only in importance to the Navy Commissioners in making possible the deployment of the country's seapower; naturally they could not guarantee English victories in every battle or encounter, but without them such possibilities would hardly have existed.[72]

Other secretarial types impress more by their variety than anything else. Sir Thomas Page (1613–81) was another academic turned administrator. He came from a quite well-to-do Middlesex family and was educated at Eton and King's College, Cambridge, where he was a Fellow from 1631 to 1675 and then Provost until his death. Although there is no sign of his having been expelled either in the Presbyterian purge of Cambridge in 1644–5 or with the imposition of the Engagement under the Commonwealth in 1649–50, he seems to have been on the Continent during the later 1650s, probably in Ormonde's service. And he was Irish Secretary for most of the Duke's first post-Restoration viceroyalty (1662–9), but was either removed

---

[72] Sainty, *Office-holders in Modern Britain*, iv, *Admiralty Officials, 1660–1870* (London, 1975); ibid., vii, *Navy Board Officials, 1660–1832*, comp. Collinge (London, 1978); for those in post between 1689 and 1697, see also Ehrman, *Navy in War of William III 1689–97* (Cambridge, 1953); and R. D. Merriman (ed.), *The Sergison Papers* (Navy Rec. Soc., 189 (1950)), and for 1702–14, id. (ed.), *Queen Anne's Navy*, (ibid., 103 (1961)).

or else withdrew under the Duke's successor, Lord Robartes. His election as Provost was at the King's command and he was knighted at the same time. Page seems to have left little mark in Cambridge, although he made substantial benefactions to King's in his lifetime and left valuable gifts to the Vice-Provost, to another Fellow, and to the University Orator in his will. This document, made in November 1680 and proved ten months later, is slightly unusual. Page had never married, and his nearest heirs were his two brothers and various nephews. He twice refers to two of the latter as 'the sons or reputed sons' of his late brother, Sir Richard, implying that their paternity was in doubt. Sir Richard, a royalist Colonel, apparently died in a debtors' prison in Paris. No mention is made in the will of Ireland or of anyone connected with it. Although, so far as the evidence shows, a loyal and honest servant of the Lord Lieutenant, Sir Thomas's tenure of office seems little more than an interlude in a successful but unremarkable university career. The unpublished eighteenth-century College history records that Page travelled much abroad and that he 'leaned to the Romish religion'.[73]

The eldest son of Secretary of State Nicholas, John (1623–1705) was either a prize mediocrity, totally unambitious, or both. During the royalist exile, he became a Signet Clerk (1655) and Clerk of the Council (1658); he was reappointed to both these offices at the Restoration and apparently held them for the rest of his life. He was created a Knight of the Bath in 1661, when he was elected to parliament for a Yorkshire seat, thanks—it is suggested—to archi-episcopal influence. He was chosen for a more or less pocket borough in his native Wiltshire for the second and third Exclusion parliaments and that of James. He received various other minor posts and rewards in

---

[73] Venn and Venn, *Alumni Cantab.*, I. iii. 294; Twigg, *University of Cambridge . . . 1625–1688*; *Cal. Clar. St. Ps.*, iv, *passim*; HMC, *Ormonde*, ns, ii–iii; *HBC*, p. 176; *CSPD, 1660s–75*; Shaw, *Knights*, ii. 210; King's College, Cambridge, Archives, College 1.21–2; Anthony Allen, 'Skeleton' MS (c.1750), III, 1301; PRO, PROB 11/367, q. 133. I am extremely grateful to Dr Arthur Owen, Dr Mark Nicholls, Ms Jacqueline Cox, and Dr John Twigg for their help with the Cambridge sources and for providing MS refs.

the course of his career and succeeded the elderly Sir Edward as head of the family in 1669. At Christmas 1684 his £250 p.a. Council salary was three and a quarter years in arrears, which of course might still have been the case even had he been a more dynamic figure. But John Nicholas seems to have made remarkably little impression on anybody, although his only biographer has done his best for him.[74]

Richard Coling (c.1630–97), disguised in the (old) *DNB* as Cooling, was a more lively, if perhaps less than wholly admirable individual. Anthony Wood believed that he was originally of All Souls College, Oxford; but, if so, in what capacity is unclear. In 1660 he became Secretary to the Lord Chamberlain of the Household, the Earl of Manchester, and thus acted as the channel through which many applications for appointments or other favours had to pass. On 5 July 1660 he told Pepys 'how he hath a project for all us secretaries to join together and get money by bringing all business into our hands'; apparently Pepys had done him a good turn when the King was being ferried over in May 1660, and this may have been connected with his obtaining the post under Manchester. Seven years later the diarist met him when Coling was the worse for drink; besides a lot of indecent talk about the King and Lady Castlemaine, he expressed his devotion to Pepys's own patron, the Earl of Sandwich, and then went on to boast about how he was 'made up of bribes', these including the horse he was riding, the boots which he was wearing, and the wine in his cellar. He was to obtain a reversion to the Clerkship of the Robes and Removing Wardrobes in 1670 but the incumbent did not die until 1680; he then held this office to 1685, and his Secretaryship almost to the end of his life. In addition he became a Clerk of the Privy Council extraordinary in 1679 and a full Clerk in 1688, being reappointed to this position after the Revolution. He wrote his will himself, referring to his first wife having been buried in Pertenhall, Bedfordshire, but he also had property interests in Shropshire, besides a house in Suffolk

---

[74] Sainty, *Secretaries of State*, 57, 93; Bodl. MSS Eng. Hist. b. 79, fos. 6v, 15, 25v; Eng. Hist. b. 99, fo. 6v; *CSPD* and *CTB*, a few scattered refs.; PRO, PC2, a few refs. *Hist. Parl.*, iii. 42–3; Gardener, 'English Privy Council'.

Street (in the west end of London). The trustees whom he
appointed were to do their very best to obtain all the arrears due
to him as a Council Clerk; he had also invested two sums of
money on the security of the Lottery Act. His assets were to be
divided between his second wife, a son, and three daughters.
Once again, without any equivalent of Pepys's Diary after the
1660s, we are left wondering whether Coling had become less
or more respectable as he got older, but perhaps he had simply
become more discreet.[75] His younger brother Benjamin
(1630s–1700) was an even more accomplished pluralist, though
at a less significant level. He was Deputy to Richard in the Lord
Chamberlain's office from 1660 to 1697, a Surveyor of the
Dresser from 1666 to 1676, Keeper of the Council Chamber
from 1674 to his death, Yeoman Usher of the House of Lords
from 1678, and Cryer of the Court of King's Bench, also Farmer
and Receiver of Fines there. His will too suggests probably
Shropshire origins, though it is unclear whether the large legacies, which he directed should come partly from the profits of
his various offices, were realistic. He had earlier also been his
elder brother's deputy as a Council Clerk.[76]

Henry Frederick Thynne (late 1640s–1705) was the third son
of a Gloucestershire knight. More to the point, he was Henry
Coventry's nephew, and became Under-Secretary to his uncle
without any other apparent qualifications in 1672, leaving this
office when Coventry retired in 1680. Meanwhile he had
obtained a reversion to the Keepership of the royal library in
1673, although he did not succeed to this office until the 1680s.
Before that took effect, he had served as an Excise Farmer and
Commissioner (1674–7); he was also Secretary for presentations

[75] DNB, 'Cooling'; Foster, *Al. Ox.*, i. 323; Wood, *Fasti*, ii. 163; Sainty and
Bucholz, *Officials of the Royal Household*, i. 2–3, 64, 88–9; *Pepys Diary*, i.
193, viii. 368–9, x, *Companion*, and other refs.; *CSPD, 1670s–1680s*; *CTB*, v.
627; E. Chamberlayne, *Angliae Notitia*, pt. i (15th edn., 1684), 189–90; Bodl.
MSS Eng. Hist. b. 79, fos. 33, 57, 60, 64v; Eng. Hist. b. 99, fo. 13v; PRO, LC
7/1; PROB 11/440, q. 180.
[76] Sainty and Bucholz, *Officials of the Royal Household*, i. 2–3, 88; Bodl.
MSS Eng. Hist. b. 79, fos. 26, 59, 61; Eng. Hist. b. 99, fo. 7; *CSPD, 1665–6 –
1683–4*; PRO, LC 7/1; PROB 11/458, q. 176; Gardener, 'English Privy
Council'.

to benefices under Lord Chancellor Guildford in the early 1680s. The most senior post which he attained was that of fifth, or junior Treasury Commissioner (July 1684–February 1685). Although Thynne retained his library post under James, his career never really took off again after he left or was removed from the Treasury. He is one of the more obscure members of a large and affluent family network, and would seem to have lacked either the drive and ability or the good luck to get any further than he did. However, his grandson was to succeed his great uncle as Viscount Weymouth, and Henry Frederick is thus the direct ancestor of the Marquises of Bath.[77]

Another talented Under-Secretary who never got very much further was William Bridgeman (*c.*1646–99), nephew of the Lord Keeper, Sir Orlando. His father was the East India Company's agent in the Netherlands during most of the Interregnum, and the family having strong royalist connections it seems that Bridgeman spent his earliest years there. However, he was sent home to be educated at Westminster and Queen's College, Oxford, and was naturalized under the Protectorate. His father died in 1659; he married into a wealthy Anglo-Dutch family and was soon able to buy a property in Suffolk, at around the same time that he entered the Crown's service as Under-Secretary to Arlington at the age of only twenty-one. He served in the same capacity under Williamson, Sunderland, Middleton, and—after the Revolution—Sidney and Trenchard, with only two brief intervals, in 1681–3 and 1689–90. He also enjoyed a sinecure office connected with the bankruptcy laws; in 1676 he became a Clerk of the Council extraordinary, being awarded a £400 annuity, to run for seven years, in recognition of his attendance on successive Secretaries of State. He succeeded as a Council Clerk in ordinary ten years later; his tenure there was interrupted for rather longer (1689–93) following the downfall of King James, perhaps through his

---

[77] *Complete Peerage*, xii/2, 585–9, 'Weymouth'; *Hist. Parl.*, iii. 565 (family tree); Sainty, *Treasury Officials*, 18, 154; id., *Secretaries of State*, 109; *CSPD, 1670s–1680s*; *CTB*, iii–v; Chamberlayne, *Angliae Notitia*, pt. 2, *The Present State of England*, 13th edn. (1684); Bodl., MS Eng. Hist. b. 79, fo. 57v; Eng. Hist. b. 99, fo. 7.

having been an active member of the 1685 parliament. The most responsible post to which he attained was that of Admiralty Secretary (1694–8); he was removed from this office, but kept the Council Clerkship until his relatively early death. John Evelyn had a high opinion of him; on proposing Bridgeman for the Royal Society, he described him as 'a very ingenious person', and on learning of his death as 'a very industrious usefull man'. We cannot tell whether he would have risen any higher if he had lived longer, but the loss of his Admiralty post suggests not.[78]

X. MEN OF MONEY AND ACCOUNTS

Those involved on the revenue and finance side of government likewise included a wide variety of individuals, rather than conforming to a single, uniform type. Colonel John Birch, for example, held a responsible post as the Auditor of the Excise, but was in many ways more of a parliamentary than an administrative figure. There certainly were career administrators, such as most of the Exchequer Auditors, whose expertise—if any— was for dealing with accounts. At the other extreme there were merchants and bankers who became involved in one way or another as Tax Farmers, Treasurers, Receivers, Paymasters, and so forth. In many instances their own, personal creditworthiness was crucial in their service to the Crown. And once again, however precisely or loosely such classfications are drawn, some individuals inevitably cross boundaries and belong in more than one category. George Downing, Stephen Fox, and a little later Sidney Godolphin are the most obvious examples of this. An example of a Tax Farmer to whom his official career

[78] *Hist. Parl.*, i. 718–19; Sainty, *Secretaries of State*, 27–8, 67; id., *Admiralty Officials*, 36, 112; Gardener, 'English Privy Council'; Bodl. MS Eng. Hist. b. 79, fos. 31v, 39, 51v, 72v; Eng. Hist. b. 99, fo. 6v; *Diary of John Evelyn*, iv. 197, v. 161 and n. 325; *CSPD, 1670s–1680s*, sev. refs.; *CTB*, iv. 131, 818; PRO, PROB 12, Admon. May 1699. For his in-laws, the Vernatti family, see *Complete Baronetage*, ii. 397–8; W. R. Scott, *Joint-Stock Companies*, ii (Cambridge 1910), 441–2, 466; Josten, *Ashmole*, ii. 574; Peter Roebuck, *Yorkshire Baronets 1640–1760 . . .* (Oxford, 1980, 18–19, 56, 367.

was subordinate, if not peripheral, was George Dashwood. His will, made in 1683 but not proved until 1691, reveals the extent of his assets: he had properties or rental annuities in at least seven different counties, and the cash legacies which he directed should be raised out of his estate totalled about £65,000, making him by seventeenth-century standards the equivalent of a multi-millionaire.[79] Family syndicates were quite a feature of the tax-farming scene. Besides the Dashwoods, there were the Calverts of Hertfordshire and the Forths, another wealthy London family.

For the goldsmith bankers who had been most deeply involved in helping to finance the Crown, the Stop of the Exchequer in 1672, when all payments due to them were suspended, was certainly a watershed, whether or not it was a turning point in the history of public finance. Edward Backwell and Robert Vyner were the greatest operators before that; after 1672 there was never again to be so narrow and deep a concentration of government borrowing. In the mid-1670s a syndicate, consisting of the London financier Sir John James, Richard and then Lemuel Kingdon, with strong Irish connections, and Major Robert Huntington of New Model fame, managed temporarily to oust Fox from financing the military forces, through their use of credit based on the excise farm. They in turn were superseded by the partnership of Charles Duncombe and Richard Kent, with Fox also staging a comeback; but massive as Duncombe's operations were, none of them was a Crown creditor quite on the scale of Backwell and Vyner.

Unlike Thomas and Robert Vyner, Edward Backwell, and Charles Duncombe, Richard Kent (*c.*1643–90) was not in the (old) *DNB* and will presumably not be in the new one. Assisted by the numerous references to him in Christopher Clay's invaluable study of Sir Stephen Fox, supplemented by an entry in the *History of Parliament* together with some additional research of my own, it is possible to offer a brief reconstruction of his

---

[79] *CTB*, i–vii; PRO, T 53/4, p. 202; *CSPD, 1682*, p. 579; PRO, PROB 11/405, q. 112. He had a nephew Sir Samuel (1643–1705; see Woodhead, *Rulers of London*, 56–7) and a cousin William (d.1671) also involved in excise farming; his own sons were Sir Robert, Richard, and George.

career. He was the third son of a minor gentry family from Wiltshire, and his county of origin probably explains his initial employment by Fox as a clerk in the Pay Office from the age of eighteen. He remained in that position until 1674, although by the later 1660s already had bank accounts in his own name with both Sir Robert Vyner and Edward Backwell; and it was the latter's cousin and at that time assistant, Charles Duncombe, who was in turn to become Kent's senior partner. It has been suggested with some plausibility that Backwell never really resumed his banking activities on any large scale after the traumatic experience of the Stop, and that Duncombe and Kent in effect took over his business. Meanwhile, through his association with Fox, Kent moved onto the administrative side of the revenue administration. He was appointed Receiver-General and Cashier of the Excise by Lord Treasurer Danby in October 1674, in place of Fox's rivals—James, Huntington, and Kingdon—his warrant from the Treasury being confirmed by patent in March 1675. However, he was very soon to be the victim of political infighting which had little, if anything, to do with his capacity as a financial administrator. In July 1675 his patent was cancelled, although his salary of £600 a year was commuted into a pension for the same amount; and the following January James and Kingdon were formally reinstated. Professor Clay was surely correct to see this as a tactical concession by Danby to his enemies in parliament. At the same time it was recorded that Kent was owed the huge sum of £250,580 by the King, and it was ordered that in spite of his removal from office his tallies were to have priority for repayment at the Excise, subject only to certain specified charges (these seem likely to have been the payments earmarked for Backwell, Vyner, and the other goldsmith bankers most severely affected by the Stop, who were in turn being pursued, indeed prosecuted by their creditors). It is most probable that Kent had had a quarter of a million pounds of his own to lend to the King: either the bulk of this was Duncombe's money, or Fox's, or more likely their joint creditworthiness had enabled them to raise this amount in the City on the understanding that it would be repaid out of the following year's excise revenue, with Kent as no more than an agent or intermediary in this process, albeit an important one. After a brief interval out of office, he was made Receiver-General of the Customs in May 1677, at the higher salary of £1,000 a year and on the same conditions as it had previously been held by Richard Mounteney, Backwell's cousin and business associate (who had been Cashier to the Customs Farmers back in 1663). This appointment almost certainly marked a successful comeback by Fox at the expense of his rivals—Sir John James and co. Kent was twice confirmed in this post and appears to have held it without a break until after the Revolution. His political sympathies are perhaps indicated by his having been elected to James II's parliament in 1685, by his not having been a member of the Whig-dominated Convention of 1689, and then by his having been re-elected in the more Tory-inclined House of 1690, although his early death, in November of that year, makes it impossible to say how he would have fared as either financier or office-holder in the changing circumstances, which led to the subsequent creation of the Bank of England (which Duncombe was to oppose). Meanwhile, back in 1682–3, both of them had invested in other offices, buying and then reselling Six Clerkships in Chancery; from 1680 Duncombe took over Kent's former post at the Excise but with the greatly enhanced salary of £1,550 p.a. Professor Clay portrays Kent as essentially a political contact man, moving between business and government circles, and at a personal level between Duncombe and Fox. While he acquired an estate in his native county and was in a position to leave substantial legacies and benefactions in his will, Kent's land purchases were not on the scale of those made by Duncombe in Yorkshire and elsewhere. His nephew, the nearest surviving heir, parted with the main property quite soon, and the family failed to leave any lasting mark in either banking, landownership, or politics.[80]

[80] West Yorkshire Archive Service, Newby Hall MSS, Add. 120, Robert Vyner's bank ledger, 10 Sept.–1 Oct. 1666; Royal Bank of Scotland MSS, EB 1/6, 1/9, Edward Backwell's ledgers (sampled entries only). I am most grateful to Mr W. J. Connor, Principal District Archivist, Claremont, Leeds, and to Ms Alison Turton, Manager, Archives, Royal Bank of Scotland for their help with

Apart from the Stop of the Exchequer, the most significant developments for royal finance were the end of revenue farming in the Customs (1671) and then in the Excise (1683). This meant that the respective boards of Commissioners for these revenues necessarily became more important, now acting like salaried managers, instead of being overseers of the tax-farmers' operations. Some of those appointed to these commissions were or had been merchants or financiers themselves. Such a one was the brother of Lord Keeper Guildford, Sir Dudley North, who is the subject of another fine recent biographical study. He was made a Commissioner of Customs in March 1684, then in July was promoted to the Treasury Commission itself, but with the appointment of a new Lord Treasurer (the first since Danby's removal from the office in 1679) North went back to the Customs Commission in March 1685, serving on this body until just after the Revolution, to April 1689. That he was made a Commissioner primarily to counterbalance the influence of Nicholas Butler, of whom the family historian, his younger brother Roger North disapproved so strongly, is possible but seems likely to be exaggerated. Sir Dudley was an economist in his own right, besides having been a successful Levant merchant, and his appointment was surely one of the best deserved of those made in Charles II's last years.[81]

Besides Nicholas Butler and Dudley North, various others of the Customs and Excise Commissioners have already been discussed, and need not be reintroduced here: for example, Downing, Huntingdon, Southwell, and Thynne. But in view of the importance of these branches of the revenue to the Crown and to the nation, a few others are also worthy of note. Sir Richard Temple of Stowe (1634–97), Bart., KB, MP was an ex-

---

access to these documents; Bodl. MS Eng. Hist., b. 79, fos. 46, 57, 62v; PRO, T 53/4; PROB 11/403, q. 47; *CTB*, iv–viii, *passim*; Clay, *Public Finance and Private Wealth*, esp. pp. 81–2, 98–103, 141–3; *Hist. Parl.*, ii. 676–7; for Backwell, Duncombe, and Vyner see *DNB* and *New DNB* (forthcoming).

[81] North was a Customs Commissioner, Mar.–July 1684 and again Mar. 1685–Apr. 1689, and a Treasury Commissioner, July 1684–Feb. 1685; Richard Grassby, *The English Gentleman in Trade: The Life and Works of Sir Dudley North, 1641–1691* (Oxford, 1994).

parliamentarian, or at least a conformist under the Republic, with political ambitions and expensive tastes. His appointment as a Customs Commissioner in 1671 is generally reckoned not to have been a reward for services rendered so much as a means of ensuring his further support in the House of Commons. He was dropped from the Commission at the end of Charles's reign, but reappointed after the Revolution. With someone so palpably lacking in both qualifications and commitment, it is no wonder that we often find the Treasury chivvying the Commissioners.[82]

By contrast Francis Millington (?1617–1693) was a Londoner, his family probably originating from Worcestershire but settled in Wandsworth (then part of Surrey). He was apprenticed in the Drapers' Company, but seems to have been an export-import merchant. Never himself an Alderman of the City, he had civic connections and financial links with Edward Backwell and Robert Vyner. He was acting as a Customs Farmer with them in 1667, and is notable as the only member of the last operative farm to have been continued as a Commissioner under the system of direct management from 1671. He was dropped from the Commission in 1681, which indicates Whiggish connections, and was not re-employed. He petitioned to be continued in office, saying that he had ceased trading in Spanish wine, and had never defrauded the King. (Commissioners were forbidden to take part in overseas trade, in order to avoid clashes of interest.) He also alleged that he had lost £10,700 through the Stop of the Exchequer; some question mark evidently remained against him, for he was summoned to appear before the Treasury Commissioners in February 1683, although he was apparently not proceeded against further. Millington's will suggests very considerable wealth. He left an endowment to Christ's Hospital, of which he was a Governor,

[82] *DNB*; *Hist. Parl.*, ii. 536–44; many refs. in *CSPD* and *CTB*; PRO, CUSTS 18/18; Hill and Cornforth, *English Country Houses . . . 1625–1685*, p. 240; Colvin, *Dictionary*, 253. Charles Cheyne, Viscount Newhaven (1625–98) was another Customs Commissioner (from 1675 to 1684) without any particular qualifications (*Hist. Parl.*, ii. 51–2; *Complete Peerage*, ix, 'Newhaven'; Bodl. MS Eng. Hist. b. 79, fo. 71v; *CTB*, v–vii, via indexes).

but tied it to provision for disabled and superannuated seamen who had been born in Wandsworth, a pointer to maritime as well as mercantile interests. Although styled Esquire by his later years and with gentry connections, he would seem to have been one of the more bourgeois of the Commissioners.[83]

Among the Excise Commissioners, Sir Denny Ashburnham (*c.*1628–97), Bart., MP, might appear comparable to Temple in the Customs, but not so. He was a cousin of the courtly Ashburnhams, John and William, and married John's daughter Frances at an early age. Having been neutral, or at least politically inactive during the Interregnum, he was presumably made a baronet in 1661 through the influence of his father-in-law; it appears likely that he had looked after the interests of his royalist relatives and had helped to preserve their property before the Restoration. He was made an Excise Commissioner in 1665, but was dropped or stood down in the 1670s, becoming instead a Victualling Contractor for the Navy (in 1671 and again in 1673–7) and for Tangier (in 1677–8). He was then reappointed to the Excise Commission, where he remained until 1689, also serving as a Hearth Tax Commissioner from 1683 to 1684 until that revenue was abolished. He incurred much odium by his courage and integrity in testifying for a group of Jesuit defendants in one of the Popish Plot trials that he knew Titus Oates to be utterly untrustworthy (the phrase 'pathological liar' was not yet current). This cost him his seat in the three following parliaments (of 1679–81), while his return to the House in James's reign together with his holding office up to the Revolution, then put paid to both his parliamentary and official careers, although there is no evidence that he actually had Catholic or Jacobite leanings. The victualling appointment suggests, if not necessarily great liquid wealth, certainly a creditworthy reputation; moreover his second wife was the daughter of a prominent puritan-parliamentarian financier of the

[83] Perceval Boyd (ed.), *Roll of the Drapers' Company of London* . . . (Croydon, 1934), 127; Beaven, *Aldermen of London*, i. 104; *CSPD, 1680–1*, p. 664; *CTB*, vii. 174, 550, 703, other refs. in vols. ii–v; BL MS Sloane 1425; PRO, PROB 11/417, q. 215.

1640s and 1650s, Sir David Watkins. Sir Denny's career is another reminder that social and ideological divisions were not always clear and neat.[84]

A more surprising appointment was that of Francis Parry (d.1702) who was a Commissioner from 1681 to 1685. His previous experience was exclusively diplomatic, as Embassy Secretary and then Envoy or Agent in Portugal (1666–80). He had, however, gained some financial experience in helping to secure payment of Queen Catherine's dowry money, which took many years to extract from the Portuguese Crown. Possibly his appointment was also due to the influence of Sir Robert Southwell, on whose staff he had served in Lisbon and who had preceded him on the Excise Commission (in 1671–9). At the end of his life Parry had a town house in St James's besides a country seat in Berkshire. He was involved in the extraction and milling of copper, while this may have postdated his service in the Excise, the two might not have been incompatible.[85]

The holders of certain key positions in the financial administration were not all equally well qualified. The first Treasury Secretary of the reign, Sir Philip Warwick, was a gifted historical and political writer, a politician of the second rank, and an utterly loyal and honest servant of the Crown, but he was no financier or accountant. Warwick had other offices, at the Privy Council and in the Signet Office, which must have cushioned him against his loss of the Secretaryship on the death of Lord Treasurer Southampton. To ask what today would be the obvious question, whether Warwick might have been more effective at the Treasury

[84] GEC, *Complete Baronetage*, iii. 195; F. W. Steer (ed.), *The Ashburnham Archives: A Catalogue* (East Sussex County Council, Lewes, 1958). *Hist. Parl.*, i. 551–2; *CTB*, i. 251, 658; iv. 753; *CSPD, 1671–2*, p. 37; *1673–5*, p. 41; Bodl. MS Eng. Hist. b. 79, fo. 71v; PRO, PROB 11/442, q. 267.

[85] For Charles Davenant (Excise Commissioner, 1678–88) contrast D. Waddell, 'Charles Davenant (1656–1714)—A Biographical Sketch', *Econ. Hist. Rev.*, 2nd ser., 11 (1958), 279–88, and Miles Ogborn, *Spaces of Modernity: London's Geographies, 1680–1780* (New York and London, 1998), ch. 5 (more favourable); see also *DNB* and *Hist. Parl.*, ii. 196. J. Foster, *Alumni Oxonienses* (Oxford, 1891–2), i. 1120; Bell, *Handlist*, 218–20; Bodl. MS Eng. Hist. b. 79, fos. 33v, 36v, 43, 68; *CSPD, 1670*, p. 59; ibid., *1671*, p. 166; ibid., *1671–2*, p. 420; *CTB*, vii. 106–8; further refs. ibid., ix, xiii, xv, xvii; PRO, PROB 11/467, q. 204.

if he had not been a pluralist, may be to misconceive the nature of the office-holding system. His successor Sir George Downing was indeed well qualified, whatever view is taken of his scheme for wider (indirect) royal borrowing.[86] The Auditor of the Receipt from the Restoration to his death in 1672, Sir Robert Long, had been an unsuccessful challenger to Hyde for primacy among the King's advisers in exile, but he recovered from this setback and appears to have been exemplary in the execution of his official duties, effectively as the manager of the Lower Exchequer. Sir Robert Howard, Downing's successor at the Treasury (1671–2) and then Long's at the Receipt (1672–98) was a near disaster in both capacities; whether or not he was personally dishonest, which remains an open question, he was culpably negligent in not detecting, or acting to prevent, large-scale fraud by one of the Tellers in the later 1670s. His successor at the Treasury, Charles Bertie (1642–1711), as we have seen, probably got the job as a close relative by marriage of Lord Treasurer Danby, but seems to have made a fair showing in it. Nor was his loss of this post on Danby ceasing to be Treasurer by any means the end of his career. Bertie had travelled abroad as a young man, and already had some diplomatic experience before going to the Treasury, and after that he was sent as Envoy Extraordinary to the German Electors and other Princes, probably to protect him from further attacks in parliament over his handling of the secret service money. He had meanwhile secured a reversion to the post of Treasurer and Paymaster of the Ordnance; succeeding to this office in 1681, he held it until his death—with one short interval at the end of William III's reign. Although only the fifth son of the second earl of Lindsey, family influence kept him in place as MP for Stamford with a break from 1678 on, and he built Uffington House nearby, presumably at least in part out of the profits of office. Not a great man, Charles Bertie's career illustrates some of the interactions between aristocratic family connections, office-holding, and politics.[87]

[86] For Downing's system see Henry Roseveare, *The Treasury: The Evolution of a British Institution* (London, 1969), 59–62; id., *The Treasury, 1660–1870: The Foundations of Control* (London, 1973), 22–6, 30–3, 39–40.

[87] HMC, *Lindsey*, introduction, p. ix; *Hist. Parl.*, i. 639–43; Tomlinson,

His successor at the treasury, Henry Guy, as we have seen, bulks a good deal larger in the history of that department, but his reputation was and still is more controversial. Less original than the unlikeable Downing, his career as a financial administrator was to be eclipsed by that of his successor, William Lowndes, who was still only a young and relatively junior Treasury clerk at the end of our period. It does appear that by the 1680s the Treasury Commissioners were beginning to have an embryonic system both of delegation downwards and of filtering upwards, although the Board still had to deal with matters which those at the top of a modern department of state would consider to be intolerably trivial. The practice of filtering and delegation grew slowly and was not formalized until long after this time; it is one of the biggest of all differences between pre-nineteenth-century and more modern administrative practice.[88] The Treasury Secretaries from 1667 on do seem to have had a little more discretionary authority than was allowed (for example) to the Clerks of the Privy Council, that is if we compare the kind of business before the King in Council with that coming before the Treasury Board.

Some financial administrators were instruments rather than managers, let alone policy-makers. Until the mid-1680s this was true of William Culliford (*c.*1640–*c.*1720). The younger son of a not very prominent Dorset gentry family, he had held minor posts briefly in the Excise and then under the Customs Commissioners. In the early 1680s he was sent on two missions to investigate the south-western ports of the kingdom (covering the coast from Dorset round to South Wales). Although still employed in the Customs, the fair copies of his reports found their way to the Treasury; he had uncovered an appalling state of laxity, incompetence, and dishonesty, such that there would have been no need to smuggle in order to evade proper payment

---

Guns and Government, 225; Sainty, *Treasury Officials*, 30; Hill and Cornforth, *English Country Houses*, 242; Colvin, *Dictionary*, 1098; *CTB*, iii–vii (esp. vols. iv and v); *CSPD*, *1673–81*. Prof. Roseveare, who knows the Treasury sources better than I do, is somewhat more critical of Bertie.

[88] I am grateful to Lord Butler of Brockwell for a helpful conversation on this point.

of the duties due on exports and imports in almost every port which he visited. Some officers were too elderly and/or infirm to carry out their duties properly, some were constantly drunk, others were simply corrupt and open to bribery by merchants and shipowners. Something of a purge followed; certainly by the eighteenth century there was more smuggling in the conventional sense because the customs service was less open to this kind of abuse. Culliford meanwhile was rewarded by promotion; and this, as we have seen, was nearly his undoing. The Irish revenues, indeed the whole financial system of that kingdom, had been in a mess for many years. Richard Jones, first Earl of Ranelagh, had been their principal manager for much of the 1670s; he was in fact an extremely adept and persuasive courtier who used his friendship with the King and leading ministers to maintain his position and to prevent proper inquiries into his failings. Another plausible Irish financial expert, Sir James Shaen, undoubtedly had the gift of tongues, and the ability to draft fluent memoranda; during his last viceroyalty Ormonde did succeed in getting rid of Ranelagh and became increasingly cynical about Shaen. Eventually, on the initiative of the Treasury Commissioners in London, the decision was taken to do away with revenue farming and management, and instead to have salaried, hands-on Commissioners in full charge. The chairman of this new body was an ex-client, by then friend and political ally of the Lord Lieutenant, Francis Aungier, Lord Longford, but the other Commissioners were completely unknown to Ormonde, most of them being sent over from England. This was the body, set up in 1682, to which Culliford was appointed in 1684, when he was nearly murdered. The Irish Revenue Commission was undermined for ideological reasons under James's viceroy, Tyrconnell, when Culliford and others returned to England. He went back to Ireland after the Revolution and the Williamite victory in the civil war there, and was subsequently accused—on both sides of the Irish Sea—of having misused his position in order to traffic in confiscated and then restored lands. By then an MP himself, he managed to weather these parliamentary storms and resumed a long connection with the Customs in England, now as a Commissioner. Almost any would-be administrative reformer was likely to lay himself open to counter-charges of dishonesty, which is not of course in itself to exonerate Culliford totally: the evidence simply does not permit of a clear-cut verdict either way. Insofar, however, as the proof of the pudding is in the eating, he definitely did not amass a great fortune, unlike, for example, Ranelagh or the first Duke of Chandos, and seems to have died a relatively poor man. He may of course have lacked the skill, as well as the opportunity, to emulate those who made fortunes on the scale of Stephen Fox and Charles Duncombe without misusing their official positions in ways which were considered unacceptable.[89]

XI. THE VIRTUOSO AS ADMINISTRATOR

The title of this Section may appear to be a contradiction in terms, but that is largely because the word virtuoso has changed its meaning. As it was used in the later seventeenth century, of someone with a wide range of interests in matters artistic and intellectual, who was versatile, discriminating, and by no means merely a superficial dilettante, I suspect that more than a few of the most senior and successful civil servants of our day would meet the definition admirably. Among those holding office between 1660 and 1685 who seem to me to qualify may be included Sir Kenelm Digby, Lord Brouncker, John Evelyn, Elias Ashmole, perhaps Sir William Petty, Sir John Hoskyns, Thomas Povey, Thomas Neale, possibly Sir Robert Howard, and Thomas Henshaw. Most of those named have already appeared in these pages, and it would burden the reader excessively to provide biographical sketches of them all.

John Evelyn was described as 'an excellent virtuoso' as early as 1668. He had been proposed for election to the Royal Society (not yet so named) in December 1660, and is counted as the thirty-eighth Fellow in order of election; he was to be the

---

[89] For Culliford see *New DNB* (forthcoming) and refs. in Chs. 2 and 3 above.

Secretary of the Society in 1672–3, and served frequently on its Council. According to the editor of his *Diary*, he twice refused the Presidency out of modesty. Although Evelyn was not a scientist as we would understand it, the range of his interests was remarkable. He wrote on gardens and fruit trees, the problem of London smog, architecture, the history of engraving, forestry and timber, notorious impostors in the three great monotheistic religions, the earth and its cultivation, navigation and commerce, medals and salads, and beekeeping. Evelyn described and illustrated beehives made by Moses Rusden 'Whom I got to be sworn the King's beemaster to Charles II: No such office before'. Although he spent much time at court, Evelyn was not a place-seeker, at least not a very persistent or successful one. He was a Commissioner for the care of the sick and wounded and the relief of prisoners in both Dutch Wars (in which he certainly did his conscientious best), a Commissioner for Trade and Plantations in 1671–4 (which at £500 a year was his most lucrative post), and finally under James II a Commissioner for the Privy Seal during the Earl of Clarendon's absence as Lord Lieutenant of Ireland (while remaining Lord Privy Seal). Readers of his *Diary* will probably conclude that the pursuit of office meant relatively little to Evelyn, who enjoyed substantial private means; as far as can be seen, being in or out did not make a great deal of difference to him as a courtier, landed gentleman, author, virtuoso, and devout Anglican.[90]

Elias Ashmole was a more original but also more erratic character. He was much more self-made and for a long part of his life in constant financial difficulties. After a visit to his house in Lambeth, Evelyn rather patronizingly recorded seeing Ashmole's library and curiosities, including his mainly astrological manuscripts, 'to which study he is addicted, though I believe not learned; but very Industrious, as his history of the Order of the Garter shows, he showed me a toade included [enclosed or

---

[90] All biographical details from *Diary of John Evelyn*, i, introduction, ch. 1; app. 1, and John E. Ingram (ed.), John Evelyn, *Elysium Britannicum* (Philadelphia, 2000), p. 276 n. 39); also Michael Hunter, *The Royal Society and its Fellows, 1660–1700*, 166–7 and via index; and Colvin, *Dictionary* 357–8.

embedded] in Amber'. Over and above their differences in personality, Evelyn was born into the upper gentry, whereas for Ashmole the status as well as the profits of office meant a lot. As Windsor Herald, his stipendiary fee was only forty marks (£26 13s. 4d.) a year; his main income there came from fees collected during visitations and in the granting of arms. By contrast the Comptrollership of the Excise was well paid, though shared between him and the courtier Thomas Chiffinch until the latter's death in 1666; but there may not have been much scope for receiving fees or other less formal payments from people using his office—other office-holders and those paying excise; the Comptroller's duty was primarily to oversee other staff. Still, at £500 a year, this was riches compared with anything to which he had been accustomed. The feast which he gave for the benefactors who had helped him in his work on the Garter provides a good idea of Ashmole's networking abilities. Those who came were Sir Joseph Williamson (Secretary of State), Sir William Swan (diplomat), Sir Charles Cotterell (Master of Ceremonies), Sir William Dugdale (Garter King-of-Arms), Sir Edward Carteret (Black Rod), John Cooke (Under-Secretary), Nicholas Oudart (ex-Secretary to the Queen of Bohemia and Latin Secretary), Tobias Rustat (Yeoman of the Robes), and Thomas Henshaw (late Resident Envoy to the King of Denmark and French Secretary). The 'Persons invited but came not' were the Bishops of Salisbury and of Lincoln, the Lord Treasurer's Secretary, the King's Chemist or 'Chemical Physician', the King's Closet Keeper, the Lord Chamberlain's Secretary, the Secretary to the Keeper of the Privy Purse, a Page of the Bedchamber, and the Vicar of St Martin's in the Fields. Whether any significance should be read into those who did and did not come, to partake of the attractive fare which was provided, I do not know. By contrast with this, Ashmole's Freemasonry would not seem to have had much to do with the advancement of his career. If we look at those admitted and others attending (on 11 March 1682) when he was the senior fellow (of his Masonic lodge), they are not particularly distinguished or influential. The high points in his official career were perhaps first the publication of his *Institution, Laws and Ceremonies of the Most Noble Order of*

the Garter (1672) and then the enlargement of his department in
the Excise, to provide for four deputies and an increased salary
for himself (in 1674 and 1677). Much of his time and energies
latterly were taken up with gaining control of the Tradescant
collection and then arranging for the creation of the Ashmolean
Museum in Oxford, first opened to the public in June 1683.[91]

Thomas Povey on the other hand is the archetype of the virtuoso who either neglected his official duties or else had no head for
them. In fairness, we should remember that he had written one of
the best statements of the neutralist case produced during the
Civil War, back in 1643. Having done well at the Restoration, he
was progressively stripped of his offices, and ended his days in
near penury. Suffice it only to quote Pepys, in 1665: 'most excellent in anything but business'. Some of the items from his collection may today be viewed at Dyrham Park, the great house built
by his nephew William Blathwayt, including a remarkable
trompe-l'oeil by Samuel van Hoogstraeten.[92]

The problem with Sir William Petty is twofold. Those sources
which say that he was a Navy Commissioner are incorrect,
based on a misunderstanding of an alleged remark by the King;
the only position which he held that qualifies him for inclusion
here was that of Irish Revenue Farmer (1675–82), though he
was also Registrar of the Irish admiralty court. And this was the
man of whom Evelyn wrote:

There were not in the whole world his equal for a superintendant of
Manufactures, and improvement of Trade; or for to govern a

---

[91] *Diary of John Evelyn* iv. 138 (23 July 1678); C. H. Josten (ed.), *Elias
Ashmole (1617–1692): His Autobiography and Historical Notes, His
Correspondence, and Other Contemporary Sources Relating to His Life and
Works* (5 vols, Oxford 1966) (cont. pagn.), 1488–90, 1699–701; *CTB*, iv. 639,
640, v. 722; Bodl. MS Eng. Hist. b. 79, fo. 58v.

[92] *DNB*; Sainty, *Office-holders in Modern Britain*, iii, *Officials of the
Boards of Trade, 1660–1870* (London, 1974), 18, 20, 112; *Pepys Diary*, vi.
215, x. *Companion*, and innum. other refs.; many refs. in *Diary of John
Evelyn*; BL Adds. MS 11,411 (his letter-book), MS Egerton 2,395; *CSPC Am
WI*, refs. 1656–1660s; other primary and secondary sources on Cromwell's
'Western design'; *CSPD, 1660s–1680s*, via indexes; *CTB*, iv and v; HMC,
Eighth Report, app. 1 (Braybrooke papers), p. 280a; *The Moderator expecting
Sudden Peace of Certain Ruine* (1643, Thomason Tracts, E89 (21); Wing, *STC,
1641–1700*, P 3042–3).

Plantation: If I were a Prince, I should make him my second Counselor at least: ... in my life never having known such a genius.

And Charles II reputedly said of Petty, 'the man will not be contented to be excellent, but is still Ayming at Impossible things'. Why then did he not find employment more consistent with his talents? One reason for his undoing was his marvellous gift of mimicry, sometimes at the expense of the high and mighty; another was his ability to outsmart other projectors and prove them wrong. A more serious criticism can, however, be found in a letter from the Earl of Essex when he was Lord Lieutenant, written to Shaftesbury (then Lord Chancellor) in 1673, when Petty was trying to procure a grant of Phoenix Park on the outskirts of Dublin for the King's mistress, the Duchess of Cleveland:

besides if we consider the man, who undertakes it, 'twill easily be fore-seen with what vigour and injustice a Grant of this nature will be pros-ecuted, for I am confident in all his Majesties 3 Kingdoms, there lives not a more grating Man than Sir William Petty; I daresay the Practices of Empson and Dudley would be found nothing in comparison of the vexations, which this poor country would suffer, if such a Grant should pass...

The other question about Petty is more obvious, but one which raises an issue of definition. Was he indeed a virtuoso at all, rather than a man of exceptionally high and varied abilities— medic, land surveyor, naval architect or ship designer, political arithmetician, and statistician—perhaps indeed a polymath, who was yet, in respect of conventional career prospects, his own worst enemy?[93]

In order to refine this definition a little further, it may be helpful to explain why I have not reckoned Samuel Pepys as a virtuoso. After all, as he recorded on 9 March 1666, 'music and

---

[93] A full bibliography would swell this note to absurd proportions. For my citations see *Diary of John Evelyn*, iv. 56–61; *Petty-Southwell Correspondence, 1676–87*, ed. Marquis of Lansdowne (1928), 281; PRO (Shaftesbury Papers) 30/24/50, fos. 154–5. Among other contemporary sources not to be missed see A. Clark (ed), *Aubrey's Brief Lives, 1669–96* (Oxford, 1898), ii. 139–49, and of modern works note E. Strauss, *Sir William Petty: Portrait of a Genius* (1954). All other accounts will be superseded when Dr Toby Barnard publishes his biography of Petty.

women I cannot but give way to, whatever my business is', and a little later that year 'music is the thing of the world that I love most, and all the pleasure almost that I can now take'. Certainly no reader of the *Diary* can doubt that its author was both exceptionally well informed and immensely enthusiastic as an amateur musician. But there was also, from 1662–3 onwards, a commitment to the duties of his office and an absolute determination to master every aspect of its business, in order to make himself indispensable, which marks him out from the others discussed here.[94] At the opposite extreme we may take the case of Sir Kenelm Digby, really a survivor from an earlier epoch, exceptionally gifted but hardly to be taken seriously as an office-holder, although he was a Revenue Trustee for the Queen Mother from 1662 until his death. John Aubrey's account of him cannot be bettered, although we should allow a little for artistic licence. Regarding his scientific pretensions, Evelyn eventually concluded that Digby was 'an arrant Mountebank'.[95] Then there was Sir Paul Neile, son of Charles I's Archbishop of York, who supervised the construction of the country's largest telescope. Despite having been a Gentleman Usher of the Privy Chamber and (in the 1670s) an Excise Appeals Commissioner, he seems to have died poorer than he started, while lacking the range of interests to qualify here.[96]

Thomas Neale, whose maternal grandfather, Sir William Uvedale, was Charles I's Treasurer of the Chamber, had wider

---

[94] *Pepys Diary*, vii. 69–70, 228.

[95] Aubrey, *Brief Lives*, i. 224–9; *Diary of John Evelyn*, iii. 48; *DNB*; num. modern biographies, among them R. T. Petersson, *Sir Kenelm Digby, the Ornament of England, 1603–1665* (1956). He had blotted his copybook by coming to terms with the Protectorate government in 1655–6, but remained Chancellor to the Queen Mother until 1664 and one of her Revenue Trustees until his death; he left his family in poor financial circumstances.

[96] *DNB: Missing Persons*; *Hist. Parl.*, i. 353–5 (though elected for the newly enfranchised borough of Newark, the House prevented him from ever taking his seat); further refs. in Ashmole, Evelyn, and Pepys via indexes; PRO, LC 3/73, fos. 11v, 15; LC 7/1; Sainty and Bucholz, *Officials of the Royal Household*, i. 146; Hunter, *Royal Society*, F5 and via index. He was a regular visitor to Shaftesbury in the Tower (*CSPD, 1677–8* refs.). In his will he describes himself as being of Codnor Castle, Derbyshire, as well as St Clements Danes, Middlesex [i.e. Greater London] (PRO, PROB 11/382, q. 22).

interests if not perhaps greater talents. He sat in every parliament but one from the 1660s to the 1690s. Having married a wealthy widow, he traded in East India Company stock and later became a London property developer. At different stages of his career he held the offices of Groom Porter, Groom of the Bedchamber, Commissioner for the Mint, Master of the Mint, Postmaster for the Plantations, and manager of the Lottery loan. There is some suggestion that, as Groom Porter, he was a professional gambler, though not necessarily a dishonest one. He was a party to one of the longest-running and costliest property law suits of the time, involving the title of the Dean and Chapter of St Pauls to much of Shadwell in East London, but he is better known for the Seven Dials development on what had been St Giles's Field. A draft bill for the parish of St Paul, Shadwell was read but rejected in the House of Lords on 25 May 1677, but compared with the dura-tion of some suits in Chancery, the final decision in King's Bench on Lady Ivie's case, given by Chief Justice Jeffreys in favour of the Dean and Chapter and Neale (in 1684), was perhaps not so long drawn out. For all this, he seems to have been more success-ful at spending than at making money.[97]

XII. ARISTOCRATS AS ADMINISTRATORS

This may seem an unlikely topic. Why should those at the very apex of the social hierarchy, below only the immediate, legiti-mate royal family, have bothered themselves with the details of official business, as against enjoyment in the exercise of patron-age and some share in policy-making? And the answer is that only some of them did so. It seems sensible to think of the peers in two categories: those born into the nobility by direct or indi-rect hereditary succession, and those raised into it by the

[97] *Hist. Parl.*, iii. 129–31, a better notice than that in *DNB*; Reddaway, *Rebuilding of London* (rev. edn., 1951), 237 n. 4; *Pepys Diary*, via index; Brett-James, *Growth of Stuart London*, 303, 343; Sir J. C. Fox (ed.), *The Lady Ivie's Trial for the Great Part of Shadwell* (Oxford, 1929), in which judgment was given on 4 June 1684; I. K. Steele, *The English Atlantic, 1675–1740: An Exploration of Communication and Community* (Oxford, 1987); Craig, *The Mint*, chs. 10–11; Challis (ed.), *A New History*, 393; HMC, *Ninth Report*, app., 96; *Lords Journals*, xiii. 125.

monarch. We might apply G. R. Elton's distinction between the first and second of the Tudor kings, Henry VIII—unlike his father—having been 'born to the purple'.⁹⁸ Of the new peers, it does not appear that George Monck, first Duke of Albemarle, concerned himself very much either with military administration in his capacity as Lord General, or with the business of running the royal stables as Master of the Horse, and he had declined to go to Ireland as Lord Lieutenant in 1660–1, though he was to resume his career as an Admiral in the Dutch War of 1664–7. Lord Craven, soon created the first Earl of Craven, seems on the other hand to have taken more pains as a kind of unspoken minister without portfolio and latterly as deputy Commander-in-Chief (after Monck's death and Monmouth's disgrace).⁹⁹ So far as can be seen, Henry Bennet Lord Arlington never troubled himself much with the domestic side of the Secretary of State's duties; hence the key role of Joseph Williamson as Under-Secretary; nor, except to assert his rights of patronage and of access to the sovereign, was he any more interested in the running of the household above stairs as Lord Chamberlain (1674–85). The man with whom he is often bracketed in the misnamed 'Cabal' ministry, Sir Thomas, created first Lord Clifford, was a very different personality and had a different view of administration; having been active in the household below stairs and then on the Treasury Commission, he was vigorous if also controversial during his brief tenure as Lord Treasurer (1672–3). Since he was criticized both for excessive harshness and for wanton liberality, it is tempting to conclude that he may have got things about right, but this would probably be simplistic. The more plausible alternative view is that Clifford was inconsistent, having been 'over-promoted' and lacking the sustained capacity needed in that great office.

⁹⁸ G. R. Elton, *England under the Tudors* (London, 1959), 71.

⁹⁹ TS handlist of the Craven MSS in the Bodl. Library (for a copy of which I am extremely grateful to Sir Howard Colvin). For his building activities see Hill and Cornforth, *English Country Houses*, 137–49; Colvin, *Dictionary*, 754, 1065, 1067, 1068. For his career in general see *DNB*; *Complete Peerage*; and countless refs. in standard sources (*CSPD*, PRO, PC 2, etc.), and for his will PRO, PROB 11/437, q. 71.

Of the other chief or leading ministers, Edward Hyde, first Earl of Clarendon, however renowned as statesman and historian, is not remembered particularly for his strictly legal work as Lord Chancellor. It is true that he issued orders for the better running of the Court of Chancery, but then so did every other Lord Chancellor and Lord Keeper of the century; and in other respects he was perhaps conscientious to a fault. Thomas Osborne, created Earl of Danby, was Lord Treasurer for nearly six years (June 1673–March 1679). At times he certainly seems to have been busier as a patron and party leader at court and in parliament than as a finance minister, but reading the Treasury Books leaves the impression that he was vigilant and by no means idle. Clarendon's younger son, Laurence Hyde, created Earl of Rochester, was not quite a chief or prime minister in the same way as his father or Danby had been, but from late in 1679 to the summer of 1684 he was extremely active as First Lord of the Treasury or senior Treasury Commissioner. While his industry is not in doubt, judgements as to his ability and his honesty have varied from his own time down to the present. In many ways the most gifted of all those raised to the peerage through service under the Crown was Anthony Ashley Cooper, first Earl of Shaftesbury. Active as Chancellor of the Exchequer from 1661 to 1672 and as a Treasury Commissioner 1667–72, and always also as a patron, he only really emerged as a party political leader after his loss of office, that is after having been Lord Chancellor (1672–4). In this latter capacity he was grudgingly praised even by his enemies for his energy and probity as the senior equity judge and head of the Court of Chancery. His brief return to high office as Lord President of the Council in 1679 does not provide an adequate basis for any further appraisal; in any case this was a non-departmental position. Shaftesbury was primarily a party leader in opposition, and formidable indeed as such, even if ultimately defeated by an even greater party leader, the King himself. Of those who rose into the peerage through their eminence in the law, Heneage Finch, first Earl of Nottingham has been seen as having been decisive in the development of equity, and should certainly be ranked highly as a legal administrator. The career and achievement of his successor, Francis North, Lord Guildford are difficult to disentangle from his younger brother's pietistic biography, almost more like a memorial to him. We may accept that he was honest and conscientious, but his impact as the head of Chancery appears to have been slight compared to that of his immediate predecessor.

An interesting and ultimately tragic case is that of Arthur, second Baron Capel of Hadham, created first Earl of Essex. Apart from one short spell as an Ambassador, his rise in the King's service was oddly delayed. As Lord Lieutenant of Ireland (1672–7), he showed himself to be by inclination more of a would-be reformer than any other viceroy of the reign; his correspondence suggests someone who grasped the point that details did matter, even if delegation was essential, and that things would not just look after themselves. While he lacked a substantial power-base, in the sense of a previous following in Ireland, and was to be recalled to make way again for Ormonde, it would be too harsh to describe him as a failure. The weaknesses of Irish financial administration have already been touched upon; in the final analysis it was the Lord Treasurer and the King who were to blame for this. Essex's second, very short tenure of high office as senior Treasury Commissioner in 1679 again showed him to be conscientious, but quickly aware of losing the King's confidence, more because of his growing association with the Exclusionist cause than because of any shortcomings in his financial management. As an administrator, he must be judged by his time as viceroy. His subsequent political career in opposition, culminating with his arrest on suspicion of treason and his probable suicide in the Tower belongs to the political not the administrative history of the reign, though I personally find it unbelievable that he was party to a plan for the assassination of the King and his brother.[100]

If we turn to the 'hereditaries', those born into the upper

---

[100] The two published volumes are only a selection of his correspondence as Lord Lieutenant: ed. O. Airy, Camden n.s. 47 (1890) and C. E. Pike (ed.), Camden 3rd ser., 24 (1913); see also *Letters* (London, 1770 and Dublin, 1773); BL MS Stowe 200–17, MS Add. 36,786; *CSPD, 1672–7*. His name was struck off the list of privy councillors (i.e. the King dismissed him from the

ranks of the peerage, there are some striking contrasts. Although he held a major office for a time, as Master of the Horse, George Villiers second Duke of Buckingham was a non-event as an administrator. James Butler, twelfth Earl and first Duke of Ormonde, though over-ready to delegate and perhaps lazy in matters of detail, besides being unquestionably loyal to the Crown, should on balance be seen as reasonably conscientious.[101] Looking back to the early years, as we have seen, Henry Wriothesley, second Earl of Southampton, had an almost impossible task as Lord Treasurer. He did his best and was certainly not idle, but it would have required almost superhuman capacity to reform royal finances at that stage in Charles's reign. Southampton, as it happens, is one of the few peers whose family fortunes have been studied in detail for the mid- and later as well as for the earlier seventeenth century. Lawrence Stone showed how the Wriothesley fortunes were restored by urban development in London (Southampton Row, etc.); even so, the Earl's income from this property (*c.* £3,500 p.a.) was less than half his salary as Lord Treasurer (£8,000 a year). Since he had no son, his London estates passed to the Russell family through one of his three daughters.[102] Moving forward to the King's last years, the third Earl of Conway, who was Secretary of State in 1681–3, was by common consent ignorant and inadequate. In

Council) on 24 Jan. 1681 (PRO, PC 2/69, p. 192), but he had left the Treasury Commission in Nov. 1679 (Sainty, *Treasury Officials*, 18, 125). I am not aware of a modern biography. Recent arguments for his having been murdered are put in R. Ashcraft, *Revolutionary Politics and Locke's Two Treatises of Government* (Princeton, NJ, 1986), 380–2, esp. n. 190, and R. L. Greaves, *Secrets of the Kingdom . . . 1677–1689* (Stanford, Calif., 1992), 219–29, 400–3; and for his having committed suicide by M. MacDonald, 'The Strange Death of the Earl of Essex, 1683', *History Today*, 451 (Nov. 1991), 13–18. For his opposition contacts see Haley, *Shaftesbury*, 441–2, 749, also 549, 556, etc. For his building of Cassiobury House, Herts. in 1677–80 see Hill and Cornforth, *English Country Houses*, 224, and Colvin, *Dictionary*, 648.

[101] See Aylmer, 'The First Duke of Ormond as Patron and Administrator', in Toby Barnard and Jane Fenlon (eds.), *The Dukes of Ormonde, 1610–1745* (Woodbridge, 2000), 115–35, and chs 1–4 and 6–8 in the same vol.
[102] Lawrence Stone, *Family and Fortune* (Oxford, 1973), 236–40; for the building of Southampton, later Bedford House, Bloomsbury see Colvin, *Dictionary*, 972; for the Earl's descendants see *Complete Peerage*, 'Southampton'.

contrast to him, Robert Spencer, second Earl of Sunderland was—like Arlington—ambitious in matters of high politics but bored by administrative detail, though the loss of most of his papers may give a misleading impression in this respect. (I am very conscious of the superb biographies written on Shaftesbury and Sunderland in the later twentieth century, and deeply regret that neither Kenneth Haley nor John Kenyon is still alive for me to consult as I write this.)

Clearly any easy generalization about grandees being too grand, or too preoccupied with other matters, to bother with administration, or effectively to oversee its direction is easily refuted. The notion of self-made men resting on their laurels once they had got to the top has a little more plausibility if we think of Edward Montagu, first Earl of Sandwich (even if his career was redeemed by a hero's death in battle). Arthur Annesley, second Viscount Valentia in the peerage of Ireland, then created first Earl of Anglesey, is a more complex case. Too much of a puritan to coast along or to idle away his time, he was still something of a failure both as Irish Vice-Treasurer and as Treasurer of the Navy but nonetheless recovered his position sufficiently to be Lord Privy Seal for more than nine years (1673–82). Although his diary suggests that he took his duties as Privy Councillor and a member of Council committees very seriously, his attendance and activity were in fact uneven to the point of being erratic. Who would have prophesied in the 1660s, even before the mid-1670s, that Essex would come to a violent end in the Tower, while Anglesey would only finally be dismissed from office because of his attack on the role of Ormonde, and so indirectly on that of Charles I himself, in their relations with the Irish Confederates nearly forty years before?[103]

Another peer by inheritance whose importance grew in the course of the reign was Henry Somerset, Marquis of Worcester, later created first Duke of Beaufort. Once promoted to high office, as Lord President of Wales and the Marches, and made a

---

[103] For Anglesey see Aylmer, 'Patronage at the Court of Charles II', in Eveline Cruickshanks (ed.), *The Stuart Courts* (Thrupp, Glos. 2000), 197–9 and nn. 7–13.

Privy Councillor, he proved assiduous both as an active supporter of royal policies and in pursuing what he perceived as his own rights and interests. He invoked the ancient, and long dormant legal action *scandalum magnatum* against those who had implied that he was favouring Papists or perhaps—even more serious—was inclined that way himself, but his claim to overlordship in part of Gwent was also involved. His creation of something like an old-fashioned regional power base in Wales and the border counties is the more remarkable in that the Court of the Marches was only a pale shadow of its former self. Worcester, then Beaufort as he became in 1682, seems to have governed Wales (if that is the right phrase to use) from his home at Badminton and not to have resided in Ludlow. His tour of Wales in the summer of 1684, in his capacity as Lord Lieutenant of all the individual counties, was recounted by one of his servants, and strongly suggests something more like a ceremonial progress than anything involving attention to administrative or legal detail. An aside may perhaps be permitted here. In 1677 the Herald Francis Sandford dedicated one of the plates illustrating his *Genealogical History of the Kings of England* to Worcester. This was a reproduction of a drawing or engraving of the famous Plantagenet tombs in Fontevraud Abbey, Anjou, when all four of the coffins with their effigies were side by side under a kind of canopy, or recessed but open tomb, rather than being set out singly in the nave as they are today. The book illustration carries the dedication to the Marquis top left and the arms of the Somerset family top right. As a Herald, Sandford would undoubtedly have known that the Somersets could claim direct descent in the male line from John of Gaunt (and so from the royal house back to 1066), but with two illegitimate unions along the way. Did he not realize how sensitive a political issue retrospective legitimization had become in the fraught atmosphere of the later 1670s?[104]

---

[104] *DNB*; *Complete Peerage*, ii. 51–2; *Hist. Parl.*, iii. 454–6; John C. Lassiter, 'Defamation of Peers: The Rise and Decline of the Action for Scandalum Magnatum, 1497–1773', *Amer. J. Legal Hist.*, 22 (1978), 216–36, esp. pp. 228–9, 231; Molly McClain, 'The Wentwood Forest Riot: Property Rights and Political Culture in Restoration England', in Susan Dwyer Amussen and Mark

XIII. ODD MEN OUT

There are some individuals who defy classification, but are too remarkable to be left out for that reason. Let us look at them in approximate order of age.

We have already met Sir John Curzon of Kedleston (c.1599–1686), first baronet. He had obtained a reversion to the Receiver-Generalship of the Duchy of Lancaster as early as 1636, and was acting in that capacity during the early 1640s. He sat for Brackley in the third parliament of Charles I and then for one of the Derbyshire county seats in April–May 1640 and again from that November until Pride's Purge eight years later. He had succeeded his father in 1632 but in the sources for the 1630s and 1640s is easily confused with Sir John Curzon, knight, of Oxfordshire, who was, however, a royalist in the Civil War. Curzon appears to have continued to act in his office, except when the Duchy's jurisdiction and separate revenue system were temporarily abolished under the Commonwealth; and, although latterly assisted by his son and heir, was still there to the end of his long life. His wife came from the wealthy and influential Crewe family of Stene, Northants. In 1672 he was said to owe the King £19,600 on his account as Receiver-

A. Kishlansky (eds.), *Political Culture and Cultural Politics in Early-Modern England: Essays Presented to David Underdown* (Manchester and New York, 1995), 112–32; N. R. R. Fisher, 'Colonel Edward Cooke of Highham (c.1622–1684) and Henry Somerset, First Duke of Beaufort: Client and Patron', *Trans. Bristol and Glos. Arch. Soc.*, 115 (1997), 245–64; see HMC, *Ninth Report*, app., 116–17, and *Beaufort and Other Collections*, 67–8, 88, 114–15 (for the attacks on him and his counter-attack, 1678–83); for the Welsh tour see T. Dineley, *An Account of the Progress of His Grace Henry the First Duke of Beaufort through Wales 1684: And Notitia Cambro-Britannica*, ed. C. Baker (priv. pr., 1864); there is also a facsimile edn. with contemporary drawings, ed. R. W. Banks (1888; repr. by photolithography 1988); Francis Sandford, *A Genealogical History of the Kings of England . . .* (folio. 1677; Wing, STC 1641–1700, S 651), pl. 64 and pp. 64–5; Anthony Wagner, *Heralds of England: A History of the Office and College of Arms* (1967), chs. 9 and 10; Sandford is also in *DNB* and appears in other standard sources. Ashmole refused to sell him the office of Windsor Herald in 1675 (Josten, *Elias Ashmole*, 203, 1418); he was a non-juror, if not a Jacobite, sold his office to the famous Gregory King, and himself died in the debtors' prison of Newgate.

General. Since Professor Douglas Chandaman omitted the Duchy revenues from his otherwise invaluable work, and since the late Sir Robert Somerville was only able to publish lists of office-holders of the Duchy in the second volume of his book (starting in 1603), I have found it difficult to follow the financial side of the story in any depth. Neither the Duchy records nor the surviving family papers take us any further. His account as Receiver-General for 1672–3, declared before the Chancellor of the Duchy on 7 July 1674, recorded his having had £1,670 10s. 4¹/₄d. in hand at Michaelmas 1673. Clearly careful of his family's future, Sir John made his will as early as 1670, confirming it in 1682, but he had by then already settled his main estate on his eldest son, who was to rebuild the family home at Kedleston, whether or not out of his father's profits from the Receiver-Generalship it seems impossible to tell. Sir John's ability to retain his office under every successive regime from the Long Parliament to James II cannot but impress.[105]

Colonel Bullen Reymes, FRS, MP (1613–72) is the subject of an engaging modern biography. Although of Dorset gentry origin, and latterly himself domiciled near the coast at Portisham, his papers have ended up in Wiltshire. Reymes spent most of the years 1631–7 abroad, but he got a good start at Court through his father having been in the service of the Villiers family. In spite of an impeccably royalist record, he was not particularly well rewarded at the Restoration, although in 1661 he became a Gentleman of the Privy Chamber and—more materially worth while—was made Vice-Admiral of the Dorset coast by James as Lord Admiral. The increasing regard in which he was held is shown by his having been sent on a confidential mission to Tangier in 1664, to report on the state of the recently established garrison there. Like John Evelyn, he was put on the

[105] GEC, *Complete Baronetage*, ii. 132–3; 'Inner Temple Admission Register' (TS), i. 390 (original fo. 477); Keeler, *The Long Parliament*, 149–50; Underdown, *Pride's Purge*, 40, 50, 251, 371; Robert Somerville, *Office-holders of the Duchy and County Palatine of Lancaster from 1603* (London and Chichester, 1972), 18; *CSPD, 1672–73*, p. 342; PRO, DL 28/13/17; PROB 11/386, q. 19; Kedleston MSS (courtesy of the National Trust. I am grateful to the Archivist, Jill Banks, for her help).

Commission for the sick and wounded in 1664–7 and again in 1672. But his most fortunate break came with the reorganization of the Great Wardrobe (resulting from Sandwich's lax management as Master and the incompetence or dishonesty of the Clerk) in January 1668. Reymes was appointed to the new office of Surveyor at the relatively high salary of £300 a year. Earlier in the 1660s he had been in a business partnership with the Pley family of Poole and Weymouth, merchants and ex-parliamentarians, for the importation and manufacture of sailcloth required by the navy. George Pley senior had contrived to keep his Collectorship of Customs at Weymouth in 1660, but was eventually forced out of it (for financial irregularities, not for his politically incorrect past); his son George junior managed to retain his Collectorship at Lyme and to avoid being held liable for his father's debts to the Crown. Reymes meanwhile fell seriously ill in the autumn of 1672 and died in December. His will is unusual in that he left a specially valuable ring to Mrs Constance Pley, whom he describes as his 'sister' and for whom he expresses most particular affection and esteem. She had in fact been an active participant in the sailcloth business. Since he also addressed George Pley senior as 'brother' and this followed the marriage of his own daughter, Tabitha to George Pley junior, these were surely terms of endearment towards his daughter's parents-in-law. Unlike Reymes's biographer, I conclude that his relationship with Constance was platonic only, though as a widower he might well have wished it otherwise. While his offices in the Privy Chamber and then the Great Wardrobe would seem to characterize him as a courtier, Bullen Reymes was essentially a provincial, but one with all-round talents and a wide range of interests.[106]

---

[106] Helen A. Kaufman, *Conscientious Cavalier. Colonel Bullen Reymes, MP, FRS, 1613–1672: The Man and his Times* (London, 1962); *Hist. Parl.*, iii. 323–5; Newman, *Royalist Officers*, no. 1203; G. D. Squibb (ed.), *Visitation of Dorset, 1677* (Harl. Soc., 117 (1977)), 58; innumerable refs. in *CSPD, 1664–72*, and in *CTB*, iii–iv; PRO, LC 3/73, fos. 12v, 14v; Bodl. MS Eng. Hist. b. 79, fo. 29v; PRO, PROB 11/340, q. 26. Captain George Pley was Clerk of the Cheque at Weymouth during the 1650s, having been a parliamentarian in the 1640s; he was an assessment and militia commissioner for Dorset; he served as acting Governor of Portland, Weymouth, and Sandsfoot Castle, and

Henry Slingsby (*c*.1621–*c*.1688) was the younger son of a Yorkshire knight. He matriculated at Oxford in 1635 but did not stay to take a degree. His next years are obscure but he was probably a junior officer in the royalist army during the Civil Wars. His career begins to be documented from 1656 when he was in exile, acting as secretary to the Earl of Bristol, but passing between the Continent and England as courier and secret agent. He then made what turned out to be a very judicious change of patrons; from the winter of 1658–9 to the spring of 1660 he was one of Edward Hyde's regular correspondents. He was well rewarded at the Restoration, which would certainly not have been so if he had remained attached to Bristol, being made a Trade Commissioner. He later also served briefly as Plantations Secretary (in 1670–2) at a combined salary of £500 a year plus £1,000 for incidental expenses; this came to an end when the then Council was wound up, not because Slingsby was dismissed. Most important of all, in 1662 he was appointed joint Master of the Mint and then, on the death of Sir Ralph Freeman in 1667, sole Master. Slingsby inherited an estate in Cambridgeshire through his wife, and he remained in his responsible and lucrative post at the Mint until he was suspended in 1680 for accounting irregularities, although he was not finally forced out of the Mastership until 1686. The Treasury Commissioners continued to pursue him for his arrears—or perhaps illicit gains—though Evelyn, a long-standing friend, thought him hard done by. His will is quite revealing, or at least suggestive, in this respect and will bear quotation:

I have no reason to fear the present King's justice and mercy to me who have served the Crowne in several considerable Offices and places with all care and faithfulness for many years all which are well known unto his Majestie and from whom there are some Thousands of Pounds that

was also Agent for the Navy Commissioners at Plymouth in the later 1650s; he was dealing in sailcloth by 1659 if not earlier (PRO, SP46/81, fo. 90; E 351/653; AO 1/605/56; Firth and Rait (eds.), *Acts and Ordinances*, ii. 661, 1323; *CSPD, 1655–9*). For Mrs Constance Pley's letters to Pepys, see *CSPD, 1665–6*, 20 Aug., 3 Sept. 1665, 16 Jan., 1 Feb. 1666. For her husband's eventual removal from office in 1679 see *CTB*, vi. 95, 402, 550. Reymes's surviving papers are in the Wiltshire and Swindon Record Office, at Trowbridge: WRO 865/11/389–475.

are justly due unto me but have reason to hope that H.M. will be pleased to consider and give order to pay the same to prevent the ruine of me and my family . . .

Slingsby had clearly persuaded himself that he was the innocent and injured party by the end of his career. How well he had run the Mint is another question, but he was evidently incapable of working out and presenting proper accounts.[107]

Roger Whitley (*c.*1618–97) is unusual in that parts of his career are very fully documented, other parts not at all. He was the younger son of a Flintshire esquire, educated at Christ Church, Oxford and Gray's Inn; he served as a royalist field officer in the Civil War and was then a very active, not to say reckless, cavalier conspirator in the 1650s. At the Restoration he was at first rewarded only with local offices and a minor reversion in the royal household, though he soon obtained a curious post for the registration of emigrants sailing to the plantations, and presumably received fees from those who did not evade this requirement. He had already been elected to parliament, and was to sit for Flint boroughs in 1660, 1661–79, 1679, and 1679–80, and for the city of Chester in 1681, 1689, and 1695–7. His first significant promotion came in the mid-1660s, when he was appointed Knight Harbinger. The notebook which he kept in that capacity tells us virtually nothing about Whitley as an individual, but conveys a strong, if hardly surprising, impression that finding and providing accommodation, when the royal court was on progress or otherwise out of town, was tedious and trying; but before resigning from this office, he had moved on to higher things.[108]

---

[107] Foster, *Al. Ox.*, i. 1345; *Cal. Clar. St. Ps.*, iii. *1655–57* (Oxford, 1874), via index, ibid., iv. *1657–60* (Oxford, 1932), *passim*, pp. 140–669, ibid., v. *1660–1726* (Oxford, 1970), 30; *Diary of John Evelyn*, iii. 335, n. 2, ibid., iv. 567; HMC, *Eighth Report, App., House of Lords MSS*, 140; *CSPD, 1670s–1680s*, from indexes; *CTB*, iii, vi–viii, from indexes; Sainty, *Officials of the Boards of Trade*, 21, 116; Craig, *Mint*, 176–8; Challis, *A New History*, 351–5; Bodl. MS Eng. Hist. b. 79, fos. 21, 33v, 61v; PRO, PROB 11/399, q. 62 (no religious prologue).

[108] *Hist. Parl.*, i. 152–4, 513, iii. 709–11; D. Hayton (ed.), *History of Parliament, House of Commons, 1690–1714* (forthcoming); Newman, *Royalist Officers*, no. 1560; Bodl. MS Facs. f 5 (original, MS Eng. Hist. g. 22,

From 1672 to 1677 Whitley served as Deputy to Arlington, who—nominally together with Lord Berkeley (something of a 'sleeping partner')—was then Postmaster General. In this capacity he was in effect manager of all the mail services in England and Wales, as well as having responsibility for the posts into and out of the country. His work in this capacity is copiously but unevenly documented. The so-called 'Peover Papers', which descended through a female heir to the Mainwaring family of Peover in Cheshire, and are now in the possession of the Bodleian Library, had previously been deposited on loan in the John Rylands Library in Manchester; but even before that, the Postmaster General had persuaded the Mainwaring family to deposit the 1670s part of Whitley's papers with his Department (in 1900), and this loan was confirmed in 1915. Meanwhile the head of the Post Office secured the services of Gertrude Girdlestone, a researcher who combined being an extremely accurate reader of later seventeenth-century handwriting with being a typist of professional standards, which was, to say the least, unusual in the 1900s. So the Post Office Archives contain both the original manuscripts and the typed transcripts. The great bulk of these comprise his out-letter books for the whole five-year period. Most unfortunately he either did not keep the letters which he received or else these have not survived. Nor, unluckily, was Miss Girdlestone commissioned to copy his two volumes of accounts, one of which is now too fragile to be consulted. The letter-books do, however, contain an enormous number of Whitley's letters to the sub-postmasters around the country (who were confusingly sometimes called deputies), and reveal his ability as a manager, balancing praise and blame, wielding as it were both carrot and stick. Not only is this much the earliest continuous and detailed body of evidence for the internal history of the postal services, but they enable us to see a

unfit for production). The notebook appears to cover the years 1668/9–72, some entries being undated, he was Harbinger from 1665 to 1673 (PRO, LC 3/73, fo. 106; LC 7/1, unpag.). For his 1650s papers see Bodl. MSS Eng. Hist. e. 308–12; and on this phase of his career, David Underdown, *Royalist Conspiracy in England, 1649–1660* (New Haven, Conn., 1960), via index.

middle-ranking office-holder in relation to his subordinates in a manner comparable to Pepys's navy and admiralty papers.

The control of the Post Office at the top level was extremely complicated. The farm had originally been vested in Arlington as Secretary of State, jointly with Lord Berkeley; when Arlington exchanged the Secretaryship for the office of Lord Chamberlain, he continued as farmer and in effect as Postmaster General, itself a source of difficulty and perhaps jealousy with the then Secretaries of State, Williamson and Henry Coventry, because of the traditional connection between their offices and the posts for reasons of security and intelligence. What happened after York resumed control in 1677 was more important for Whitley's future career. According to one source, he offered his services to the Duke but requested additional powers to hire and fire the deputies or sub-postmasters. This was rejected, and Philip Frowde, son of the Sir Philip who had earlier shared responsibility with Arlington's unlikeable elder brother, Sir John Bennet, took over day-to-day management of the office, though there are two variant versions of a survey of the whole system, prepared for James soon after this, by one Thomas Gardiner, who became Comptroller of the Inland Posts while Frowde held this position for the Foreign Posts. Such of Whitley's accounts as are usable are difficult to interpret; they purport to show a final balance in his favour, of money due to him from the Crown, but the account never seems to have been officially 'declared' or enrolled in any Exchequer series. Considerable sums are shown as having been invested by him in the East India Company, which suggests that Whitley himself regarded these as legitimate profits (unless we are to suppose him to have been quite remarkably naïve as well as dishonest).[109]

Then followed what is in many ways the worst documented part of his whole career. Following Professor J. R. Jones, J. P. Ferris in the *History of Parliament* suggests that Whitley

[109] Post Office Archives, Ref. 1/7–9 (TS copies and index); 1/10–11 (originals from Dartmouth MSS and Royal Archives respectively); Post 94/9–10. I should like to thank the staff at Freeling House, Mount Pleasant for their friendliness and help with these materials.

veered towards the opposition during the final session of the Cavalier Parliament. As so often in such cases, it is impossible to know whether he became a Monmouthite because James had turned him out of the Post Office, or because as a sincere Anglican he was increasingly alarmed by the prospect of a Popish successor. Be that as it may, his support for the Exclusionist cause was to cost him a great deal of money and might well have cost him his life. In his home territory of Cheshire and North East Wales, he had together with other members of his family been involved in collecting and accounting for various taxes during the 1660s and 1670s. And at times some of them (though not particularly Whitley himself) had been under investigation for alleged failings in this capacity. Another financial responsibility, however, was the immediate, or anyway proximate, cause of his undoing. He was appointed as one of the Commissioners to disband and pay off the regiments which had been raised in 1677–8 and then sent over to Flanders as part of Charles II's pretended intention to enter the continental war on the Dutch side against France, although at the same time other units of volunteers had been sent across to fight on the French side. The Disbanding Commissioners, as they were known, themselves later became the object of Treasury scrutiny for alleged malversation, supposedly for having pocketed part of the money meant for the demobilized officers and other ranks. But it was a quite different episode which might have been literally fatal to Whitley. When the Duke of Monmouth was on a political progress in Cheshire, the Exclusionists turned out in strength to greet him; and Whitley was seen to bow so low that he was accused of having knelt to the Duke in order to kiss his hand—an honour which should only have been paid to a legitimate royal Prince, and a gesture which thus had treasonable implications. The incident was reported to Secretary Jenkins by a local Tory on 11 September 1682. The financial screws soon began to be tightened on Whitley. In December 1682 the King in Council ordered his 1664 commission for registering emigrants to be cancelled, 'as being found to be of no use, but rather a prejudice to his Majesties Service'. According to retrospective evidence from the

1690s, he tried to get his account as a Disbanding Commissioner passed by presenting it on oath to the Chief Baron of the Exchequer in September 1683. It may seem suspicious that what he purported to have received from the Chamberlain of the City (another of the Commissioners)— £9,046 18s. 10¹/₂d. —is balanced by payments totalling exactly this amount; but since the account gives the precise amounts paid to individual officers and units, Whitley would have had to be a very systematic (and ill-advised) liar if the account was not substantially truthful. The following year proceedings were begun against him in earnest, both for having improperly converted Post Office funds to his own use and for having fiddled the disbanding accounts.[110]

It was this which inaugurated the last and in one way much the most fully documented phase of his career. In the spring of 1684 Whitley began a detailed day-to-day diary which he kept up until very shortly before his death in 1697. It tells us little about the proceedings in the Commons when he was himself an MP (in 1689–90 and again in 1695–7), but much about his attendance on various committees of the House when he was not a Member (in 1685). Not the least remarkable fact about this text is that someone should have started to keep a diary at the age of sixty-six and have gone on until he was seventy-nine. While he was usually attended by some of his immediate family (a son, more often daughters, and latterly granddaughters), on his constant journeys between Chester, London, and Tunbridge Wells, Whitley had been a widower since his early forties, and there is no evidence of any close relationship thereafter. While he was certainly convivial and sociable, as well as being very much of a family man, he disapproved of drunkenness, especially in those who were supposed to be carrying out their offi-

---

[110] Jones, *First Whigs*, 12; *Hist. Parl.*, ii. 710; John Ferris, 'Official Members in the Commons, 1660–1690', in J. S. Morrill, P. A. Slack, and D. Woolf (eds.), *Public Duty and Private Conscience in Seventeenth-century England* (Oxford, 1993), 296; *Statutes of the Realm*, 31 Charles II, c.i, cl. xviii (appointment of Sir Gilbert Gerrard, Bt., Whitley, Col. J. Birch and Sir Thomas Playfair, Chamberlain of the City, as Disbanding Commissioners, 1679. To receive 2d. poundage and no more.); *CSPD, 1682*, pp. 387–9; PRO, PC 2/69, p. 598; AO 1/312/1238.

cial duties; he might almost be described as a 'Puritan of the Right', and in this bears some resemblance to his greater and more tragic contemporary, Arthur Capel Earl of Essex. In the sheer amount of his entertaining he reminds one of C. M. Bowra's description of himself as 'a man more dined against than dining'.[111]

Not only did Whitley have to mortgate much of his property and to borrow heavily from the Whig bankers Clayton and Morris (possibly also from the Tory financier Charles Duncombe), in order to pay the massive composition exacted from him by the Treasury for his alleged misuse of post office moneys back in the 1670s: his papers and other belongings were searched, and the firearms which were found in his Cheshire home confiscated. Moreover, under the terms of the revised charter granted to the city of Chester (in operation 1683–8), he was specifically barred from taking any part in municipal affairs or of holding any office there. This is not so surprising when we bear in mind that his relations by marriage, the Gerrard family, were leading Whig activists, and when the diary shows that his political associates in London included the redoubtable John Wildman, who had debated against Henry Ireton at Putney nearly forty years earlier when Whitley was a royalist field officer. Perhaps indeed he started keeping the diary, with its extraordinarily detailed record of whom he saw and talked with, when and where, partly as a safeguard against possible future charges of treason or lesser offences. More than once he records his suspicion of individuals whom he met, and notes having been careful what he said in front of those either whom he did not know or whom he did know and did not trust. In the aftermath of the Rye House Plot and then of Monmouth's Rebellion (of which he records his strong disapproval, not least on the grounds that the Princess Mary and her husband the Prince of

[111] Bodl. MS. Eng. Hist. c. 711. Once, when he had just returned from London to Chester, Whitley recorded the wife of one of his tenants as having 'brought my wife a present' (fo. 62, 26 Aug. 1686), but I have found no other evidence that he ever remarried and conclude that the entry is meant ironically; 'we' in the diary invariably refers to his immediate attendants at any given time, family, or otherwise.

Orange had a stronger claim to the throne than the Duke), it was a time when many people had good cause to feel insecure. Indeed if William's attempt on England had failed, or if he had been defeated in Ireland, it is unlikely that a victorious James would have been particularly merciful. And this was someone who had risked his life in battle and on the scaffold for the royal cause in the 1640s and 1650s. Having become a good Orangist, once it was clear beyond any doubt that William was going to succeed in his bid for the throne, Whitley was not only elected for Chester in the strongly Whig Convention Parliament of 1689 but was also elected as mayor of the city under its restored charter. His relations with the urban community suggest a kind of gentry populism. Having lost his parliamentary seat in the Tory reaction of 1690, his final re-election in 1695 might be described as a triumph of spirit over body. With rapidly failing health and stamina, his attendance and participation were poor to the point of being derisory: demonstrating the futility of trying to hang on in public office too late in life. Having got his armoury back in 1689, he specified in his will that the weapons both offensive and defensive should descend with the ownership of his house at Peele. The King actually stayed there with Whitley on his way back from Ireland after the Boyne campaign in 1690, but perhaps rather surprisingly William did not dub his host a knight. Did a slight lingering Monmouthite taint remain?[112]

The youngest of these stubborn individualists, Silas Taylor (1624–78) was the eldest son of a leading Herefordshire parliamentarian. He and his father Sylvanus were both authors and antiquarians; hence the inclusion of Silas in John Aubrey's *Brief Lives*, although there are some oddities in the latter's account, which in turn is based partly on the work of the Oxford anti-

---

[112] Besides diary entries see *CTB*, vii. 894, 1481, viii. 195, 460–2, 582, 866. Of his total net debt, calculated at £22,892 by the Treasury, £7,631 was to go to Philip Frowde, the rest to the King. For the disbanding accounts see *CTB*, vi. 58, 62, *et seq.*, ibid., vii. 1053; after the Revolution, the sum of £9,047, allegedly due on these was remitted in full (see n. 110 above); he was also granted £500 royal bounty for the cost of rebuilding the common hall at Chester, undertaken in his capacity as Mayor (*CTB*, ix. 134–5, x. 1350).

quary Anthony Wood. Aubrey says that Taylor's father 'left him a pretty good estate', but Sylvanus did not die until 1667, and he had already had to disgorge the church lands which he had acquired during the Interregnum several years before that. It is by no means clear that the manors of Bosbury, Colwell, and Coddington were actually his to bequeath to Silas (as specified in his will), whereas his younger son Sylvanus junior was left the manor of Lucton on which taxes were still being paid by him in 1663. Since one of Sylvanus senior's daughters was made sole executrix of his will, it seems likely that father and eldest son were not on particularly good terms. How far should we accept Aubrey's account of Silas having purloined priceless medieval manuscripts from Worcester and Hereford cathedrals, and then having tried to sell one back to the King for £120 and refusing an offer of £100 for another? First we need to review his circumstances at and immediately after the Restoration. At that stage he was a client and dependant of Sir Edward Harley (1624–1700), KB, MP, son and heir of the well-known puritan Sir Robert. The Harleys were presbyterian parliamentarians who had been in opposition or at least out of public life under the Republic. This relationship explains the survival of Taylor's collections relating to Herefordshire among the Harleian manuscripts in the British Library. It also explains the post which he held as Commissary and Paymaster for the English garrison at Dunkirk, of which Harley was the first royal Governor (in 1660–1). Sir Edward's virtual withdrawal from public life from 1662, on grounds of religious and moral principle, in effect left the unfortunate Taylor without a patron. He may have crossed over to Virginia briefly in 1661–2 to look for possible openings; certainly he was to seek appointment as Engineer on the establishment there some years later. Aubrey may well be correct that it was Sir Paul Neile who obtained for him the post which he was to hold from 1665 to his death, as naval Storekeeper at Harwich, to repay the kindness which he had shown to many royalists when he was a sequestrator in the 1640s and 1650s. In this capacity Taylor was on the Navy's payroll and answerable to the Board of Commissioners in London; his great hope was that Harwich would be elevated to the status of a full-scale naval dockyard, thereby affording him some prospects of promotion. But, although there was a temporary itinerant Commissioner based there during the latter stages of the Dutch War (1666–7), this was not to be. And it was to Under-Secretary, and then Secretary of State Williamson that Taylor had to answer as unofficial (and hence unpaid) 'intelligencer' covering that sector of the coast and the narrow seas. For much of the time he reported at least weekly, frequently more often than that. How far he did this from fear of being proceeded against for his earlier activities, how far to curry favour with a potential new patron is unclear. He scarcely received thanks for his pains, let alone any more tangible reward. When directed to go over to the Netherlands on an espionage mission, he had to point out that he did not have even the basics of the Dutch language. Harwich, however, was the English terminal for the ferry and mail services from Zealand and Holland, and thus a key point in Williamson's intelligence network. Ultimately Taylor was an isolated, if not a pathetic, figure. Yet his letters, including a splendid description of the King's visit in Harwich in 1668, have a certain sparkle and liveliness almost to the last, even when he is complaining about non-payment of his wages or other neglect. He was not without gifts as a musician, though Aubrey thought more highly of his musical gifts than did James Duke of York. And, besides the sorry story of the church manuscripts, Aubrey was told by Taylor in a letter that 'I should be glad to assist in the common-wealth of learning, if it lay in my power' (12 August 1672). With more ample means, he might indeed have blossomed as a virtu-oso; as it was, his career underlines the lack of career prospects for a talented individual with a chequered past and without the necessary patrons or other connections to offset this.[113]

[113] *DNB*, 'Silas Domville'; Foster, *Al. Ox.*, i. 1462; Wood, *Ath. Ox.*, ii (1692), 464–5; Aubrey, *Brief Lives*, ii. 254; *Hist. Parl.*, ii. 494–7 (for Sir Edward Harley); *Correspondence of Hartlib . . . with Governor Winthrop . . .* (Boston, 1878), 14, letter from Henry Oldenburg to John Winthrop, Oct. 1661; HMC, *Portland* iii (*Harley Papers*), 251, 262; Bodl. MS Aubrey 13, fo. 207; *Pepys Diary*, 29 June 1668; *CSPD, 1668–9*, pp. 9–10 (Taylor to Pepys, describing the King's visit, 8 Oct. 1668); PRO, PROB 11/324, q. 71 (his father's will; a third son, Gabriel is mentioned but was left nothing; Silas himself died intestate); *Herefordshire Militia Assessments of 1663*, ed.

XIV. CONCLUSION

In drawing the threads together at the end of this chapter we need to look at the subject in two distinct ways. There are two very broad and general questions to be asked: what difference did these crown servants make to the process of state formation, or indeed to other aspects of the country's history; and what was the significance of crown service for them as individuals, members of families, and constituents of social groups? An attempted answer to the first of these questions will be best reserved to the next and final chapter of this book; the second requires to be briefly addressed here.

Looking at the selected crown servants of 1663, 1673, and 1683, it was clear that office-holding acted as a positive factor for wealth and even more so for status. And it would be very strange if this had not been so. We can, however, have no means of telling how these same individuals would have fared had they pursued other, alternative careers, for example in law or trade. It was certainly not a period when fortunes were easily made, or even improved through landownership and agriculture alone, though clearly exceptions to this can be found at all levels from wealthy peers and gentry to modest freeholders and tenant farmers. Service in the armed forces of the crown and in the expanding overseas empire carried proportionately greater risks of premature death in battle and from disease, but also the possibility of dramatic enrichment and upward social mobility. Although his career was only just beginning to get off the ground by the beginning of 1685, John Churchill, first Duke of Marlborough is the most striking example, if not exactly typical. If we survey those in the civil employment of the Crown, it is easy to pick out a handful of families who made it to the top and established themselves at or near the apex of English society: the

M. A. Faraday (Camden 4th ser., 10 (1972)), pp. xi–xii, introduction, p. 25; *CSPD, 1664–78*, via indexes, for his letters to Williamson and to the Navy Board (until 1673); PRO, ADM 106/282, 290, 299, 311 (via indexes, for 1673–5; not checked for 1675–8); W. R. Powell, 'Silas Taylor of Harwich (1624–78). Naval Affairs, Espionage and Local History', *Essex Archaeology and History*, 25 (1994), 174–84.

Annesleys (until into the eighteenth century), the Bennets (but not in the direct male line), the Finchs, the Godolphins, the Hydes, the Osbornes and perhaps a very few others. If we look at the next level down, and ask ourselves which crown servants of any moment as administrators raised themselves and their families to a significant extent, the answer is less clear. Thus one generation later, on the death of his son George, William Clarke's inheritance passed to two Oxford Colleges. Perhaps the clearest such cases, of new and lasting family fortunes, are those of George Downing, Stephen Fox, and William Blathwayt. Some courtly families prospered more lastingly than others: certain branches of the Seymours, the Ashburnhams, Wyndhams, Killigrews, and Progers are among the most obvious. Further down the official hierarchy, it becomes more difficult to track families forward for more than a generation. Types to follow in this way would include the Exchequer Auditors, such as Sir Edmund Sawyer, Richard and William Aldworth, and Brooke Bridges; the successive Surveyors-General Sir Charles and William Harbord; and John Birch of the Excise.

A strong case could also be made for family continuity in some legal offices, like the Henleys as Chief Clerks of King's Bench, also the Clerks of the Crown in that court. In Common Pleas, the holders of the offices of Chirographer, Custos Brevium, and the three Prothonotaryships would be the ones to follow forward; likewise in Chancery those holding the Clerkship of the Crown and the Six Clerkships. Such rather impressionistic selections could be extended across the range of courts and departments, most certainly including the Under-Secretaries of State and Treasury Secretaries. Evidence from surviving wills and other, often very miscellaneous sources, strongly suggests that—even below this level—among the lowest ranks of those included in our selections, there must have been families of office-holders who either rose appreciably within the middle class or even penetrated the lowest level of the gentry.

It may fairly be asked how the Crown servants of 1660–85 compare in these respects with their equivalents earlier and later. For reasons which hardly need to be spelt out again, no close or exact comparison is possible with 1649–60, because the careers of too many State's servants of the Republic were cut short by the Restoration. More of a parallel can be established with the King's servants of 1625–42. Here, however, the differences in the economic and demographic contexts, as well as in the political and religious climates, make it difficult to compare like with like. This could only be overcome, or disregarded, if we were to assume that the changed circumstances more or less cancelled each other out in their effects; that is the end of long-term inflation and population growth, together with the consequences of all that happened between 1642 and 1660. This is a risky, not to say rash way of proceeding. Thus we might agree that landownership and the law offered proportionately fewer opportunities and attractions after 1660 than they had done before 1640; as against this, finance and trade, colonization, and naval and military service provided more by way of alternative means to greater wealth and social enhancement. If we were to count in all Charles II's mistresses and their offspring under the heading of those enjoying royal favour (but not necessarily holding office as defined here), this might be set in the balance against the quite extraordinary gains which accrued to the Villiers and a very few other court and ministerial families (such as the Carrs or Kers, Cranfields, Howards, Westons, and Wentworths) from the 1610s to the 1630s.[114] But these families and individuals were by definition untypical, whether under the earlier or the later Stuart monarchs. If we try to take a broader view, we observe the same relative fluidity within an essentially hierarchical social system, indeed one with some hereditary 'caste-like' tendencies, where service under the Crown provided one of the upward routes for advancement but by no means an infallible or universal one, either in the years 1625–42 or 1660–85. Office could and sometimes did precipitate the decline or even downfall of families and individuals, even if this was rare compared to the reverse phenomenon. I began this research expecting to find that holding office under the Crown made proportionately more difference to more individuals and

---

[114] Stone, *Crisis of the Aristocracy*, ch. 8 and app. 19.

families after 1660 than before the Civil War. At least with my terminal date of 1685, such a hypothesis cannot be sustained and is probably better discarded.

XV. A VERY LAST WORD ON PROSOPOGRAPHY

The historical technique of collective biography, seeking to collect, verify, and present a minimum amount of information about the lives and careers of a relatively large number of people has by now been long established both in history and in applied social studies. Since my own first, halting steps towards extending this method to seventeenth-century office-holders, it has been successfully applied to many other social groups and categories in early-modern times, including even the humblest inhabitants of some English villages.[115] At the risk of tedium, it is worth repeating that this is one technique for improving historical understanding by deepening and extending our knowledge of the past. It is not a substitute for other approaches, such as individual biography in depth, local and family histories, political narrative, constitutional analysis, intellectual, religious and economic history, or cultural studies—to mention but the most obvious. No one will have much use for this book, nor indeed for the two others to which it is intended as a sequel, who rejects entirely the prosopographical method as an acceptable and worthwhile instrument for the historian. Yet its validity can be accepted without having to make excessive claims for it, and certainly without neglecting or denigrating other equally valid ways of approaching the past. Integrating all these approaches in order to write what is sometimes called 'total history' is altogether another matter and remains an ideal to which most of us can only aspire without ever seriously expecting to attain it.

[115] See works by Alan Macfarlane, Margaret Spufford, Keith Wrightson, and others, published 1970s–1990s.

5. Conclusion

1. SYMBOLS AND EMBLEMS OF STATE

Many historians have emphasized the importance of symbols and ceremonies as a feature of government and an aspect of state power. Whether these were of greater significance in the seventeenth century than in the twentieth and the twenty-first centuries need not concern us here. It is, however, hard to believe that two civilized powers of today would regard a maritime dispute over saluting the flag as a *casus belli,* though stranger things have happened in our time. The English claim to sovereignty over the narrow seas around the shores of these islands (but extending far outside what have come to be defined as territorial waters in modern international law) was symbolized by the demand that vessels of all other nationalities should strike their flags and dip their topsails to the ships of the English Crown (or State—for the Commonwealth had applied this doctrine with at least equal vigour). Samuel Pepys indeed extended this to the seas hundreds of miles away from Britain when he roundly condemned Captains Cloudesley Shovell and Matthew Aylmer for having struck their flags to the admiral of a Spanish fleet off the southern coast of Spain. Fortunately, neither officer suffered the fate of Admiral Byng in the next century.[1]

---

[1] The fullest treatment of this subject still seems to be T. Wemyss Fulton, *The Sovereignty of the Sea: An Historical Account of the Claims of England to the Dominion of the British Seas and of the Evolution of the Territorial Waters: with Special Reference to the Rights of Fishing and the Naval Salute* (Edinburgh and London, 1911). See Edwin Chappell with W. Matthews (eds.), *The Tangier Papers of Samuel Pepys* (Navy Rec. Soc., 73 (1935)), 114, 151, 167, 184, 186, 189, 191, 197, 203, etc. If Pepys had had his way and Aylmer had been executed, the present author would not have existed, being a direct descendsnt of Matthew.

Disputes for precedence between the ambassadors of foreign monarchs in London provide another example of such bids for primacy. The French and Spanish Crowns both claimed the foremost place; and, no doubt, if the Emperor had been regularly represented at the English court, his envoys would have done so too.[2]

Many of the Crown's servants were involved in the symbolic expression of royal authority within the realm, that is in relation to the King's own subjects. Flags, canopies of state, statues, escutcheons, uniforms, coins, seals, and titles were all changed as quickly as possible on the King's return in 1660. Charles and his Council were forced to recognize that it was simply not feasible to call in the entire republican coinage overnight, and that the Mint needed more time to produce replacement coins. In general, however, the process was rapid and thoroughgoing. The Office or College of Arms (the Kings, Heralds, and Pursuivants) enjoyed a halcyon period of activity with the collection of extra fees. The same was true of the clerks and others involved at the Signet, Privy, and Great Seals. Years ago the late E. P. Thompson suggested that part at least of the purpose of the Judges going round on assize was to impress and overawe as well as to dispense justice.[3] More recently other historians have rightly emphasized the determination of the restored royal government to make the King's long delayed coronation, in 1661, as splendid and memorable an occasion as was humanly possible.[4] The officially encouraged re-erection of maypoles in towns and villages around the country was perhaps directly related to the manifestations of royal authority and state power. However, the close and complex interrelationship of church and state, with a restored royal supremacy as well as an Anglican enforced uniformity, means that we should

[2] Roderick Clayton, 'Diplomats and Diplomacy in London, 1667–1672', Univ. of Oxford D.Phil. thesis (1995).

[3] See D. Hay, P. Linebaugh, and E. P. Thompson (eds.), *Albion's Fatal Tree* (1975) 27–9.

[4] Ronald Hutton, *The Restoration: A Political and Religious History of England, 1658–67* (Oxford, 1985); Paul Seaward, *The Cavalier Parliament and the Reconstruction of the Old Regime, 1661–1667* (Cambridge, 1989).

certainly think of the outward trappings of the restored episco-
palian church as an integral part of the same process.[5]

The Lords Lieutenant were literally the monarch's mini-
viceroys in the counties. The holders of these new positions and
their often more active Deputies had ceased to act since the
1640s; appointments were all *de novo*.[6] The offices of the annually selected sheriffs and the justices of the peace had by contrast
survived through the Interregnum, but there were predictably
sweeping changes in the composition of the commissions during
the years 1660–2. Thereafter the overall picture of relations
between the Crown and the JPs seems to be one of temporary
harmony, followed from the 1670s by the successive purges
which were to continue even after the Revolution of 1688–9.[7]
Parallel with this, the purging of city and borough corporations
is familiar as an integral part of the more strictly constitutional
settlement following the King's return.[8] This may, however, also
be seen as a successful reassertion of aristocratic and gentry
hegemony over the urban middle class. Finally, the first years of
Charles II's actual (as opposed to *de jure*) reign witnessed the
most lavish creation of titles since the reign of James I; these
extended from Monck's dukedom down to mass knightings
often of minor cavalier gentlemen whose other claims to reward

---

[5] I. M. Green, *The Re-establishment of the Church of England, 1660–1663*
(Oxford, 1978); John Spurr, *The Restoration Church of England, 1646–1689*
(New Haven, Conn., and London, 1991).

[6] Victor L. Slater, *Noble Government: Stuart Lord Lieutenancy and the
Transformation of English Politics* (Athens, Ga., 1994).

[7] Lionel K. J. Glassey, *Politics and the Appointment of Justices of the Peace,
1675–1720* (Oxford, 1979); also Norma Landau, *The Justices of the Peace,
1679–1760* (Berkeley, Calif., 1984); S. K. Roberts, *Recovery and Restoration
in an English County: Devon Local Administration, 1642–1670* (Exeter,
1985); Anthony Fletcher, *Reform in the Provinces: The Government of Stuart
England* (New Haven, Conn., and London, 1986); Andrew Coleby, *Central
Government and the Localities: Hampshire, 1649–1689* (Cambridge, 1987),
and other regional and local studies numerous beyond citation.

[8] W. C. Costin and J. S. Watson (eds.), *The Law and Working of the
Constitution*, i, *1660–1783* (1952), 15–17; J. P. Kenyon (ed.), *The Stuart
Constitution, 1603–1689*, rev. edn. (Cambridge, 1986), 351–3, for the
Corporation Act of 1662; also Paul D. Halliday, *Dismembering the Body
Politic: Partisan Politics in England's Towns, 1650–1730* (Cambridge, 1998),
but see Perry Gauci, *Politics and Society in Great Yarmouth, 1660–1772*
(Oxford, 1996) for a more qualified view.

or compensation it was impossible to satisfy. Thus of the ninety-five peerage creations between the Restoration and the end of the reign, nineteen date from 1660–1. Even allowing for promotions within the peerage, and life titles granted to ladies, this works out at only marginally fewer annually than the early Stuart creations of 1603–41. Charles II created no fewer than 219 new baronetcies between May 1660 and December 1661, excluding eleven baronets of Ireland and six of Scotland. Besides sixty-eight Knights of the Bath created at his coronation in April 1661, he dubbed 309 knights in 1660–1; the median annual number of baronets created for the rest of the reign was only about eight, and for knights some twenty-eight or -nine.[9]

The written and spoken word were also symbolic. The republican act requiring all legal documents to be written in English, as well as in normal current handwriting, and for court proceedings to be in English, was not one of those re-enacted as a statute with royal authority, and was not to be reintroduced until well into the next century. The majesty of state and of law was perhaps felt to require an element of mystery, but the vested interest of lawyers and legal office-holders was no doubt an additional factor. There was also a systematic campaign to recover records and other documents, including those of the committees which had been set up by what were now regarded as the rebel and usurping authorities of the 1640s and 1650s. This was partly for retributive purposes, for example to bring to justice those who had trafficked in royal and church property, or were still seeking to conceal their illicit gains. The Registrar of the Dean and Chapter of Westminster Abbey, Francis Royley (who was a cousin of the Assistant Keeper of the Records,

---

[9] Lawrence Stone, 'The Inflation of Honours', *Past & Present*, 14 (1958), 45–70 and id., *The Crisis of the Aristocracy, 1558–1641* (Oxford, 1965), ch. 3, 'The Inflation of Honours', app. 3, p. 755, app. 5, p. 757; J. C. Sainty (comp.), *Peerage Creations, 1649–1800: A Chronological List of Creations in the Peerages of England and Great Britain* (Parliamentary History, occ. ser. 1 (1998)); *Complete Baronetage*, microprint edn., H. Montgomery-Massingberd (Gloucester, 1983); W. A. Shaw, *Knights of England* (2 vols., London, 1906), where my figures include dubbings by Irish viceroys, but these were relatively modest under Charles II.

William Ryley, but had changed his name) took a particularly active part in this. He subsequently became involved in the government's intelligence network, which explains why his private correspondence is to be found in the state papers. An attempt to return the Scottish royal and other public records to that kingdom ended in disaster, when the ship carrying them was wrecked on its way north, with the loss of eighty-five hogsheads of documents; fortunately for Scottish property-owners and for future historians of Scotland, some were saved.[10]

Another highly symbolic act was the exhumation of Oliver Cromwell's body, together with those of Henry Ireton and John Bradshaw, from Westminster Abbey, followed by their dismemberment and public display. The bodies of other prominent parliamentarians, republicans, and Cromwellians were also removed from the Abbey, and had to be reburied elsewhere. This was in addition to the trials and executions of living regicides who had not escaped overseas to Europe or America. Ex-rebels as such could not of course be punished, due to the major role of one-time parliamentarians and Cromwellians in bringing about the Restoration in a peaceable and orderly way.

A more constructive manifestation of restored royal power, whether or not more successful in its effects, was Charles II's well-known claim to the sacred healing powers of his royal predecessors. The practice of touching for the King's Evil, in order to cure scrofula, has been traced back to the rivalry between the French and English monarchies in the thirteenth century (and not, as used to be supposed, to much earlier, pre-Conquest, times).[11] The organization of the touching process under Charles is well documented except for the early part of

[10] Sir Archibald Primrose to Lauderdale, 19 June 1661 (*The Lauderdale Papers*, Camden ns, 34 (1884), 64).

[11] Marc Bloch, *Les Rois thaumaturges: étude sur le caractère surnaturel attr-ribué à la puissance royale particulièrement en France et en Angleterre* (Paris, 1924; new edn., with preface by Jacques le Goff, Paris, 1983); (pl. iv, from a print of 1684, shows Charles II in action, not looking as if he was enjoying it very much); Keith Thomas, *Religion and the Decline of Magic* (London, 1971), 177–8, 192–8, 204–6; Frank Barlow, 'The King's Evil', *Eng. Hist. Rev.*, 95 (1980), 3–27; Noël Woolf, 'The Sovereign Remedy: Touch-pieces and the

his reign. According to the records kept by successive Clerks of the Closet, and preserved in the Exchequer, during his last sixteen years (from April 1669 to the end of 1684) he touched the staggering total of 28,983 persons, or an annual average of 1,811. Individuals, whether children or adult, were not meant to come back after one touching; how effectively this was enforced is not clear, but these figures certainly suggest a symbolically successful activity whatever the therapeutic reality.[12] On the other hand, the King's decision to forgive Colonel Thomas Blood for his theft of the royal regalia from the Tower, probably in order to strengthen the government's hold over a valuable double agent, indicates a more cynical realism in such matters.[13]

Medals could be struck for a variety of reasons. Many were in honour of individuals, but this was not limited to the high and mighty and could extend to quite obscure people, such as an apothecary for his skill in embalming the bodies of the dead. Often they were to commemorate particular events; these included the King's marriage, the naval victory over the Dutch in 1665, the Great Fire, the progress of overseas colonization in 1670 (inscribed '*Diffusus in orbe Britannus*'), and the founding of Christ's Hospital mathematical school in 1673, besides the thousands of 'touch-pieces' for issue to those on whom the royal hands were laid.[14]

Dates were also added to the quasi-sacred calendar. Celebrations of his father's martyrdom and of the King's own birthday and entry into London (30 January and 29 May

King's Evil', *British Numismatic J.* 1979, 49 (1980), 99–121 and pl. xix–xxii (I am most grateful to Nicholas Mayhew for this reference, and for showing me touch-pieces in the Ashmolean Museum's collection).

[12] PRO, E 407/85 i (loose folded sheets), giving numbers of those touched and of medals handed out, Apr. 1669–Dec. 1685 (I have excluded the first year of James II from my total).

[13] A. Marshall, 'Colonel Thomas Blood and the Restoration Political Scene', *Hist. J.*, 32 (1989), 561–82; also his *Intelligence and Espionage in the Reign of Charles II* (Cambridge, 1994).

[14] J. Pinkerton, *The Medallic History of England* (London, 1802), 87, 89, pls. xxxi–xxxiv; E. Hawkins, A. W. Frank, and A. Grueber, *Medallic Illustrations of the History of Great Britain and Ireland to the Death of George II*, i (London, 1885), Charles II, nos. 1–291; *CSPD*, 1682, p. 102.

respectively) again underline the unity of church and state, likewise the tendency to play down Gunpowder Plot Day and the date of Queen Elizabeth's accession (5 and 17 November respectively) with the periodic banning of fireworks and bonfires. Symbols were of course also open to use by the Crown's opponents, as with the Pope Burnings, the wearing of green ribbons, and so forth.[15] The Crown's calling in of charters by the use of the ancient legal action of *Quo Warranto*, particularly in the early 1680s, might also be thought of as a symbolic act. I should be more inclined to see it as a reminder that royal authority over corporate bodies was absolute, yet at the same time rested in this way on a thirteenth-century statute, not merely on exercise of the prerogative. Unlike his father, Charles did not indulge in futile antiquarianism by asserting his rights through such measures as knighthood fines, forest laws, or the summoning of the Great Council of Peers (all but the last mentioned being in any case illegal under the legislation of 1641). The only statute which he calculatedly broke was his own Triennial Act of 1664.

It is not easy to assess the importance of all this for the inhabitants of the country as a whole. Compared with his royal predecessors and successors, such success as Charles achieved surely depended more on practical political skills, including his choice of men to serve him.

---

[15] Tim Harris, *London Crowds in the Reign of Charles II: Propaganda and Politics from the Restoration until the Exclusion Crisis* (Cambridge, 1987); O. W. Furley, 'The Pope-burning Processions of the Late Seventeenth Century', *History*, 44 (1959), 16–23; J. R. Jones, *The First Whigs: The Politics of the Exclusion Crisis, 1678–83* (Oxford, 1961); Mark Knights, *Politics and Opinion in Crisis, 1678–1681* (Cambridge, 1994) is a more measured treatment than Jonathan Scott's *Algernon Sidney and the Restoration Crisis, 1677–1683* (Cambridge, 1991), in spite of the fascinating new material which this work contains. Sidney, like Edmund Ludlow, was a positive propaganda asset in the King's hand.

II. POLICIES, TASKS, SUCCESSES, FAILURES

Some undertakings and activities of government are generic, in the sense of belonging to the very definition of a state. Yet even these reflect the specific circumstances and objectives of particular governments at different times in history. Thus we might say that the preservation of law and order, the prevention of crime and the enforcement of justice are inherent to the very nature of any state. But we might well want to go on to qualify this, for example, by adding that for many states at the beginning of the twenty-first century the most intractable problems in this respect arise from the activities of international terrorists and drug smugglers, which of course is not to deny the existence of other more traditional types of crime against persons and property. Members of Charles II's government were at least as much concerned with the supposed threat from irreconcilable puritans and republicans, both at home and abroad, who wished to undo the Restoration, as they were with murder, assault, highway robbery, burglary, theft, forgery, coining, pickpocketing, and the rest. Occasionally the two merged together in the minds of the authorities, as with the activities of the so-called Levellers of Warwickshire in 1670, whereas in 1675 it seems to have been clearly recognized that the riot by the East London silk workers was economic (if also potentially xenophobic) and not ideological in motivation.[16] Although there were no major changes in the general system of law enforcement, new crimes were created by the Navigation Laws and by the extension of the Game Laws. Historians of crime and punishment have shown that over a longer period of time the number of hangings was tending downwards, even when on paper the severity of the law was increasing.[17]

---

[16] Although a great deal has been written since, Max Beloff, *Public Order and Popular Disturbance in England, 1660–1714* (Oxford, 1938; repr. edn., London, 1963) remains in many ways the best account.

[17] J. M. Beattie, *Crime and the Courts in England, 1660–1880* (Oxford, 1986; Cynthia B. Herrup, *The Common Peace: Participation and the Criminal Law in Seventeenth-century England* (Cambridge, 1987); J. A. Sharpe, *Crime in Early Modern England, 1550–1750* (1984) and his

The threat from puritans, republicans, and levellers might have been expected to diminish with the passing of time after 1660. But when the continuing discontents of surviving radicals from republican days merged with the frustrations of the Whig-Exclusionist political opposition, especially after the dissolution of Charles's last parliament at Oxford in April 1681, resort to some kind of violence again seemed a real possibility. If credibility is given to all the Crown's witnesses and to the whole prosecution case against the so-called Rye House Plotters and their aristocratic allies in 1683, the King and his brother only escaped assassination by a fortuitous change in the date and route of their return from Newmarket to London. As with the Fifth-Monarchist rising in London at the beginning of the reign (in January 1661) this proved of enormous propaganda value to the Crown, not least in helping to discredit the earlier allegations by Titus Oates and others of a Popish Plot to murder the King and replace him by his brother, as well as to justify extreme measures against the political opposition.[18] The long-drawn-out campaign against what was perceived as the excessive and stubbornly maintained independence of the City of London eventually culminated in the recall of the city's charter (in January 1683), by any standards one of the King's greatest political victories.[19] In terms of actual military strength, the peacetime standing army was progressively (though not continuously) enlarged over the course of the reign.[20] At the same time royal authority continued to depend on co-operation with the peerage and the gentry (less the hard core of Whigs and Exclusionists). James II's reign was to demonstrate this beyond any reasonable doubt.

Judicial Punishment in England (1990), which provides the best brief summary.

[18] Since Doreen J. Milne's pioneering study, 'The Results of the Rye House Plot and their Influence upon the Revolution of 1688', *TRHS*, 5th ser., 11 (1951), 91–108, much has been written on this. Besides the works already cited (by Haley, Kenyon, Miller, Scott, Knights, *et al*), see Louis B. Schwoerer, 'The Trial of William Lord Russell (1683): Judicial Murder?' *J. Legal Hist.*, 9 (1988), 142–68.

[19] J. Levin, *The Charter Controversy in the City of London, 1660–1688* (1969), and many refs. in other histories of the reign already cited.

[20] John Childs, *The Army of Charles II* (1976).

Security against internal upheaval is often but not invariably linked to protection against external attack. Here the dominant influences were the two wars with the Dutch (1664–7 and 1672–4) and England's relations with the greatest contemporary power in the Christian world, France under Louis XIV. Enough has already been said about the contribution of the Navy Board, the other Navy Commissioners, and their various subordinates, as well as the dockyard officers and other personnel, and the Ordnance Office, together with the Victualling Contractors and their agents, in preparing the fleet for active service and battle with the enemy.[21] Near the end of the earlier war, after the Medway disaster of June 1667, there was a sudden invasion scare, leading to the hasty raising of new regiments and other rather frantic preparations, though there is little evidence of the Dutch ever contemplating more than perhaps one or two small-scale amphibious raids. Nor had French participation in this war on the Dutch side (in 1666–7) posed any great threat of this kind. At no stage was there any real danger of the country being successfully invaded by foreign forces until the King's brother had been on the throne for more than three years. Soon after the beginning of James's reign, the defeat of attempted invasions by Monmouth and Argyll might be said to have demonstrated the strength of his inheritance from his elder brother. If these victories had been handled with more political acumen and judicial moderation, the security of the state would have been increased (as, in the very short run, perhaps was the case).

Charles's government twice appeared to be poised, ready for full-scale military intervention on the Continent. In 1673 an English army was mustered and prepared to invade the Netherlands, if the combined Anglo-French fleet won a sufficiently decisive victory over the Dutch navy to assure uninterrupted control in the narrow seas. This did not happen. The following year England pulled out of the war altogether, and most of the additional regiments which had been recruited for

[21] My account of the Ordnance Office and its personnel, in Chs. 2 and 4 above, should be supplemented by Tomlinson, *Guns and Government*, esp. ch. 1.

this projected campaign were demobilized or at least stood down. In 1677–8, by contrast, the government prepared a substantial expeditionary force, which was actually transported across to Flanders, ostensibly to attack France in alliance with the Dutch. It is highly unlikely that the King and his closest advisers had any serious intention of becoming involved in the war; whether their motives for this elaborate—and quite expensive—pretence had more to do with putting pressure on Louis XIV to make peace with the Dutch or to satisfy public opinion at home, it is hard to know. At the administrative level the key figures in such military preparations included the Secretary-at-War, the Muster-Masters, and the Ordnance Office. If Matthew Locke has been portrayed as a somewhat colourless character here, we should perhaps remind ourselves that most of us might appear a little unexciting if we were preceded by William Clarke and followed by William Blathwayt. In 1671 Monck's brother-in-law Sir Thomas Clarges had been replaced as Commissary-General of Musters by two obscure members of the Howard family: Sir Cecil, who is said to have been a younger son of Lord Howard of Escrick and had been with the royal court in exile, and Henry, the fourth son of the Earl of Suffolk, to which title he was himself to succeed in 1691, his elder brothers all having died. Their qualifications seem more as courtiers than as military administrators. Perhaps fortunately, the financial side of these preparations was largely in the hands of the ubiquitous and highly capable Stephen Fox, at least until the winter of 1678–9, although (as we saw near the end of the last chapter), the Disbanding Commissioners appointed by parliament also became involved, to their own detriment in Colonel Whitley's case.[22]

[22] In 1678 a warrant was issued to Clarges as Commissary-General (*CSPD, 1678*, p. 125), but I can only think that this was an error by a clerk. See *Hist. Parl.*, ii. 74–81, to be preferred to *DNB*. For Cecil Howard see Le Neve, *Knights*, 40; Shaw, *Knights*, ii. 222; PRO, LC 3/73, fo. 13; Bodl. MS Eng. Hist. b. 79, fo. 28v; he had ceased to act by 1680 but left no will. For Henry see *Complete Peerage*, xii/1, 470–1; *CSPD, 1679–80*, p. 629. For the two of them as Commissaries, there are numerous other refs. in *CSPD* and *CTB*. On the 1678 expedition see Childs, *Army*, ch. 10.

Apart from brief and localized colonial campaigns, the only sustained land warfare in which England was engaged took place in North West Africa. The defence of Tangier against the Moroccans was a constant administrative, financial, and military preoccupation, involving several of the Crown's servants, such as Pepys, Povey, Reymes, Pepys's rival John Creed, Hewer, and Shere, from the initial garrisoning of Tangier in 1662 until its final evacuation in 1684. Although the fighting was intermittent rather than continuous, it was fierce and by no means always went in England's favour. Disease also took a heavy toll of the forces stationed there.[23]

The overseas empire did expand, but only to a limited extent. Apart from the decision to retain Jamaica (captured from Spain in 1655), and the transformation of Barbados and the Leeward Islands from being proprietary to crown colonies, the other additions to England's American empire were Carolina, which was granted to proprietors in 1663, and New York, which after its capture from the Dutch in 1664 was granted to the King's brother, and after its brief recapture by the Dutch in 1672–3, regranted to James as part of the peace settlement in 1674. The largest and most surprising proprietary grant was that made in 1682 to the Quaker William Penn, son of Sir William the Admiral and then Navy Commissioner, partly in recognition of the Crown's debt to his father. The factories or trading posts on the West African coast were in the charge of the Royal African Company, which in theory had a monopoly of the infamous transatlantic slave trade, although this was proving irresistibly attractive to independent, or 'interloping', traders in human cargoes. English posts, little more than toeholds as yet, on the shores of southern Asia, including Bombay within a few years of its acquisition by the English Crown from Portugal, were part and parcel of the East India Company's trading monopoly; uniquely this body was also solely responsible for security, such as the provision of convoy escorts, at least anywhere east of the

---

[23] The fullest account remains Enid M. G. Routh, *Tangier: England's Lost Atlantic Outpost, 1661–1684* (1912), but on the military side it is superseded by Childs, *Army*, chs. 6 and 7. Many of the loose papers in PRO, CO 279 (Tangier Papers) are in a confused state and difficult to use.

Cape of Good Hope, and even in the South Atlantic. Thus, after its reoccupation in the 1670s, the tiny and remote island of St Helena belonged to the Company rather than the Crown. Understandably, greater pressure could be put on the government to take action against interlopers in the Indian Ocean and even further east that was the case with the slave trade; besides, by this time many top people had money invested in East India stock.

In view of all this, it is surprisingly difficult to assess the importance of the colonial empire in the minds of the King and his Councillors, or to estimate what priority they gave it. There is a lot of surviving evidence about the successive commissions and committees for trade and the plantations. And, if we take at their face value the voluminous privy council items, together with all the materials now calendared in the *State Papers Colonial* and the other uncalendared Crown Office series in the Public Record Office, we should conclude that this was one of the Crown's foremost concerns.[24] But a nagging doubt remains. Just as economic historians have become more sceptical about identifying a body of coherent, consistent policies, and designating these as 'mercantilism', so the quest to identify and define a single English imperial or colonial policy has some of the same characteristics as staring at Lewis Carroll's Cheshire Cat. That it took from 1664 to 1683 to bring about decisive action against the recalcitrant Massachusetts Bay Company, is one indicator of this. Hesitations and changes of policy towards further expansion in the Caribbean is another; as is the relatively modest scale of naval protection afforded to the mainland American settlements and for the convoying of transatlantic trade. Attempts to exploit colonial resources for timber and other naval stores were indeed pursued quite persistently, yet it seems that domestic and Baltic supplies continued to be the more important.

[24] See also the pioneering but now rather dated monographs, C. M. Andrews, *British Commissions, Committees and Councils of Trade and Plantations, 1622–1675* (Baltimore, Md., 1908; repr. New York, 1970) and R. P. Bieber, *The Lords of Trade and Plantations, 1675–1696* (Allenstown, Pa., 1919).

The question of trade, however, brings us to a more consistent priority of the royal government. Whether the attempt to maximize the country's exports while ensuring an adequate flow of imports was always a means to the end of augmenting royal revenue, or was seen as a way of increasing national wealth and prosperity, is something of a circular argument. Setting aside the direct taxes voted by parliament, normally for the armed forces in wartime or during preparations for war, the customs duties on foreign trade, together with the excise taxes levied on certain imported commodities, were immensely important for the buoyancy of the Crown's regular revenue. All this has been admirably spelt out by C. D. Chandaman and need not be repeated here. But the economic and political consequences of the so-called Navigation Acts were not entirely straightforward and predictable. The clauses of these various measures which related to colonial trade, rather than to shipping as such, led to a series of vexatious disagreements between London and Dublin. Whereas there was no doubt that (until 1707) Scotland was excluded from the benefit of the trade laws which prescribed that all colonial imports, wherever their place of origin, must pass through England, and that most of the major colonial export products had to be trans-shipped and pay duty in England, even if they were bound for continental Europe, and that England for this purpose included Wales and Berwick-on-Tweed (but excluded the Isle of Man and the Channel Islands), the status of Ireland was damagingly ambiguous. Indeed, it seems to have changed in this respect on at least three occasions during the course of the reign. The 1660 Act appears to have included Ireland among the permitted destinations for ships carrying colonial exports; then the Act of 1663 prohibited the unloading there of the so-called 'enumerated commodities' (tobacco, sugar and its by-products, dyestuffs, etc.). But the wording of this statute was so unclear that the exclusion of Ireland had to be spelt out again in 1671, with an Act which lapsed in 1680 and which was not re-enacted until 1685. The issue behind all this was that colonial merchants and shipowners wanted Ireland to qualify because one of the estuaries or harbours there was often the nearest and safest haven after the ocean crossing; the Irish government naturally wanted this too because their own revenue farmers or commissioners would thereby collect the duties payable on the goods carried in such ships. On the other side, the English Customs Commissioners, usually backed by the Treasury, insisted that all colonial cargoes must come to England and the duties be paid there; failing that, if ships were genuinely driven into Irish ports by storms, bond must be given, so that the full duty would be payable when they did reach England, none of the cargoes having been unloaded in Ireland. Even after 1680 the Privy Council was sending orders to the Lord Lieutenant and his Council as if the statutory prohibition was still in force. These disputes illustrate how different branches of a government can pull in contrary directions.[25] All this was over and above the strenuous efforts of Edward Randolph, backed by his superior William Blathwayt, to have the trade laws and the shipping clauses observed at the colonial end, above all in New England, and so to increase royal revenue in this way too.[26]

How much difference it would have made if the King had felt like Evelyn and had appointed Sir William Petty to a top financial position is anybody's guess. My own feeling is that he would very quickly have got at odds with other senior ministers and, like Sir William Coventry in 1667–9, would not have lasted long. Petty was a great champion of indirect taxation, which he wanted to be levied on services as well as goods, much like VAT today. The not very successful Law Duties (forerunner of the later Stamp Taxes) of 1671–80 might be seen as an attempt to implement something like this (though not undertaken by Petty). In addition, the longer-lasting Hearth Tax of 1662–89 was a levy of which he strongly approved. According

[25] The fullest account which I have found is in L. W. Harper, *The English Navigation Laws: A Study in Social Engineering* (New York, 1939; repr. 1964), app. 1, p. 397 n. 35; see also L. M. Cullen, *Anglo-Irish Trade, 1660–1800* (Manchester, 1968), 2, 37–8; and refs. in *CTB*, iii–vii (for the order by the King in Council of Feb. 1681, vii. 52–3).

[26] See M. G. Hall, *Edmund Randolph and the American Colonies, 1676–1703* (Chapel Hill, NC, 1960) and Jacobsen, *William Blathwayt*, also S. S. Webb, 'William Blathwayt Imperial Fixer', *William and Mary Q.*, 25 (1968), 3–21 and 26 (1969), 373–415.

to Chandaman, this was just becoming really efficient, while some of the earlier opposition to it had subsided, when it was abolished immediately after the Revolution.[27] Apart from the general unpopularity of what was often called the 'chimney money', another issue which had divided members of the government and MPs was whether industrial forges and furnaces should be assessed: were they 'hearths' within the meaning of the various Acts on which the tax rested? In particular the cutlers of Hallamshire in South Yorkshire maintained a prolonged opposition to having their installations assessed, but it was correctly perceived that if they had their way and were made exempt, the same question would arise with ironmasters and other metal workers elsewhere, Worcestershire and Nottinghamshire being mentioned in particular.[28]

There were three principal administrative innovations during Charles's reign which had major fiscal implications. Two of these have already been discussed: Downing's scheme for Treasury orders or assignments (1665–72), described by Professor Roseveare,[29] and the end of tax-farming, the importance of which some may think I have overestimated. The third was the large-scale and long-lasting increase in the use of *sol* tallies by the Exchequer (which, unlike *pro* tallies, carried no named payee), as in effect a further kind of credit instrument; this has been fully explained by Professor Chandaman, although some of the technicalities are difficult to follow.[30]

Although Chandaman included Issues from the Exchequer (and Assignments on future revenues) in his tables of half-yearly totals, along with those for royal or public revenues, he did not attempt to treat Crown expenditure in any detail.[31] There is plenty of evidence to show awareness by ministers and lesser

[27] C. D. Chandaman, *The English Public Revenue, 1660–1688* (Oxford, 1975), ch. 3.
[28] Ibid., 99–100, 102; *CTB*, v. 159–60, 465–6, 472, 479, 675; ibid., vii. 541–2, 582–3.
[29] See notes on Downing's system in Ch. 4, sect. x, above.
[30] Chandaman, *English Public Revenue*, app. 1, 'The Revenue Accounts, Credit Techniques, and related Exchequer Procedures', 281–302.
[31] Ibid., app. 3, 'Exchequer Receipts and Issues, 1660–1688'. Note too the word *Revenue*, and not Finance, in the title of his book.

officials of the need for economy in public spending, indeed for severe retrenchments. The problem was at least threefold: arising from the King's generosity, where he had more in common with his grandfather than with Charles I; the general level of spending, including what arose from waste and dishonesty; and the Crown's extraordinary commitments, almost exclusively naval and military. In a gloomy, almost plaintive letter to the King, of July 1663, Lord Treasurer Southampton expressed his fear of growing dependence on the House of Commons and thus on the classes represented there, in particular constituents of the borough members.[32] This was followed very shortly by drastic reductions in what was allocated for the royal household and for pensions, although most of these economies were in practice reversed over the next few years. And little more was attempted, let alone achieved, until the appointment of the Treasury Commissioners on Southampton's death in 1667. In July a special Retrenchment Committee was set up, consisting of these Commissioners and five other Privy Councillors. Specific reductions in all the major spending departments were ordered the following January and on 18 March 1668 the Committee laid out a 'list of sums to which the several branches of the revenue [*sic*] are now to be limited'. This was intended to peg ordinary expenditure at £629,568 16s. 8d. annually. All pensions from the Crown were ordered to be stopped in May, and over two years later those of the King's servants whose pay was in arrears were ordered to be paid for one year only; there were certain listed exceptions, while over and above these the King invariably intervened on behalf of those brave men and women (or their families) who had helped him to escape, and so had saved his life, after the battle of Worcester in 1651. An alternative programme of unknown authorship, also dating from 1668, had proposed severe all-round economies, but at the same time the payment of more generous salaries to all the King's servants, at the price of perquisites and other gains from office being abolished; perhaps not surprisingly, this scheme was

---

[32] Dorset Record Office, Fox–Strangways papers, D/FS I, Box 272, 3rd vol., fo. 47r–v.

never pursued further. Yet a third, variant set of proposals can be dated to the same year.[33]

Naturally none of this was happening in a political vacuum. The Dutch War came to an end in 1667, but this led to the additional costs of demobilization; having rejected the Accounts Commission issued by the King in March 1667, the House of Commons insisted on the appointment of independent 'Commissioners for taking public accounts', who were to continue in being for up to three years and to report on their findings.[34] Of the nine individuals appointed to this body, none was a member of the House of Lords and only three were sitting MPs; none was a central office-holder, although one (Giles Dunster) was later to hold a senior position in the Excise and another (Sir George Savile, Bart.) was to attain the highest ministerial level (when he was Earl, then Marquis of Halifax). The Commissioners were specifically charged with discovering whether money which had been voted by parliament for the carrying on of the Dutch War had been diverted and misused for other purposes. Their final report is a slightly disappointing, anti-climactic document, but none the ess repays careful reading. It was only signed by five of the original nine Commissioners, and a committee of the House of Lords rejected their accusations against Sir George Carteret (as Navy Treasurer) in two overwhelming votes of eleven and ten to one. The prorogation of parliament on 19 December 1669 then brought all proceedings to an end.[35] This must also be put into the context of ministerial changes: the fall of Clarendon and the formation of the so-called 'Cabal' ministry. A special Irish Retrenchment Committee of Privy Councillors and others was appointed in January 1668,[36] criticisms of Ormonde for his fail-

[33] CSPD, 1667, p. 338; 1667–8, pp. 202, 287–8, 292 (PRO, SP 29/236/193, i–vi); CTB, ii, 336, ibid., iii. 620; ibid., vii. 1651–2, and app., ibid., v. 2646–50 (both calendared with Treasury Books of 1680s but clearly belonging to 1668).

[34] Statutes of the Realm, v. 624–7; CSPD, 1667–8, p. 90 (see Kenyon, Stuart Constitution, 392); for the King's earlier, abortive commission, see Lords Journals, xii. 54, 57; PRO, SO 3/16, p. 83.

[35] HMC, Eighth Report, app., pp. 128–9 and annexed doc. pp. 129–33; Lords Journals, xii. 255, et seq.

[36] CTB, ii. 232.

ure to control expenditure more effectively, for his alleged condoning of profligacy if not corruption among his subordinates, and for his own possible involvement in such malpractices, all formed part of the ostensible grounds for his recall and replacement as Lord Lieutenant, which was followed by the appointment of a powerful Council committee, from which he was pointedly excluded, to investigate all aspects of royal finances in Ireland since the Restoration; this body was in turn succeeded by a standing Commission on Irish Affairs, of which he was still not a member as late as September 1672, though he was added to it the next month.[37]

Not long after the presentation of the Accounts Commissioners' report, the two Treaties of Dover were signed, and the country once again committed to preparing for war against the Dutch. In all this, Crown servants such as Pepys and Fox were important executive instruments, but except for Downing as Treasury Secretary (and then as Ambassador to the Netherlands States-General), there is no evidence that any of them took any part in formulating or initiating this new policy. Moreover, on the strictly financial side of government, partly because written records do not show individuals talking to themselves, or even discussing things with a single colleague (in this case the Chancellor of the Exchequer), there is less evidence about plans for controlling, let alone reducing expenditure under Lord Treasurers Clifford (1672–3) and Danby (1673–9). With the return to a Board of Treasury Commissioners (in 1679–84) this was to change again. Perhaps because of growing doubts about the competence, if not the probity of the two Edward Griffins (father and son), as successive Treasurers of the Chamber, attention was now focused more sharply on the Household above Stairs than had been the case earlier. Although in itself trivial, it was symptomatic that the Keepers of the royal cormorants were still extant in 1679, although their suppression had been ordered in 1667; strict orders for a much reduced Chamber establishment were issued in September 1680. Another small, if not exactly corroboratory piece of evidence

[37] PRO, SP 44/34, fos. 182v–90r; *CSPD, 1672–3*, p. 39.

relates to one of the offshoots or sub-departments of the Chamber. Sir Gilbert Talbot, the long-serving Master of the Jewel House, reckoned that the value of his office had been cut by £1,300 p.a. over the twenty years 1660 to 1680.[38] The Mint, the Tower, and the Ordnance Office were likewise the objects of Treasury scrutiny leading to reforms, during the last years of the reign. At the time of his death, Charles II's finances were in a healthier state than they had ever been before, at least until 1684. And, whatever their political and psychological impact may have been, the notorious French subsidies played only a modest part in this recovery; gross receipts in *livres* were equivalent to an average of c.£75,000 p.a. in the 1670s, rising to just over £80,000 p.a. in 1681–5.[39]

In some areas of what we should today think of as national policy, more depended on those involved at the local level, and on private generosity, than on direct state intervention from the centre. This was largely true of poor relief, of measures taken to avoid famine conditions arising after harvest failures, and of steps taken to maintain fuel supplies in exceptionally cold winter weather. Attempts to prevent any further outbreaks of the plague after the terrible final visitation of 1665–6 did require vigilance and strict enforcement by customs officials and others in the seaports, organized on a national basis.[40] Action during and after the Great Fire of London in September 1666 affected officials, such as Pepys and others, including the central bureaucracies of the London Customs and the Excise, both of which had lost their premises. Special priority was given to the building of a new Customs House, but basically the rebuilding of London involved what would today be called the interface between the public and private sectors. Granted that Christopher Wren's and others' proposals for a fundamentally

[38] *CTB*, vii. 1648, 1664; ibid., vi. 687; 'Memoir upon the King's Jewel House by Sir Gilbert Talbot', ed. H. Ellis, *Archaeologia*, 22 (1829), 114–23.

[39] For a succinct, and to the best of my understanding definitive, treatment see Chandaman, *English Public Revenue*, 134–5.

[40] Paul Slack, *The Impact of Plague in Tudor and Stuart England* (1986), esp. ch. 12; for the contrast with other forms of social amelioration see his *From Reformation to Improvement: Public Welfare in Early Modern England* (Oxford, 1999).

new layout of the city were not to be realized, the speed and completeness of physical reconstruction and attendant economic recovery were truly remarkable. In the aftermath of the Fire, certain of the Judges incurred additional responsibilities in the special Fire Court; as was pointed out many years ago, the heaviest burden in this was borne by two ex-Cromwellians and one ex-neutral (John Archer and Christopher Turnor, and Matthew Hale respectively).[41]

At this stage, the reader may fairly expect some assessment of the contribution made by office-holders, below the top level of councillors and ministers, to the various branches of state activity. In this regard, it is surely the central secretariat, the armed forces, the nascent colonial empire, and the revenue administration, together with the system of public credit, which stand out. Many of the most interesting among the major figures involved in these areas, have I hope already been sufficiently discussed.

The areas where Charles II's government could be said to have been least successful were religion and the succession. To put it crudely, the King lost on points in the former case, and won (in the short-run) by a knock-out in the latter. The price which he paid to save Danby's life and to defeat the Exclusionists entailed losing some of his ablest and most valuable servants, temporarily including Stephen Fox. Whether or not he ended his reign with a more efficient administration, to underpin his policies, than he had started with, remains open to debate. J. R. Western thought so, and saw this as an important factor in the potential which existed for a successful royal absolutism. On this score we may perhaps end by quoting the great Marquis of Halifax in one of his political essays: 'An exact Administration, and good choice of proper Instruments doth insensibly make the Government in a manner absolute without assuming it.' However, in another essay, appearing in his papers just before this one, he had also pointed out:

If men of Business did not forget how apt the tools are to break or fail, they would shut up shop. They must use things called *Men* under

---

[41] T. F. Reddaway, *The Rebuilding of London after the Great Fire* (1940; 2nd rev. edn., 1951); *Pepys Diary*, x, *Companion*, 138–40, 517–18, 632–5.

them, who will spoil the best Scheme that can be drawn by Human Understanding.[42]

III. CONTINENTAL PARALLELS?

Use of the phrase 'royal absolutism' suggests the need for a comparative view across later seventeenth-century Europe. Charles II's contemporaries included his cousin Louis XIV of France, Frederick William (the 'Great Elector') of Brandenburg-Prussia, Charles XI of Sweden, Frederick III and then Christian V of Denmark, and Leopold I of Austria. It seems worth exploring, even at a superficial level, the similarities and differences between these states and England, to see whether any meaningful parallels can be found.

The recovery of the French monarchy after the disturbances of the Fronde (1648–53), followed by the so-called Personal Rule of Louis XIV from 1661, suggests at a first glance a definite resemblance to the Restoration in England. But Colbert's great drive to reduce the number and significance of venal office-holders, even if its effects were largely to be reversed later, has no parallel even in the work of the Treasury Commission of 1667–72. Moreover the French Estates General had not met since 1614, and the practical limits to royal power were different from those experienced by any English ruler—whether Charles I, Cromwell, Charles II, James II, or William III. The size and diversity of France, the continuing strength of provincial institutions, and (according to some historians) the effects of faction and venality within the royal court and the central administration constituted features for which there was no parallel on this side of the Channel, unless perhaps in the resistance met by James II in the county lieutenancies and commissions of the peace, to his policies during 1686–8. Whatever the

[42] George Savile, Marquis of Halifax, 'Political Thoughts and Reflections', in *Complete Works*, ed. W. Raleigh (Oxford, 1912), 219 and 218; J. R. Western, *Monarchy and Revolution: The English State in the 1680s* (1972), esp. chs. 3–5, a posthumous work of much insight and originality.

force of these restraints on the effectiveness of the central government and on the king's unfettered power, it is not necessary for us to enter here into the debate as to how absolute a ruler Louis really was. Common sense tells us that his power was of a different order from anything attained by the English monarchy, even in the 1680s. Which country was the better governed is quite another question, and one which involves too many value judgements to allow of any simple answer. To give but one example, the speed and efficiency with which Colbert and other servants of the King built up the French navy was the envy of English ministers and officials. On the other hand, Louis's constant wars, and the overburdening of French society with excessive taxation and military service which resulted, can leave little if any doubt in which of the two countries most ordinary people would have preferred to live. Moreover the persecution of the Protestant, Huguenot, minority in the 1670s and 1680s, exceeded in both severity and scale the measures taken in England against either ex-Puritan dissenters and Quakers or Catholics (except for the actual victims of the Popish Plot hysteria, which could be said to have demonstrated the English monarchy's weakness rather than its strength).[43]

The rulers of the time who most indisputably achieved an increase in monarchical power were the successive kings of Denmark and the Great Elector of Brandenburg-Prussia. In the Danish case this was initially fuelled by an anti-noble reaction, to which we might conceivably find a parallel in Yorkist or early Tudor England, but categorically not in that of Charles II. In the case of Frederick William's scattered and varied dominions, his crucial victories were over the provincial and particularly the urban institutions which stood in the way of his taxing powers. As with the French *intendants*, the role of centrally appointed administrators at the local level has only the most limited and partial parallels in the case of England.

The Swedish experience was a little more complicated. The

---

[43] The literature is vast and its flow shows no sign of diminishing. For a general overview see R. Bonney, *L'Absolutisme* (Paris, 1989), and—putting the case most strongly for the limits on royal power—Roger Mettam, *Power and Faction in Louis XIV's France* (Oxford, 1988).

Crown undoubtedly achieved a recovery of power under
Charles XI, initially at least with the support of almost all social
groups and classes except the high nobility, who were felt (probably rightly) to have abused their position during the long
minorities of Christina and Charles himself, punctuated only by
the short interval of Charles X's reign. The Swedish monarchy's
advance towards near absolutism in the 1670s and 1680s was
not a myth or an optical illusion, but its brittle nature was to
become evident in the reign of Charles XII, and even more so
with the return to constitutional government after his death in
1718.[44]

The successes achieved by Leopold I in consolidating control
over his empire were likewise real and not illusory. But the
extraordinary diversity of his dominions makes any attempt at
a close comparison extremely tenuous. It may be tempting to
equate Austria with England, Hungary with Scotland, and
Bohemia-Moravia with Ireland, in a kind of three-kingdoms or
multiple-monarchies model. But we soon run up against difficulties in this: the Habsburgs were more nearly absolute in their
own home territories of Austria, and more restricted by the
continuing power of the estates in Hungary, the exact opposite
of the Scottish-English situation. The conquest and rigorous
subordination of the Czech lands after 1618–20 does provide a
closer parallel with the fate of Ireland after the attempted war
of liberation in the 1640s, but even this breaks down if we look
at the religious situation in the two cases. Insofar as the Czech
resistance to Austrian rule had been partly motivated by religious differences, the remains of Hussitism and the more recent

    [44] K. J. V. Jespersen, 'Absolute Monarchy in Denmark: Change and
Continuity', *Scandinavian J. Hist.*, 12 (1987), 307–16; T. Munck, *The
Peasantry and the Early Absolute Monarchy in Denmark, 1660–1708*
(Copenhagen, 1979); F. L. Carsten, *The Origins of Prussia* (Oxford, 1954),
chs. 13–16, and F. L. Carsten (ed.), *The New Cambridge Modern History*, v,
The Ascendancy of France, 1648–88 (Cambridge, 1961), ch. 23; id., 'The Rise
of Brandenburg'; Michael Roberts (ed.), *Sweden's Age of Greatness,
1632–1719* (London, 1973), and Roberts, *Essays in Swedish History* (London,
1967); Ragnhild Hatton, *Charles XII of Sweden* (London, 1968); Arne
Losman, Agnete Lundström, and Margarete Revera (eds.), *The Age of New
Sweden* (Stockholm, 1988).

Protestant elements there were thoroughly suppressed, if not actually extirpated, following the victory of the Habsburgs and the Counter-Reformation Catholic Church. By contrast, even the most brutal agendas for English rule in Ireland did not seriously envisage the complete destruction of the Catholic religion; indeed, the English knew, even if they were reluctant to admit this openly, that the great majority of the Irish people would never convert to Protestantism. Here, as in Poland from the late eighteenth to the late twentieth century, the Catholic faith of the people was in effect the form assumed by ethnic and cultural nationalism in resistance to alien rule. According to the most recent and best history of the Habsburg monarchy, there was relatively little by way of ethnic feeling between Germans and Czechs; furthermore, if socio-economic changes are taken into account, as well as more narrowly constitutional ones, the greatest beneficiaries following the destruction of Bohemian autonomy were the great nobles, Czech as well as German. This seems to bear only slight comparison with the conflict of Saxon and Gael in Ireland. The Hungarian-Scottish parallel has a little more cogency in this respect, since surviving Calvinism was linked to the stubborn defence of Magyar constitutional rights against Habsburg centralization. But the further that we pursue this line of thought, the more artificial does any close, sustained comparison between Charles and Leopold become.[45]

To take this kind of inquiry any further, we need to identify the elements which most sharply differentiated these various state systems from that of Restoration England. The relative efficiency and honesty of the Crown's servants, as these have been defined here, while obviously one important factor, was by no means the only one, or even necessarily the most decisive. In determining the potential for absolutism, we must also take into account the monarch's law-making capacity and ability to raise taxes without being fettered by representative institutions, even where these still existed; the relations of centre and locality, and

[45] R. J. W. Evans, *The Making of the Habsburg Monarchy, 1550–1700: An Interpretation* (Oxford, 1979), for the Emperor Leopold, ch. 4, and more generally on 'The Centre and the Regions', pt. 2, chs. 5–8; also J. P. Spielman, *Leopold I of Austria* (London, 1977).

in particular the presence or otherwise of centrally appointed magistrates, tax collectors, and other functionaries at the local level; and finally the role of the military within the territorial state as well as on its frontiers.[46] In the English case, we are brought back to the excise collectors and other lesser officials, and in the seaports to the customs service, as portents of things to come, albeit that even by the 1680s the excise administration was still only at a formative stage.

We must also beware of being too mechanical in the application of such criteria. Many of these apparent prerequisites for successful royal absolutism can also be found in later seventeenth-century Spain; yet the mainspring of effective governance at the top was sadly lacking under Charles II, Spain's last Habsburg monarch. At the other extreme, the constitutional structure of the United Provinces of the independent Netherlands was so utterly different, being more like that of a confederation than a unitary state, that any attempt to work out parallels or comparisons is probably futile, although its economy was even more advanced than that of England and its culture more distinctively bourgeois. Such superficial and no doubt rash generalizations as those offered here will serve to demonstrate the limits of what can be achieved by comparing the central bureaucracies and their personnel in different countries at around the same date, even when some of the problems experienced by the respective states and their rulers do not look so very different.

---

[46] Wolfgang Reinhard (ed.), *Power Elites and State Building* (Oxford, for the European Science Foundation, 1996), ch. 4: Aylmer, 'Centre and Locality: The Nature of Power Elites', and ch. 6, Robert Descimon, 'Power Elites and the Prince: The State as Enterprise'. In fairness, it should be pointed out that the series, in which this is one of seven volumes, on *The Origins of the Modern State in Europe*, was intended to cover the whole time span from the thirteenth to the eighteenth centuries. For a non-specialist trying to keep track of the most important works appearing on European history, the Historical Association's *Annual Bulletin of Historical Literature* (var. eds. (London to 1973; Oxford 1974–)) is an invaluable guide.

IV. BUREAUCRACY, SOCIAL STRUCTURE, AND THE STATE

Many points of likeness and difference between the Crown's servants of 1660–85 and the King's servants of 1625–42 or the State's servants of 1649–60 have already been suggested in earlier chapters and in section II of this one.

To go much further in this direction is inevitably to offer more opinions than facts. The contrast with those nearer in time is the easier to draw. Historians who see the Cromwellian Protectorate as having been halfway or more back to hereditary monarchy will tend to emphasize the continuity of policies, methods, and personnel in 1660. That at least thirty-seven out of 127 of the State's servants known to have been alive in May 1660 (from a random sample of 200), and twenty out of a selection of 100 particularly important republican administrators were to hold office at some time after the Restoration might seem to support such an interpretation.[47] Yet the differences are surely much more striking. With obvious and important individual exceptions, Charles II's servants were more upper-class, less puritan, less self-made, and less committed to ideals of public service than the men of 1649–60. While their enemies often emphasized hypocrisy as the sovereign failing of the Puritans, there were certainly Anglican and Catholic hypocrites too; moreover, genuinely sincere and upright individuals can likewise be found across the chronological and ideological divides.

Comparing the servants of Charles II with those of his father lends itself to less by way of clear contrasts. In spite of cuts in the size of the household departments, and the abolition of the prerogative courts (including the Court of Wards and Liveries), there were more of them. The moves away from life tenure and the tendency towards higher salaries, which could both be seen as legacies of the parliamentarian-republican administrative system, may have made the Crown's servants after 1660 more susceptible to political pressure from above. At no time before

---

[47] Aylmer, *State's Servants*, tables 26 (p. 196) and 41 (p. 208).

1687–8 did the later Stuart kings forfeit the loyal support of so many of their servants as Charles I had of his by 1640–2. Those holding office after the Restoration might be characterized as having been more knowing, more easy-going, less well educated (in spite of the Royal Society)more sectarian but less deeply religious than their predecessors before the Civil War. Not living in a period of monetary inflation, they were under less financial pressure; but in both eras family circumstances, the accidents of mortality, and the attributes of character and personality were frequently decisive in determining the fortunes of individuals and their dependants. The relative profitability of land and the alternative sources of wealth changed significantly. Over the course of sixty years a wider choice of career patterns had opened up with the growth of empire and of the armed forces; the other professions were still small, except for the law and the church, but there were more architects, surveyors, and book-keepers or accountants, and probably more medics than earlier in the century. While the King's servants of 1625–42 had the Commission on Exacted Fees and Innovated Offices and the proponents of 'Thorough' to keep them on their toes, the Crown's servants of 1660–85 had for parts of the reign the Treasury Commissioners and briefly the Public Accounts Commissioners breathing down their necks. None of Charles II's ministers inspired as much fear as Thomas Wentworth Earl of Strafford had done, but both Clarendon and Danby in their time perhaps aroused as much hatred.

Patronage and connection remained the most powerful influences on appointment and promotion. If age at entry to office was on average slightly higher in 1660–3 than in 1625–42, this was due to the forced interruption in the careers of many royalists during the intervening years. In all three epochs, office-holding was a more generally positive factor for enhancing people's status than for making them dramatically richer. None of the three regimes was what is nowadays sometimes called a 'kleptocracy'. On the other hand none would have met the standards required in the public service today, or even those which were gradually established from the 1780s to the 1870s; the State's servants of 1649–60 came nearer to doing so, at least in some respects. By definition we cannot know what the system and its personnel as it existed in the 1630s would have looked like by the 1660s–1680s without the intervening events of 1640–60. Beyond reasonable doubt, the Restoration and its aftermath constituted a successful counter-revolution, but a return to things exactly as they had been was impossible. If we take into account the individuals and methods carried over from the 1650s, the commitment to a maritime empire and the continued shift away from household government, the Interregnum had a positive legacy as well as generating a reaction against puritanism, republicanism, and military rule. Insofar as Charles II's regime was more secure at the end of his reign than at the beginning, the two most obvious reasons were the exclusionist Whigs having overreached themselves and the much greater buoyancy of the revenues resulting from peace and relative prosperity, although fiscal and administrative changes had also contributed to the King's new-found solvency.

When I was studying the servants of Charles I back in the later 1950s, the intellectual climate was very different from that of today. In my own case, one seminal influence was the work of the then Yugoslav dissident, Milovan Djilas. His book, *The New Class*, like James Burnham's *The Managerial Revolution* and other works in the same genre, argued strongly and persuasively that control of the state apparatus and management of the means of production were more important than the actual ownership of property in determining the distribution of power in modern societies. From a quite different and more technically academic direction, there was the impact of G. R. Elton's first (and in some respects most original) book, *The Tudor Revolution in Government*, which postulated a decisive shift having taken place towards a more bureaucratic and departmentalized central government in England under the direction of Thomas Cromwell in the 1530s. In addition to this, it seemed necessary to test the challenging hypothesis of H. R. Trevor-Roper (now Lord Dacre) that office-holding and court connections were the crucial elements in improving the fortunes of the landed gentry, rather than entrepreneurial skills and frugality, as R. H. Tawney and Lawrence Stone had proposed. The years

1625 to 1642 also needed to be set in a longer-run chronological perspective, and England had to be considered comparatively, in relation to other states of early-modern Europe, besides drawing more remote parallels in time and place. Since then it has become clearer to me that bureaucracy, if not in Karl Marx's sense a fragment of 'false consciousness', is more a circular or fluctuating historical phenomenon than one characterized by linear development.[48] Meanwhile, when I was completing my study of the State's Servants of 1649–1660, around 1970, my concern was in large part to see how far the men and the methods of republican rule differed from those of royal administration before the Civil War. But this was against a background of changing priorities within my own subject, with the growth of interest in local, social, and cultural history. At the turn of the twentieth and twenty-first centuries, the intellectual climate is again much changed. But even if traditional political, constitutional, and administrative history seem to be even further out of fashion, a revival of interest in the State has certainly been evident during the last ten or twenty years.

And in that context, the place of the years 1660 to 1685 in the history of the English State and of the nascent British Empire still seems to be of enough interest and importance, even—dare I say it—of enough contemporary relevance, to merit closer scrutiny. As my old tutor Christopher Hill was fond of saying, the historian should concentrate on trying to explain what did happen in the past, rather than what did not happen. So, whether or not it was inevitable being left to speculation, we must accept the fact of the Restoration and of all that followed from it. We must accept too that, while Charles II defeated his opponents and was thus succeeded by his brother, and not by his nephew and niece or by his own illegitimate son, James II soon came unstuck and was replaced by William III and Mary II in 1688–9, with all the further consequences which flowed from this. It has become fashionable among some historians to speak and write of the 'long eighteenth century', extending from

[48] For a further attempt to work out some of these problems see Aylmer, 'Bureaucracy', in *New Cambridge Modern History*, xiii, *Companion Volume*, ed. Peter Burke (Cambridge, 1979), ch. 6.

1688, or even from 1660, all the way to 1832. This has included playing down the importance of the Revolution Settlement and its aftermath. First advanced by J. P. Kenyon, this argument has been taken much further by Professor Jonathan Clark. In his most recent pronouncement, 'state formation' is explicitly limited to territorial definition and consolidation. I have tried, clearly in vain so far as Professor Clark is concerned, to make the case for a wider, more comprehensive meaning.[49] While exceedingly difficult to define at all precisely, the case for the state as 'culturally formative' remains compelling. Be this as it may, even if the social, religious, and constitutional consequences of the Revolution in 1688 are thought to have been exaggerated by so-called Whig historians, we still have to explain the rise of England, subsequently of Great Britain, to world power. If the administrative underpinning for this process was already well laid, at least in part, by the end of Charles II's reign, thanks to the work of those discussed here, the necessary fiscal reconstruction was still substantially to be achieved after 1688. As already intimated, we cannot know whether or not the creation of the national debt and the Bank of England, the evolution of the Land Tax, the extension of the Customs and above all of the Excise revenues would all have happened under James II and James III; the fact is that these developments did come about under William and Mary and their successors. Professor Clark is clever enough to have foreseen these objections to his argument and to have fore-armed himself against them; some of his followers and admirers I fear may not be.

Much has been made in several recent books and articles of the enhanced military capacity of the English, and then British state, arising from its much increased financial strength. This in turn rested on the twin pillars of heavier taxation and the

---

[49] J. C. D. Clark, *English Society, 1688–1832: Ideology, Social Structure and Political Practice during the Ancien Regime* (Cambridge, 1985); and, most recently, 'Protestantism, Nationalism and National Identity, 1660–1832', *Hist. J.*, 43 (2000), 249–76, esp. 249–50; for a different approach see Aylmer, 'The Peculiarities of the English State', *J. Hist. Sociol.*, 3 (1989), 91–108, and Philip Corrigan and Derek Sayer, *The Great Arch: State Formation, Cultural Revolution and the Rise of Capitalism* (Oxford, 1986).

creation of the Bank and the long-term funded debt. For understanding the new financial system of the 1690s and after, the
works of Professor P. G. M. Dickson and of Dr D. W. Jones are
fundamental, with a longer chronological perspective being
provided by the articles of Professor Patrick O'Brien, the most
relevant of which has already been cited in Chapter 3 above. But
it is Professor John Brewer's strikingly original and on the whole
very persuasive book, *The Sinews of Power*, covering the years
1688 to 1783, which has been most influential in its use of the
term 'military-fiscal' or 'fiscal-military' state. Some historians of
continental Europe have used the phrase 'from domain to tax
state', to describe the long-term transition between the thirteenth and the eighteenth centuries. As a broad and general
description of the changes in the fiscal basis of government this
is unexceptionable. On the other hand, the term 'military-fiscal
state' applied to Hanoverian Britain is in slight danger of hard-
ening into a shibboleth. For all the war-making capacity demonstrated from 1689 to 1815 and the imperial and naval
hegemony to which the country attained—and which it was to
retain until the later nineteenth century—Britain was hardly a
'military state' in the same sense as Frederickan Prussia or
Bonapartist France. In the subsequent collaborative volume, on
Britain and Germany, which he has jointly edited, Professor
Brewer has contributed an extremely interesting social analysis
of eighteenth-century revenue officers—to be precise of excise
officials out 'in the field' rather than the bureaucrats at headquarters. Moreover, in his own and other chapters there is an
altogether more subtly nuanced treatment of these problems,
besides very generous acknowledgement to my own writings.[50]

Other, more recent contributors to these debates have tended
to push the chronological emphasis further back, into the mid-

[50] P. G. M. Dickson, *The Financial Revolution, 1689–1756* (London, 1967);
D. W. Jones, *War and Economy in the Age of William III and Marlborough*
(Oxford, 1988); John Brewer, *The Sinews of Power: War, Money and the
English State, 1688–1783* (London, 1989); J. Brewer and Eckhart Hellmuth
(eds.), *Rethinking Leviathan: The Eighteenth-century State in Britain and
Germany* (Oxford, for the German Historical Institute, London, 1999). Note
also valuable chs. by Thomas Ertman, John Childs, Joanna Innes, Paul
Langford, and others.

seventeenth if not the later sixteenth century. This has required heavy reliance on being able to construct reliable indices for the quantitative burden of the state on society, using the figures arrived at by Professor O'Brien and Dr Hunt (cited here, in Chapter 3, section XVII) in combination with those in histories of public finance (Chandaman for 1660–88) or else taken direct from Exchequer and other public records. Without wishing to downgrade the importance of the Civil Wars (of 1642–52), the three Anglo-Dutch Wars (of 1652–74), the second Anglo-Spanish War (of 1655–60), or even the first one (of 1587–1604), there is a danger of slipping unintentionally into a kind of teleological determinism here, as much as there is in political and constitutional history (according to revisionist critiques of so-called Whig and Marxist historians). The development of the new revenue and credit system, the enhanced role of parliament and the continued shift towards ministerial and away from royal government cannot be thought of as a continuous process from 1588 or even from 1640 to 1714 and after. Britain's rise to global power remains a more difficult historical phenomenon to explain than her subsequent decline from the 1880s to the 1960s. Drs Braddick and Wheeler have both made valuable contributions to this ongoing debate; whether they have permanently changed the whole historiographical landscape it is too soon to say. Many historians have helped us towards a better understanding of the issues involved. Besides those authors already mentioned, the first two volumes of the *Oxford History of the British Empire* ought also to be read and pondered.[51]

In conclusion we should return briefly to central government and its personnel. Apart from the works of Professors Beattie

[51] Michael J. Braddick, *The Nerves of State: Taxation and the Financing of the English State, 1558–1714* (Manchester, 1996); James Scott Wheeler, *The Making of a World Power: War and the Military Revolution in Seventeenth-century England* (Thrupp, 1999); *Oxford History of the British Empire* (gen. ed. William Roger Louis), i. Nicholas Canny (ed.), *The Origins of Empire: British Overseas Enterprise to the Close of the Seventeenth Century* (Oxford, 1998), ii, Peter J. Marshall (ed.), (Oxford, 1998). Dr Braddick's newest book, *State Formation in Early Modern England, c.1550–1700* (Cambridge, 2000) opts for a 'long seventeenth century' and, in his own words, 'is principally concerned with the impact of the state in English villages and wards' (p. 27).

and Bucholz on the royal household and Professor Baugh on the navy,[52] we still lack sufficiently detailed studies for the first half of the eighteenth century (or indeed, if preferred, for the period from 1689 to 1760) to make possible any detailed estimate of continuity or contrast with the men and methods of Charles and James IIs' time. There are valuable studies of the Land Tax administration by Professors W. R. Ward and Colin Brooks,[53] but that arm of the eighteenth-century financial structure was always exceptional in being more in the hands of local landowners, that is to say run mainly by amateurs, compared with the Excise and the Customs, which were emphatically not run by metropolitan and provincial businessmen; hence the particular value of Brewer's work on excise officers. Geoffrey Holmes's chapter on civil administrators in his study of the period 1680–1730 is really too general and impressionistic to provide a substitute, while my own articles looking forward into the eighteenth century are too slight to support any firm hypothesis.[54] In the latest volume of the *New Oxford History of England* series, Dr Julian Hoppit takes a very favourable view of the growing state bureaucracy after 1688. He may be right to do so; however, Lowndes, Blathwayt, and Godolphin are the only individuals whom he names, and he also records the malversation by James Brydges, first Duke of Chandos, to the tune of £600,000, as Paymaster of the Forces.[55] The works of

---

[52] J. M. Beattie, *The English Court in the Reign of George I* (Cambridge, 1967); R. O. Bucholz, *The Augustan Court: Queen Anne and the Decline of Court Culture* (Stanford, Calif., 1993); Daniel Baugh, *British Naval Administration in the Age of Walpole* (Princeton, NJ, 1965).

[53] W. R. Ward, *The English Land Tax in the Eighteenth Century* (Oxford, 1953); Colin Brooks, 'Public Finance and Political Stability: The Administration of the Land Tax, 1688–1720', *Hist. J.*, 17 (1974), 281–300.

[54] Geoffrey Holmes, *Augustan England: Professions, State and Society, 1680–1730* (London, 1982), chs. 8 and 9; Aylmer, 'Office-holding, Wealth and Social Structure, c.1580–c.1720', in F. Braudel (ed.), *Domanda e Consumi: Livelli e Strutture (nei secoli XIII–XVIII)* (Florence, 1978), given as a paper at the Datini Institute in Prato, 1974; 'From Office-holding to Civil Service: The Genesis of Modern Bureaucracy', *TRHS*, 5th ser., 30 (1980), 91–108.

[55] Julian Hoppit, *A Land of Liberty? England, 1689–1727* (New Oxford History of England (gen. ed. J. M. Roberts) Oxford, 2000), 125–6, 377. There were certainly other administrative scandals in the 1690s, but this is not the time or place to discuss them at length.

Professor Paul Langford have a great deal else to tell us about
the eighteenth century, but not much about the kind of men in
the service of the Crown as it has been defined here.[56]
Without, I hope, reading too much into his invaluable studies,
there is a suspicion at least that it was becoming more difficult
for those without property or the right connections to get very
far, than had been the case in the seventeenth century. Had
society at least in this respect become slightly more oligarchic?
That must not lead us to exaggerate its openness before 1689
(except perhaps from 1642 to 1660). My own guess is that the
navy and the revenue services at least did remain relatively
open to talent, and that otherwise Britain's rise to world
power could simply not have come about.

Looking back briefly, rather than forward, how should we
sum up? Given the extraordinary parsimony of the Queen
herself and the shocking meanness of her parliaments and her
taxpaying subjects, we must continue to marvel at the achievements of the Elizabethans, even if state power and personal
profit through privateering often became dangerously
confused.[57] As to the early Stuarts, the Ship Money fleets were
among the more remarkable successes of Charles I's rule without parliament, though much good this did him. The whole of
the Interregnum, in particular the years of republican rule from
1649 to 1653, continues to stand out, not as aberrant so much
as unique: for all the English Republic's failings and limitations, a door was briefly ajar, sliding to again under the
Protectorate, and then slammed firmly shut in 1660. Yet not so
as to put the clock back to 1640; fortunately that is never
possible in history. The part played by one-time servants of the
Long Parliament, the Commonwealth, and Oliver in the service
of Charles II, and the continuing measure of openness to talent
have, I hope, been adequately documented in these pages. It is
sometimes said that countries get the governments which they

[56] Paul Langford, *A Polite and Commercial People, England 1727–1783*
(ibid., Oxford, 1989), and id., *Public Life and the Propertied Englishman
1689–1798* (Oxford, 1991).
[57] Penry Williams, *The Later Tudors, 1547–1603* (ibid., Oxford, 1995).

deserve—an excessively harsh judgement on humanity, so it has always seemed to me. Do rulers and governments get the servants that *they* deserve? With all faults, as the saying goes, maybe so.

Index

Monck, George (*cont.*):
  and Lord Lieutenancy of Ireland
    12, 51
  and restoration of Charles II 12,
    163
  illus. **Pl. 20**
Monmouth, Duke of, *see* James,
    Duke of Monmouth
Monmouthshire 141
Montagu, Edward, Earl of
    Manchester 12, 81, 157, 199
Montagu, Edward, 1st Earl of
    Sandwich 11, 12, 21, 82, 83,
    114, 116, 150, 199, 224, 228
  as Ambassador 187
Montagu, Ralph 186, 192
monuments, funeral 126, 127, 128,
    129
  of office-holders at: Ashburnham,
    East Sussex 128; Christ's
    College, Cambridge 130;
    Croome, Worcs. 130; Farley,
    Wilts. 126; Jesus College,
    Cambridge 130; Ramsbury,
    Wilts. 128; Ravenstone,
    Bucks. 130; St Olave's
    London 130
Moore, Jonas, snr 184, 185
Moore, Jonas, jnr 184
Morgan, William, *et al.* 141, 142
Morland, Sir Samuel 150
Morrice, William 12, 154
Mounteney, Richard 107, 205
music 25, 130, 217
  Master of the King's 70
musicians, court 25
  amateur 218, 238

Narborough, Sir John 179
national income (NI) 133–4, 136
Navigation Act(s) 32, 54, 250, 256
Navy the 44, 62, 73, 139, 145–6,
    180
  benefits in kind for officials 110
  Charles II, interest in 66–7
  officials' absence 98
  officials' salaries 136
  seagoing officers 106
  secrets, naval 180, 182
  shore administration 139

supplies 111
technicians in 184
wages, unpaid 36
Navy Commissioners of 63, 110,
    111, 139, 159, 179–83, 197,
    252, 254
  as Comptroller of Victualling
    Accounts 49
  extra, in charge of royal dock-
    yards 180
Navy Office or Board 46, 47, 49,
    100, 101
  office location 100–101
  officials of: Clerk of the Acts 46,
    73, 130, 140; Clerk of the
    Cheque 48; Comptroller 46;
    Inspector of Naval Accounts
    112; Master Attendant 48;
    Master Shipwrights 48, 73;
    Ship's Cook 98; Storekeeper
    48, 77, 237; Surveyor 47,
    181; Treasurer 46, 102, 103,
    158, 224, 260; Victualler 80
  see also Admiralty, Lord
    Admiral; Pepys, Samuel
  illus. **Pl. 11**
Navy Victualling 80
  contractors 209, 252
  farming of 48
  office 48
Neale, Thomas 213, 218
Neile, Sir Paul 218, 237
Netherlands, The 17, 32, 179, 191,
    193, 201, 238, 252, 261,
    268
New College, Oxford 76
New York 53
Newcastle 33
Newmarket 67, 99, 100, 251
Newton, Sir Isaac 41
Nicholas, Sir Edward 11, 12, 76,
    158, 198, 199
Nicholas, Sir John 198–9
Nicholson, Francis 176
Norfolk 191
North, Council of the 55
North, Sir Dudley 206
North, Francis, Baron Guildford 18,
    125, 206, 217, 221
North, Roger 125, 126, 176, 206

Whitehall 15, 48, 67, 100, 193
  illus. **Pl. 8, 9**
Whitley, Col. Roger 39, 40, 80, 83,
  116, 230–6, 253
widows 39, 56, 85, 86, 115, 118,
  151, 218
Wildman, John 38, 235
William, Prince of Orange 20, 157
  and Mary 165, 175, 176, 195,
  235, 272
William III 67, 82, 94, 128, 134,
  137, 186, 210, 264
Williamson, Sir Joseph 83, 89, 167,
  169, 191, 201, 215, 232
  Appoints own deputy for licens-
    ing publications 97
  fee paid on promotion 107–8
  Fellow of Queen's College,
    Oxford 16
  minor appointments, requests to
    76
  record keeper, intelligence collec-
    tor 17, 76, 193, 194
  £1,600 for Clerkship offered to
    90
  sale of Clerkship 91
  Secretary of State 16
  self-made 194
  Under Secretary of State 16
  see also Secretary of State
wills and bequests 56, 136, 141,
    147–51, 164, 180, 240
  made by: Beale, Bartholomew
    150; Coling, Benjamin 200;
    Coling, Richard 199; Clarke,
    William 150; Curzon, Sir
    John 227; Dashwood, George
    203; Dereham, Thomas 191;
    Downing, George 150;
    Doyley, Sir William 115;
    Godolphin, Sir William 187;
    Kent, Richard 205;
    Millington, Francis 207;
    Morgan, William (4) 141–2;
    Morland, Samuel 150;
    Montagu, Edward, Earl of
    Sandwich 150; Page, Sir
    Thomas 197–8; Pagitt,
    Justinian 86; Pindar,

Matthew 150; Reymes, Bullen
    228; Slingsby, Henry 229–30;
    Sylvius, Gabriel de 191–2;
    Taylor, Sylvanus 237;
    Whitley, Roger 236
  see also officers, wealth of;
    Prerogative Court of
    Canterbury
Wiltshire 198, 204, 227
Winchester, Hants. 100
Winchilsea, Earl of, *see* Finch,
    Heneage
Windsor, Berks. 45, 67, 100
  Receiver of the Castle at 120
Wood, Anthony 78, 199, 236
Woods and Forests:
  officers 120
  Surveyor of 184
Woolwich 48, 79, 110–11, 159
Worcester cathedral medieval MSS
    237, 238
Worcester College, Oxford 193
Worcester, Marquis of, *see* Somerset
    Henry
Worcestershire 155, 207, 258
Works, King's (or Office of) 21, 94,
    145
  Surveyor of the 184
Worsley, Dr Benjamin 53, 121
Wren, Sir Christopher 184, 262
Wren, Matthew 77, 103
Wriothesley, Thomas, Earl of
    Southampton 11, 28, 34, 76,
    97, 104, 172, 223, 259
  death of 209, 259
Wyche, Sir Cyril 189–90
Wyche, Sir Peter 78, 189–90
Wylde (Wild), Robert 91
Wyndham family 154, 240
Wyndham, Sir Hugh 166

Yard, Robert 169
Yarmouth 89, 167, 179
Yeomen of the Guard 20, 25, 158
Yeomen of the Robes 130
  see also Wardrobe
York 45, 55
Yorkshire 115, 174, 198, 205,
    229